Attitudes towards death have changed dramatically over the centuries, not least because ideas about what happens after death have changed. The Victorians were not only obsessed with the subject of death, bereavement, and funeral rituals; they also speculated on the nature of heaven and hell, and argued about the related theme of divine judgment.

In this book Michael Wheeler looks at the literary implications of Victorian views of death and the life beyond, and the fear and hope embodied in the theological positions of the novelists and poets of the age. His analyses of each of the 'four last things' of Christian theology – death, judgment, heaven, and hell – and their part in nineteenth-century thought draw on a wide range of sermons, tracts, biographical writings, anthologies of sacred poetry, and popular 'guides to heaven' from 1830 to 1890, in addition to the more established canon of Victorian literary and theological writings. He shows that many nineteenth-century poets and preachers, novelists and Bible commentators are engaged in a shared act of interpretation in the face of death and bereavement, when language comes under great strain but can also draw upon traditional sources of consolation.

A revised and abridged version of Professor Wheeler's award-winning study of 1990, *Heaven, Hell and the Victorians* is a major exploration of a central dimension of Victorian life and thought.

Heaven, Hell, and the Victorians

Heaven, Hell,
and the Victorians

Michael Wheeler

Professor of English Literature and Director of the Ruskin Programme
Lancaster University

CAMBRIDGE
UNIVERSITY PRESS

Published by the Press Syndicate of the University of Cambridge
The Pitt Building, Trumpington Street, Cambridge CB2 1RP
40 West 20th Street, New York, NY 10011-4211, USA
10 Stamford Road, Oakleigh, Melbourne 3166, Australia

Originally published as *Death and the future life in
Victorian literature and theology* by Cambridge University Press 1990 and
© Cambridge University Press 1990

This abridged edition published 1994 and
© Cambridge University Press, Cambridge

Printed in Great Britain by Bell & Bain Ltd, Glasgow

A catalogue record for this book is available from the British Library

Library of Congress cataloguing in publication data

Wheeler, Michael, 1947–
[Death and the future life in Victorian literature and theology] Heaven,
Hell, and the Victorians/Michael Wheeler.
p.   cm.
Includes index.
ISBN 0–521–45565–0 (paperback)
1. English literature – 19th century – History and criticism.
2. Death – Religious aspects – Christianity – History – 19th century.
3. Theology, Doctrinal – Great Britain – History – 19th century.
4. Future life – Christianity – History – 19th century. 5. Future life in literature.
6. Heaven in literature. 7. Death in literature. 8. Hell in literature. I. Title.
PR468.D42W4   1994
820.9'354–dc20   94–787   CIP

(ISBN 0 521 30617 5 1st edition)

ISBN 0 521 45516 2 hardback
ISBN 0 521 45565 0 paperback

WV

For Joshua, Charlotte, and Emily

Contents

Illustrations

Preface

Heaven, Hell and the Victorians is a revised and abridged version of my earlier study entitled *Death and the Future Life in Victorian Literature and Theology*, published by Cambridge University Press in 1990. Apart from alterations throughout the text designed to make certain literary and theological concepts more accessible to a wider readership, the main difference between the two books is that this new version omits the detailed studies of four literary texts that formed Part Two of the original. In a new Conclusion, however, I briefly discuss the relevance of some of the Victorian ideas and conventions associated with death, judgment, heaven, and hell to these four texts by Tennyson, Dickens, Newman, and Hopkins.

My work on this fascinating area began in the mid-1970s, during an investigation of the background to Dickens's use of apocalyptic biblical allusions. I found that nineteenth-century theological controversies concerning eternal punishment and the future life had been thoroughly investigated by Geoffrey Rowell, in his excellent book on *Hell and the Victorians* (1974). Surprisingly, however, no large-scale work on the literary implications of this crucial, but now somewhat inaccessible, area of Victorian thought and belief had been carried out. A long period of research followed, during which many sermons and tracts, biographies and reminiscences, anthologies of sacred poems for mourners and popular guides to heaven were examined, as well as the relevant canonical works of the period, both theological and literary.

As the work went on it became clear that a number of different books could have been written, each reflecting a particular aspect of, or approach to, this large area of interest. First, there was the possibility of emphasizing the social history of death, as John Morley does, for example, and relating this to both the theology and the literature of the period. Secondly, a more 'thanatological' study would have focused upon death and bereavement as rites of passage, taking the work of

Victor Turner, Elisabeth Kübler-Ross, and Philippe Ariès as points of departure, and considering certain ideas and images of a future life as projections of the experience of those rites. Thirdly, it would have been feasible to carry out a comprehensive survey of all those ideas and images in the Victorian period, of the kind that Colleen McDannell and Bernhard Lang have since done more selectively in their history of heaven in the West. Would-be readers of all three unwritten books will, I hope, find some material of particular interest to them in the chapters that follow. I have concentrated, however, on re-examining the theological questions associated with death, judgment, heaven, and hell in the nineteenth century, and showing how these questions are reflected in the work of the creative writers.

It is perhaps a sign of our times that three leading literary critics have in recent years turned their attention to the relationship between literature and theology: Northrop Frye in *The Great Code*, Frank Kermode in *The Genesis of Secrecy*, and George Steiner in *After Babel*. The work of these three critics reflects something of the range of pressing and challenging topics which are of concern to both disciplines, including the study of language, narrative, and myth, and which are the subject of the journal *Literature & Theology*. I wish first to acknowledge my debt to the increasing number of scholars now working in the field of literature and theology, and particularly to my former colleagues on the journal – David Jasper, Terry Wright, Nicholas Sagovsky, Alison Milbank, John Milbank, and Mark Ledbetter.

Versions of sections of Chapter 1 have appeared in the form of conference papers published by the Macmillan Press Ltd, and edited by David Jasper and T. R. Wright: 'Tennyson, Newman and the Question of Authority', in *The Interpretation of Belief: Coleridge, Schleiermacher and Romanticism* (1986), and ' "Can These Dry Bones Live?"': Questions of Belief in a Future Life', in *The Critical Spirit and the Will to Believe: Essays in Nineteenth-Century Literature and Religion* (1989).

I am indebted to the following institutions: Lancaster University and its Humanities Research Committee, for granting funds for special research leave, 1986–7, and for a term's study leave in 1989; the Institute for Advanced Studies in the Humanities, University of Edinburgh, for awarding a Visiting Fellowship, Michaelmas 1986; and The British Academy, for awarding a research grant for that term. Also to the librarians and staffs of the British Library, London; the Bodleian Library, Oxford; Cambridge University Library; Edinburgh University

Library; the Harry Ransom Humanities Research Center, University of Texas at Austin; Lancaster University Library; Lincolnshire Central Reference Library, Lincoln; the National Library of Scotland, Edinburgh; New College Library, Edinburgh; St Deiniol's Library, Hawarden; and Stonyhurst College Library. I would like to thank a number of individuals who have helped me with patience and kindness: A. S. Byatt; Arthur Sale; at Lancaster, John Andrews, Pat Armitage, Chip Coakley, Davina Chaplin, Keith Hanley, Vimala Herman, Carole Lord, Denis McCaldin, Alan Robinson, Patrick Sherry, and David Webb; at Edinburgh and St Andrews Universities, Michael Alexander, Ian Campbell, Evelyn Carruthers, Peter Jones, and Karl Guthke; and particularly Andrew Brown, David Carroll, Alison Milbank, and Christopher Walsh, whose continued support and enthusiasm have sustained me. Ruth Hutchison assisted with the revisions for this new version with characteristic skill. The dedicatees, and their mother, know how profoundly grateful I am to them, in so many ways.

MDW

✦✦✦✦

Introduction

> The hand of the Lord was upon me, and carried me out in the
> spirit of the Lord, and set me down in the midst of the valley which
> was full of bones.
>
> And caused me to pass by them round about: and, behold, there
> were very many in the open valley; and, lo, they were very dry.
>
> And he said unto me, Son of man, can these bones live? And I
> answered, O Lord God, thou knowest.
>
> (Ezekiel 37.1–3)

A young lady leans over a gravestone, the other side of which is an
open grave and the exhumed remains of one John Faithful which lie
exposed on the earth. She stands in a sunlit churchyard, close to the
ivy-clad church and beneath a spreading chestnut tree. She wears a red
dress, a straw bonnet trimmed with flowers, and a black shawl. To the
late twentieth-century viewer, Henry Bowler's *The Doubt: 'Can These
Dry Bones Live?'* (illustration 1) typifies 'Victorian religious doubt', the
neutrality of the lady's expression and her unfocused gaze suggesting
that, from her own perspective, the stark reality of these 'dry bones'
has thrown the hope of life after death into doubt. But the question is:
for how long?

For the observant visitor to the Royal Academy in 1855, this genre
painting in the Pre-Raphaelite style contained more signs of hope of
resurrection than signs of death and corruption. Unlike the lady
standing behind the gravestone, the Victorian viewer could read and
interpret the message of the familiar inscriptions on the two gravestones
in the foreground ('I am the Resurrection and the Life' (John 11.25) and
'Resurgam'), and could relate these to two traditional symbols of new
life and resurrection – the germinating chestnut on the flat stone, and
the butterfly which sits on the skull.[1] So the Victorian viewer could read
the subject's doubt as only fleeting, whereas such an interpretation is

less obvious today. Had Christina Rossetti visited the Academy that year (she was in fact ill, and probably missed the show), she might well have thought about the individualism of Bowler's application of the text from the story of the valley of dry bones in Ezekiel 37. (She herself was to apply it in a more orthodox way to the Conversion of the Jews in a poem written four years later.[2]) She would certainly have understood Bowler's use of a tradition of analogy between scriptural revelation (the texts on the gravestones) and nature (the chestnut and the butterfly) that came down to the Victorians from Bishop Butler and the eighteenth century, a subject to which we will return in Chapter 1.

Bowler's painting was intended as an illustration to Tennyson's *In Memoriam* (1850), the most important poem of the Victorian period on the subject of death and the future life. T. S. Eliot's famous observation that the poem's faith is a 'poor thing', but its doubt 'a very intense experience'[3] has proved to be influential in the late twentieth century: one eminent modern critic argues, for example, that '*In Memoriam* is seldom specifically Christian'.[4] Yet at the turn of the twentieth century, Frederic Harrison had disparagingly described Tennyson's poems as 'exquisitely graceful re-statements of the current theology of the broad-Churchmen of the school of F. D. Maurice and Jowett'.[5]

Similarly with Dickens, whose more sceptical side in matters of religion has been emphasized by most recent critics. Yet even in his last completed work, *Our Mutual Friend* (1864–5), the central symbolic actions of rising and falling – worked out in the novel's social climbing and abrupt descents, the amassing and removal of dust heaps, a cityscape of airy rooftops and dark labyrinthine streets, and a river of drownings and rescues – is underpinned with a theological understanding of the fall, baptism, and man's redemption through love. The novel affirms the hope of a future life in Christ in ways which place Dickens in the same liberal Broad Church tradition as the Tennyson of *In Memoriam*, for all their differences within that tradition.[6]

For many critics in the modern, mainly secular western world, religion in historical literature is something of an embarrassment, and particularly Victorian religion in Victorian literature. The more strongly held the religious faith, the more violent can be the reaction against it. Take, for example, a famous moment of crisis in Victorian religious poetry, when the tall nun is drowning in Gerard Manley Hopkins's *The Wreck of the Deutschland* (written 1876) and the poet struggles to share in and describe her vision:

> But how shall I . . . make me room there:
> Reach me a . . . Fancy, come faster –
> Strike you the sight of it? look at it loom there,
> Thing that she . . . There then! the Master,
> *Ipse*, the only one, Christ, King, Head:
> He was to cure the extremity where he had cast her;
> Do, deal, lord it with living and dead;
> Let him ride, her pride, in his triumph, despatch
> and have done with his doom there.[7]

Now compare two modern interpretations of the stanza. One critic argues that for Hopkins, preparing for ordination as a Jesuit priest, the nun's miraculous visitation by Christ, in which she apprehends in her drowning and gasping for breath the *Ipse* or very self of her 'Master', was specifically eucharistic, the word *Ipse* being associated with the minor elevation in the mass.[8] Another, less sympathetic towards the poem's Roman Catholic content, describes this as 'the orgasmic stanza', where Hopkins makes the tall nun's death 'resemble a combination of sexual intercourse and a cavalry charge'.[9]

This study on *Heaven, Hell and the Victorians* sets out to work with the grain of the writers discussed rather than against it; to do more reconstruction (of the historical context) than deconstruction (of the literary text); to read the ambiguities of Victorian religious terms as features of a shared language of consolation; and to argue that this consolation was grounded in a specifically Christian hope, and was not merely a symptom of evasion, repression or wish-fulfilment in the face of death and bereavement. In terms of subject-matter the emphasis falls on re-examining nineteenth-century theological questions associated with death, judgment, heaven, and hell (the 'four last things'), and showing how these questions are reflected in the work of the creative writers. But the word 'reflected' suggests some kind of gap or separation between theology and literature, whereas the Victorian interpretative project discussed in this book was often in fact shared by creative writers and theologians in their engagement with the great mysteries of death and the future life, and with the challenges associated with those mysteries in the nineteenth century, including problems of evidence, authority, and language.

Eschatology – the study of the four last things – was a highly controversial subject in the Victorian Age, as even a glance through any collection of religious tracts or indeed serious general periodicals of the period will reveal. In the absence of definite and coherent teaching on heaven and hell in the New Testament, a wide range of doctrinal positions, each based upon a few individual texts, were defended on sectarian lines. Four conflicting views on eternal damnation were current in the 1870s, for example, and two ideas of heaven – as community or as a place of worship – proved difficult to reconcile. Some of the radical truth claims in the New Testament concerning the future life, which had always seemed either enigmatic or contradictory, now became questionable in the light of the Higher Criticism of the Bible, which raised new questions about the origin and authenticity of some of the most familiar New Testament stories of healing and raising from the dead.

In grappling with eschatological themes and debates in particular, theologians and creative writers reopened some of the key questions concerning the nature of religious belief and language. Both preachers and poets, for example, confronted the problem of finding a language which could convey an idea of the transcendent in an increasingly scientific-materialist world. The sense of the miraculous captured in the biblical account of a girl being raised from the dead in a house in first-century Palestine is difficult to transfer to a suburban villa where the doctor is expected, in Victorian fiction. Hans Frei, in his study of the relationship between realist narrative and the 'Eclipse of Biblical Narrative', shows how in the second half of the eighteenth century (in Britain the period of the rise of the novel) a great reversal had taken place in German biblical criticism: interpretation had become a matter of 'fitting the biblical story into another world with another story rather than incorporating that world into the biblical story'.[10] The Victorian novelist or poet who attempted to write of the 'invisible world' in a secular form and from a this-worldly perspective faced a similar challenge. In the attempt to speak of that which is 'beyond words' or to narrate the unnarratable, such as death and the future life, language comes under great pressure, and communication – in deathbed scenes, for example – can break down. As we will see later, however, one of the great paradoxes associated with these themes is that it is precisely at such moments of breakdown that the possibility of faith manifests itself.

At the centre of these concerns lies a tension between two models of reality. What we can label 'horizontal' models are based on our day-to-day human experience of moving through a world of clock time and solid objects. In contrast, 'vertical' models, which are predominant in the Bible, tell God's story rather than our story, and are often 'catastrophist' and interventionist in terms of time and history, rather than 'gradualist' and neutral. For example, in Victorian deathbed and graveyard scenes the dying person passes from life to death (or the 'next world', depending on one's perspective), via an ambiguous phase in which a 'horizontal' process of decline is marked off by two disruptive (and 'vertical') moments: that in which death is anticipated, and the moment of death itself. In the Victorian Age, highly conventionalized social customs and funerary rituals eased the transition from the deathbed to the bed that is the grave, and consolatory Christian literature emphasized the continuities between this life and the next, and particularly the idea of heaven as community. Yet the burial service in the Book of Common Prayer did not reinforce these manageable stages of separation for Victorian mourners. Rather it consoled them, as it had their ancestors, through affirmations of faith which are based upon some of the most challenging paradoxes and contraries in the New Testament, including passages from John and 11 and 1 Corinthians 15, which speak of life in death, of incorruption in corruption, of rising in descending. Such paradoxes and contraries are finally resolved only through faith.

The horizontal dimension of temporal process and deferral comes to the fore in the Victorian realist novel, and 'the sense of an ending'; in millenarian epic poems on 'the course of time'; and in doctrines of purgatory and the 'intermediate state' between death and the last judgment, whereby final divine dispensations are deferred. In moments of spiritual crisis, however, whether in fiction, poetry, or spiritual autobiography, the horizontality of everyday existence is disrupted as a person experiences some kind of vision of judgment, as in Browning's *Easter-Day*, for example. But whereas death and judgment are problematic subjects for the writer because of their contradictory or ambiguous nature as process in and through time, heaven and hell present the quite opposite problem of being fixed states. How can one write about states that are changeless and 'beyond words'? In practice, Victorian poets and hymn-writers exploit in new ways the creative tension inherent in

Christian tradition where the kingdom is described as being both here *and* elsewhere, and paradise as both now *and* not yet.

In the chapters that follow, each of the four last things is discussed in turn, drawing upon a wide range of material from the period 1830–90, some of which is familiar – novels by the Brontës and George Eliot, poems by Browning and Arnold, autobiographical works by Newman and Carlyle, and paintings by Martin and Millais – and some unfamiliar – tracts by Father Furniss of Dublin, the literary and devotional works of Revd Edward Henry Bickersteth, Vicar of Hampstead, and the memoirs of Catharine Tait, wife of a future Archbishop of Canterbury. Suggestions are offered in a short Conclusion as to how the concepts, models, and methodologies identified in the book inform four of the best known major works of Victorian literature which address the subjects of death, judgment, heaven, and hell.

First, however, in order better to understand the mind and imagination of an educated Victorian viewer of Bowler's *The Doubt* or reader of Tennyson's *In Memoriam*, we need to review a number of questions relating to the Bible – its teaching, authority, and language – which were live issues in the nineteenth century.

A LIVELY HOPE

> Blessed be the God and Father of our Lord Jesus Christ, which according to his abundant mercy hath begotten us again unto a lively hope by the resurrection of Jesus Christ from the dead,
> To an inheritance incorruptible, and undefiled, and that fadeth not away, reserved in heaven for you,
> Who are kept by the power of God through faith unto salvation ready to be revealed in the last time.   (1 Peter 1.3–5)

This is the opening of a doxology, or liturgical form of praise, for the risen Christ, and its tone is necessarily direct and authoritative. The epistle of which it is a part was addressed to young Christian communities which could expect to suffer cruel persecution, and offered a radiant message of hope for those who were committed to a difficult pilgrimage: the future is to be anticipated in joyful expectation, and embraced in certainty. This was not the place in which to introduce commentary upon the nature of the 'last time', or of Christ's promise of eternal life. Each of the key terms in the passage, however, would have had a very specific resonance for its first readers, and was to be the subject of much detailed exegesis in the nineteenth century, as we will see in later chapters. 'Lively' or 'living', for example, suggests a divinely inspired hope, since life is God's prerogative.[11] 'Hope' was a recognized technical term of the Pharisees, used by Paul in his testimony to the Sanhedrin in Jerusalem: 'I am a Pharisee, a son of a Pharisee: of the hope and resurrection of the dead I am called in question' (Acts 23.6). These words caused a dispute between the Pharisees, who believed in the resurrection of the body, and the Sadducees, who denied it. The concept of the resurrection of the body was an apocalyptic hope current in traditional Palestinian Judaism at the time of Christ, and often came into conflict with that of the immortality of the soul and a future life immediately after death, in Hellenistic Judaism.[12] Although the matter is still contested, most theologians today consider resurrection to be the basis of sound doctrine, as the whole person is thereby raised to new life, and no final separation between the body and the soul is implied.[13] At a time when persecution was an imminent threat, as in I Peter, teaching on the resurrection of the body would have been sharply relevant.

The closing words of verse 5, 'in the last time' (*en kairō eschatō*; NEB 'at the end of time') introduce the concept of the *eschaton*. The nineteenth-century term 'eschatology' has been used in several different but related senses.[14] In this book it will be used in the traditional sense of 'death, judgment, heaven, and hell' (*OED*), and the science or study of these four last things. In I Peter the end of all things is said to be 'at hand' (4.7). The apostles lived in the end-time, as Christ had already died and been raised from the dead. Thus, paradoxically, the 'lively hope' of the doxology is already an 'eschatological blessing'.[15] (Similarly, New Testament metaphors of 'first fruits' and an 'earnest' of blessings to come, associated with the gift of the Holy Spirit, emphasize a continuity between eternal life as a present possession and as a future promise.)[16]

For the first Christians, the end-time was to be completed in the *parousia* ('coming' or 'presence'), usually identified with the return or second coming of Christ.[17] Jesus's own teaching on the *parousia* had been received as a definitive prophecy of the imminent end of the present world order, and of the coming of the kingdom. As the decades passed, however, without the hoped for *parousia* being fulfilled, the question of the state of the dead between their 'falling asleep' and the general resurrection became increasingly pressing, and Christian writers encountered difficulties in harmonizing the idea of a post-mortem existence with God, in heaven, and Jewish eschatology which looked to the final judgment. (In the Middle Ages, Roman Catholic teaching on purgatory was to draw upon patristic writings which grappled with the same problem.) The writer of the Second Epistle of Peter (which has no connection with the first) anticipates 'that there shall come in the last days scoffers, walking after their own lusts, And saying, Where is the promise of his coming? for since the fathers fell asleep, all things continue as they were from the beginning of the creation' (2 Peter 3.3–4).

Paul tackled these and other difficulties in the finest chapter on the subject of death and the future life in the Bible, 1 Corinthians 15, where he wrote to members of the church in Corinth who shared the hostility of Hellenistic Judaism towards the resurrection of the body:

But if there be no resurrection of the dead, then is Christ not risen.
. . .
For if the dead arise not, then is not Christ raised:
And if Christ be not raised, your faith is vain; ye are yet in your sins.
Then they also which are fallen asleep in Christ are perished.
If in this life only we have hope in Christ, we are of all men most miserable.

(1 Corinthians 15.13, 16–19)

Paul, a Pharisee before his conversion, would have believed in a *general* resurrection. His analogy, however, of the sowing of the 'bare grain' (15.37) denotes a quality of relationship, not of substance, in the Christian scheme, and he avoids description of the *modus operandi* of resurrection: 'It is sown a natural body; it is raised a spiritual body' (15.44).[18] Similarly, the last judgment is a mystery: 'Behold, I shew you a mystery; We shall not all sleep, but we shall all be changed, in a moment, in the twinkling of an eye, at the last trump' (15.51–2). It is thus implied that not all who read the epistle will have died when the trumpet sounds. Like the writer of 1 Peter, Paul addresses those who are 'waiting for the coming of our Lord Jesus Christ' (1 Corinthians 1.7).

In the interim, however, the early church had to wait and to endure, 'knowing that tribulation worketh patience; And patience, experience; and experience hope: And hope maketh not ashamed' (Romans 5.3–5).[19] This hope is 'for that we seek not' (Romans 8.24–5), and Paul writes to the Colossians of 'the hope which is laid up for you in heaven, whereof ye heard before in the word of the truth of the gospel' (Colossians 1.5). For Paul, the four last things are mysteries hidden with God, and his teaching on the Christian hope speaks to the pilgrim church of the new covenant, going forward in confidence into 'that we see not'. 'Paradise' was for him 'now and not yet'.[20]

In the New Testament the object of the Christian hope remains indefinite: outside the Book of Revelation there are no detailed descriptions of the future life. One explanation for the infrequency and generality of Jesus's teaching on the subject in the gospels is that he took life after death for granted.[21] His reported sayings on the four last things, his raising of Lazarus from the dead, and his teaching on the kingdom are in various ways difficult to interpret. The description of the last judgment in Matthew 25, for example, modifies Jewish apocalyptic by suggesting that groups of individuals rather than nations will be judged, and judged according to their works. But no reference is made to Christ's redemptive act in dying upon the cross.[22] The final verse of the chapter ('And these shall go away into everlasting punishment: but the righteous into eternal life'), the subject of much heated debate in the nineteenth century, may have been a Matthean addition, recalling Daniel 12.2. The story of the raising of Lazarus from the dead poses more problems than it solves, as Tennyson knew:

> Behold a man raised up by Christ!
> The rest remaineth unrevealed;
> He told it not; or something seal'd
> The lips of that Evangelist.[23]

Most of Jesus's teaching on the kingdom is conveyed through parables, a form in which the truths of the gospel are at once proclaimed, through accessible stories, and hidden, through concealed meanings available only to insiders.[24] Even the most direct teaching is suggestive rather than explanatory. In the farewell discourses in the fourth gospel, for example, words which have encouraged not only ecumenists but also those who look to the unification of all world faiths ('In my Father's house are many mansions', 14.2) are followed by the unequivocal saying, 'no man cometh unto the Father, but by me' (14.6).

The Book of Revelation, on the other hand, presents difficulties of interpretation of a different order, for what James Hastings called 'the "Divina Commedia" of Scripture' can be read as all too literal a description of the events of the *eschaton*.[25] In the nineteenth century many believed that the seven seals and the four horsemen, the dragon, and the lake of brimstone were more than chiliastic symbols. At the end of the century, one theologian acknowledged the fact that the Revelation had 'suffered many things from the strained ingenuity of the dogmatic interpreter'. He himself focused upon the *parousia*, the 'objective, visible return' of Christ, as the 'decisive event of the future' in his analysis of the book.[26] Northrop Frye, however, reminds us of the problems associated with an 'objective' reading: 'The author speaks of setting down what he has seen in a vision, but the Book of Revelation is not a visualized book in the ordinary sense of the word, as any illustrator who has struggled with its seven-headed and ten-horned monsters will testify.'[27] Inspired by the Book of Revelation, many Victorian illustrators and painters, poets, novelists, and preachers attempted to combine sublimity with realism, the visionary with the matter-of-fact, in their portrayals of the last days.

In contrast to those who searched the New Testament for evidence of the location and dimensions of heaven, Friedrich Schleiermacher, the great Protestant theologian of the early nineteenth century, wrote on the subject of the future life:

all the indications [the Redeemer] gives are either purely figurative, or otherwise so indefinite in tenor that nothing can be gathered from them more than what for every Christian is so much the essential thing in every conception he may form of existence after death, that without it such existence would be mere perdition – namely, the persistent union of believers with the Redeemer.[28]

The one statement of Jesus which may be said to summarize the gospel message also underlines the grounds of the Christian hope, but without offering Martha, the sister of Lazarus, a mental picture of the future life: 'I am the resurrection, and the life: he that believeth in me, though he were dead, yet shall he live: And whosoever liveth and believeth in me shall never die' (John 11.25–6).

The lively hope of resurrection in Jesus Christ was reflected in the new tone of early Christian funerary inscriptions in the Roman catacombs.[29] Meditating on these, Walter Pater's Marius became 'as by some gleam of foresight, aware of the whole force of evidence for a certain strange, new hope, defining in its turn some new and weighty motive of action, which lay in deaths so tragic for the "Christian superstition"' (*Marius the Epicurean*, 1885; 21). Expressions of Christian hope often spring from suffering or persecution, and are eloquent testimony of faith among the bereaved. For Victorian Anglicans, and for many nonconformists,[30] it was in the order for the Burial of the Dead in the Book of Common Prayer (1662) that New Testament teaching on the Christian hope was encountered most dramatically and memorably. The words from the fourth gospel quoted above – 'I am the resurrection and the life' – affirmed in the opening sentence the doctrine on which the funeral service was based. From 1549 onwards, the lesson which followed had been taken from 1 Corinthians 15, beginning at verse 20.[31] The final collect refers to Christ's teaching, by his 'holy Apostle Saint Paul', that we should 'not be sorry, as men without hope, for them that sleep in him'. 'Our hope' is that our brother or sister 'rests' in Christ. Edward Henry Bickersteth, Vicar of Hampstead and later Bishop of Exeter, who is to figure prominently in this study as a prolific Evangelical writer on the subject of the four last things, commented on the burial service: 'It is throughout the language of holy hope.'[32] This is the theme of Bickersteth's meditations on the Order for the Burial of the Dead, entitled *The Shadowed Home, and the Light Beyond* (1875), which was written to console the bereaved between a death and a burial. Anthologies of verse fulfilled a similar function in the nineteenth century. A collection of *Sacred Poems for Mourners* (1846), for example, edited by Priscilla Maurice (F. D. Maurice's sister), followed the sequence of the burial service, offering simple reflections on the words of the prayer book and the New Testament teaching and symbolism which they embody. 'Life through Death', by Richard Chenevix Trench, a future Archbishop of Dublin, begins: 'The seed must die, before the corn appears / Out of the ground, in blade and fruitful ears.'[33] 'The Linden Trees', written by one L. C. Briggs and published in the *Illustrated Book of Sacred Poems* (1867) is also typical of the sentimental graveyard tradition of the period:

> While that blest word,
> 'The Resurrection and the life,' is heard,
> And they repeat
> The hopes of those who trust in heaven to meet,
> And rest for aye at the Redeemer's feet.[34]

The indefinite nature of New Testament teaching on the future life, which is reflected in the Book of Common Prayer, allowed Victorian preachers and poets considerable latitude of interpretation, and the idea of heaven as a blessed home or country in which friends and loved ones meet is the most characteristic of the age.

Far more contentious was the question of judgment and God's elect. The words spoken over the dead in the Book of Common Prayer – 'in sure and certain hope of the Resurrection to eternal life' – were the subject of much debate in the 1860s during a prolonged series of ecclesiastical exchanges on the subject of liturgical reform, to which Dickens refers in *Our Mutual Friend* (1864–5).[35] C. J. Vaughan, for example, Vicar of Doncaster and later Dean of Llandaff, drew attention to the dilemma of the minister who 'must give thanks to God for the sure and certain hope of another world by the grave of the drunkard or the adulterer'.[36] The effect, however, of removing the words 'sure and certain', either compulsorily or at the discretion of the priest, would in Vaughan's view be worse than keeping the time-honoured phrase, even though it was considered by some to be complacent, and to hint at the possibility of universal salvation. The nature and scope of the Christian hope in the New Testament were matters of general interest and concern in the nineteenth century, but it was often in the familiar words from the burial service, spoken over the body of a dear brother or sister departed, that a subject of universal significance was brought home to individual mourners.

Heaven, that long home or blessed country, represented for many Victorian writers and thinkers the fulfilment of their Christian hope. Ruskin, for example, claimed a special place for hope in the Christian scheme, and specifically in relation to heaven. In his commentary on the sculptures on the capitals of the Ducal Palace in Venice, which portray the three virtues, he writes:

Of all the virtues, this is the most distinctively Christian (it could not, of course, enter definitely into any Pagan scheme); and above all others, it seems to me the *testing* virtue, – that by the possession of which we may most certainly determine whether we are Christians or not; for many men have charity, that is to say, general kindness of heart, or even a kind of faith, who have not any habitual hope of, or longing for, heaven.[37]

J. M. Neale's hymn 'The world is very evil' encourages belief in heaven, a 'sweet and blessed country, / The home of God's elect':

> Strive, man, to win that glory;
>   Toil, man, to gain that light;
> Send hope before to grasp it,
>   Till hope be lost in sight . . .[38]

And one of H. W. Baker's hymns in *Hymns Ancient and Modern* begins:

> There is a blessed home
>> Beyond this land of woe,
> Where trials never come,
>> Nor tears of sorrow flow;
> Where faith is lost in sight,
>> And patient hope is crown'd,
> And everlasting light
>> Its glory throws around.[39]

This kind of affirmation – 'There *is* a blessed home' – is typical of Victorian hymnody. As we have already seen, however, New Testament teaching on the future life presents numerous problems of interpretation. Nineteenth-century eschatological controversies focused upon the conflict between the certainty of the hope affirmed in the Bible and the prayer book, and the uncertainties of biblical evidence. But before that conflict is examined in more detail, in relation to the treatment of death, judgment, heaven, and hell in Victorian literature and theology, two other issues must be considered; for questions relating to both biblical authority and the limits of religious language were both urgent and challenging in the years from around 1830 to 1890.

THE QUESTION OF BIBLICAL AUTHORITY

The debate in the 1860s over the words 'sure and certain hope' in the burial service raised the familiar problem of religious authority. As the forms of service printed in the Book of Common Prayer do not have the same authority as the creeds and the thirty-nine articles of the Church of England, what authority do these words have? Is this sure and certain hope grounded in the New Testament, and does the New Testament itself have divine authority? To what extent can individual biblical texts on the subject be received as authoritative? Article VI states that 'Holy Scripture containeth all things necessary to salvation', and article XX that although the church has 'authority in Controversies of Faith . . . yet it is not lawful for the Church to ordain any thing that is contrary to God's Word written, neither may it so expound one place of Scripture, that it be repugnant to another'. The substance of both these articles figured prominently in discussion on the question of the authority of scripture in the nineteenth century, a large and complex subject which was often closely linked to the specific issue of the future state.

As the question of authority will be central to my later discussion, its salient points should be briefly outlined here.

For Bernard Ramm, 'revelation is the key to religious authority'. Whereas the Roman Catholic Church bases its authority upon God's revelation (contained in oral tradition and the scriptures) and his 'one true Church', the Protestant principle of authority is defined by Ramm as 'the Holy Spirit speaking in the Scriptures': 'there is an external principle (the *inspired* Scripture) and an *internal* principle (the witness of the Holy Spirit). It is the principle of an objective *divine* revelation, with an interior divine witness.'[40] In the early nineteenth century the Tractarians agreed with the Roman Catholics that authority lay in the Bible and in tradition, and in his *Lectures on the Prophetical Office of the Church* (1837), for example, John Henry Newman, one of the leading lights of the Oxford Movement, argued that freedom of private judgment in the interpretation of scripture without reference to tradition would lead to latitudinarianism.[41] Newman was writing at a time when many practising Christians in Britain believed in the inerrancy of the Bible as the inspired word of God.[42] The whole question of authority, however, was to be thrown into the melting-pot over the subsequent twenty-five years.

It has been suggested that if Coleridge's *Confessions of an Inquiring Spirit*, published posthumously in 1840, had been more widely read, much of the misunderstanding over the interpretation of the Bible in the later nineteenth century might have been avoided.[43] Although perhaps exaggerated, taking insufficient account of the strength of more conservative approaches to the Bible in the nineteenth century, this proposition does accurately reflect the value of Coleridge's contribution to the debate on authority among Protestants. Coleridge affirms the Protestant principle of authority (based upon the reading, in faith, of the inspired scriptures), while attacking what he calls 'Bibliolatry'. He encourages his Friend to read the contents of the Bible 'with only the same piety which you freely accord on other occasions to the writings of men, considered the best and wisest of their several ages!'[44] Those who believe in the literal truth of every word of the Bible fall into error through the practice of 'bringing together into logical dependency detached sentences from books composed at the distance of centuries, nay, sometimes a *millennium*, from each other, under different dispensations, and for different objects'.[45]

Coleridge, however, was ahead of his time, having been one of the first Englishmen to recognize the significance of German biblical criticism. It was not until the 1860s, during the controversy following the publication of *Essays and Reviews* (1860), that this kind of approach to biblical interpretation made a considerable impact upon the public mind. In his brilliant article on the interpretation of scripture, Benjamin Jowett argued, like Coleridge, that the Bible should be read like any other book, and that passages from one part of the Bible should not be applied uncritically to other passages.[46] Now the orthodox position on 'life everlasting' and 'everlasting fire' had traditionally been based upon a number of scattered biblical texts (including Isaiah 33.14, Daniel 12.2, and Matthew 25.46), and the Athanasian Creed. The application of historical critical methods to the Bible therefore strengthened a liberal challenge to the doctrine of everlasting punishment, and it is no coincidence that the two contributors taken to law were Rowland Williams (on 'Bunsen's Biblical Researches') and H. B. Wilson (on the question of eternal punishment). The connection was stated explicitly in the declaration of nearly eleven thousand clergy, both Tractarian and Evangelical, that the Church of England believed in the inspired scripture and taught, 'in the words of our Blessed Lord, that the "punishment" of the "cursed" equally with the "life" of the "righteous" is "everlasting"' (Matthew 25).[47]

The new questions concerning the authority of the Bible which arose in the 1860s threw many thinking people into a state of near panic. They had to choose between the excesses of the radical Tübingen school and the blinkered conservatism of English scholarship.[48] The English scene was dominated by Edward Bouverie Pusey (Regius Professor of Hebrew and Canon of Christ Church, Oxford), a leading Tractarian who countered the late dating of Daniel with the observation that Christians, unlike 'the critics', believed that miraculous prophecies could happen, and by H. P. Liddon (prebendary of Salisbury and later Pusey's biographer), whose Bampton lectures of 1866, entitled *The Divinity of Our Lord,* attempted to refute Renan, Baur, and Strauss.[49] The middle ground, however, was soon taken by three scholars – Lightfoot, Hort, and Westcott – who came to be known as the 'Cambridge Three', and whose biblical criticism was as rigorous as that of the Germans. Lightfoot, moreover, managed to explode the more exaggerated claims of the Tübingen school.[50]

The contributors to *Essays and Reviews* had known that there was a gap between doctrine preached by the Church of England and the actual beliefs of educated people. In *Literature and Dogma* (1873), Matthew Arnold took the argument further, stating that '*the masses* are losing the Bible and its religion', largely as a result of Protestantism's having made the Bible 'its fixed authority'.[51] Interestingly, the issues of biblical authority and the nature of the future state are again drawn together in Arnold's preface to the popular edition.[52] His attack on the 'mechanical and materialising theology' of his day was extended in *God and the Bible* (1875), a sequel to *Literature and Dogma*, where he claimed that Jesus's words to Martha were intended to 'transform' the materialist Jewish concept of the resurrection of the body, but that his words provided the basis for the evolution of a miracle story 'exactly effacing the truth which [he] wished to convey'.[53] Our 'hope of immortality', our 'common materialistic notions about the resurrection of the body and the world to come', are 'in direct conflict with the new and loftier conceptions of life and death which Jesus himself strove to establish'.[54] As a moralist and an idealist, Arnold rejects the view, based upon a literal reading of the Bible, that Christianity is nothing but a promise of paradise to the saint and a threat of hell-fire to the worldly man, based on the authority of Christ who rose from the dead and ascended into heaven.[55] 'Of Biblical learning', he writes, 'we have not enough.'[56]

Critics of *Lux Mundi* (1889), edited by Charles Gore, a leading High Churchman, believed that the opposite was now true, and that of biblical learning we had too much. In his own essay on 'The Holy Spirit and Inspiration', Gore adopted Plato's idea of authority as a 'necessary schooling of the individual temperament' which 'leaves much for the individual to do'.[57] He uses the word 'myth' in relation to the Bible's earlier narratives, before the call of Abraham, and welcomes the results of historical criticism where it is fairly used.[58] The controversy which ensued has been fully documented and need not be rehearsed here.[59] By the end of the century Dean Farrar of Canterbury could assert in *The Bible, Its Meaning and Supremacy* (1897) that no scholar of note questioned the main conclusions of the 'Higher Criticism', and that it was better for Christianity not to base the Bible's authority on an idea of biblical infallibility. Rather, the doctrine of the Church of England is that 'Scripture *contains* the word of God'.[60]

F. W. Farrar, author of *Eric; or, Little by Little* (1858) and the famous *Life of Christ* (1874), was himself one of the major contributors to nineteenth-century debates on the future life. In his famous sermons on *Eternal Hope* (1878) he had argued that the 'common view' of everlasting punishment, which he abhorred, was based partly upon mistranslations in the Authorized Version, and that the common view was the product of what he later described in *The Bible, Its Meaning and Supremacy* as 'the wresting of texts'. In this later work he quoted Coleridge's *Confessions of an Inquiring Spirit,* and predicted that the printing of the Revised Version (1881–5) in paragraphs instead of verses would gradually help to dissipate the 'delusion' that the Bible 'was originally written in that atomistic form' enshrined in the Authorized Version.[61] The doctrine of 'eternal torment' had often been 'proved' by Isaiah 23.14, yet 'even a moderate study of the context might have sufficed to show that the verse has not the most remote connexion with that terrific dogma'.[62]

In *The Bible, Its Meaning and Supremacy,* Farrar quoted Newman: ' "The *translated Bible,*" Cardinal Newman says with reluctant admiration, "is *the stronghold of heresy.*" '[63] In Farrar's view, the Bible's influence on literature, and specifically on Wordsworth, Tennyson, Browning, George Eliot, Carlyle, Newman, and Ruskin, had been 'invaluable and supreme'.[64] For some Victorian writers who addressed themselves to the subject of the future life, however, the question of the authority of the translated Bible was pressing.

ANALOGY AND THE LIMITS OF LANGUAGE

Behind these arguments concerning translation and proof texts lay a series of fundamental problems associated with the nature of religious language itself. (Readers who do not wish to engage with such problems can move on at this point to the discussion of the Lazarus story on p. 22.)

Nineteenth-century literalists based their conceptions of heaven and hell on the narrow ground of one or two isolated biblical texts, and thus on a limited range of analogues and symbols. The same was often true of those who attempted to portray heaven and hell imaginatively, in verse or prose. Indeed, the realist novelist or painter was in certain respects in a more difficult position than the theologian. Chris Brooks examines religious symbolism in the novels of Dickens, the paintings of the Pre-Raphaelites, and the architecture of Butterfield, and finds in all these artists' work a 'mode of the Victorian imagination' which he describes as 'symbolic realism'. This mode, he argues, is grounded in typology, 'the technique of biblical exegesis, Patristic in origin, whereby events and persons in the Old Testament are interpreted both as historically real and as divinely ordained prefigurations of events in the New Testament, most centrally, of the life of Christ'.[65] Thus typology is a particular version of symbolic realism which allows 'events to be read as simultaneously real and symbolic'.

Brooks's study focuses upon aesthetics, and does not explore the closely related subject of analogy, and the inheritance of Joseph Butler's *Analogy of Religion* (1736) in the Victorian period.[66] Butler's seminal work profoundly influenced thinkers as varied as Coleridge, Newman, Keble, and Maurice. The book opens with a chapter entitled 'Of a Future Life', in which Butler examines the 'presumption or probability' of a future existence for man in the light of the 'analogy of nature, and the several changes which we have undergone', and other examples of transformation such as that of the worm turning into the fly.[67] James Buchanan, Professor of Systematic Theology at the Free Church New College, Edinburgh, wrote a treatise entitled *Analogy* in the 1860s which was based upon Butler, but which applied the word more widely. Following Butler, Buchanan commented that some analogous facts are 'applicable to such truths as are common to Natural and Revealed religion', and argued that the 'doctrine of a future state of existence after death belongs to this class'.[68] He defined analogies as

a sort of rational imagery, by which the nature and relations of things 'seen and temporal' are made to symbolize those which are 'unseen and eternal'. 'Earthly things' become the exponents and types of 'heavenly things'.[69]

Perhaps the most influential statement on analogy in the nineteenth century, however, was Coleridge's in *Aids to Reflection* (1825), where he compares it with metaphor:

Analogies are used in aid of *Conviction*: Metaphors, as means of Illustration. The language is analogous, wherever a thing, power, or principle in a higher dignity is expressed by the same thing, power, or principle in a lower but more known form. Such, for instance, is the language of John iii.6. *That which is born of the Flesh, is Flesh; that which is born of the Spirit, is Spirit.* The latter half of the verse contains the fact asserted; the former half the *analogous* fact, by which it is rendered intelligible. If any man choose to call this *metaphorical* or figurative, I ask him whether . . . he regards the divine Justice, for instance, as a *metaphorical* term, a mere figure of speech? If he disclaims this, then I answer, neither do I regard the words *born again*, or *spiritual life*, as figures or metaphors. I have only to add, that these analogies are the material, or (to speak chemically) the *base*, of Symbols and symbolical expressions; the nature of which is always *tau*tegorical (i.e., expressing the *same* subject but with a *difference* in contra-distinction from metaphors and similitudes), that are always *all*egorical (i.e., expressing a *different* subject but with a resemblance) . . . [70]

Coleridge's description of analogy as a means of expressing some 'higher dignity' which is the object of conviction via a 'lower but more known form' can be applied to the analogue, or parallel relationship between, sleep:waking (the analogous fact) and death:resurrection (the fact asserted), which was to be the 'base' of much of the religious symbolism in the apologetics and the consolatory writings of the Victorian Age. Central to Coleridge's argument, and to the claims of Victorian eschatology, is the belief that the analogical language of the New Testament renders intelligible a higher reality than that which is susceptible to scientific-materialist analysis.

Typology and analogy, then, were both seen in the nineteenth century as means by which language could transcend its human limits, and point towards 'heavenly things'. Whereas typology, however, could easily be adapted to nineteenth-century progressive or developmental models of creation, analogy, traditionally understood by less imaginative thinkers than Coleridge as reflecting a static, divinely ordered cosmos, adapted less well to a world in which language, including biblical language, came to be understood as a human construction. The question of the function and limits of religious language has, of course, continued to exercise twentieth-century theologians and literary critics. In his Bampton Lectures entitled *The Glass of Vision* (1948), Austin Farrer distinguishes between the 'great images' and 'subordinate images' of the Judaeo-Christian tradition, and argues that Christ himself expressed thought in certain dominant images, such as the 'Kingdom of God' and the 'Son of Man', and, in historical time, 'clothed himself in the archetypal images, and then began to do and to suffer'.[71] In his fourth lecture, Farrer considers how it is that these images are able to signify divine realities, and argues that 'analogy is the proper form of metaphysical thought, in the realm of *thought* there is no getting behind it'.[72] In a later lecture he states that 'faith discerns not the images, but what the images signify: and yet we cannot discern it except *through* the images'.[73] Farrer's ideas have aroused considerable interest. H. D. Lewis, for example, devoted a chapter of his study on *Our Experience of God*

(1959) to 'Experience and Images', and more recently Farrer has figured in the debate between Helen Gardner and Frank Kermode over the interpretation of Mark's gospel, Farrer's central text in *A Glass of Vision*.[74]

In *God-Talk* (1967), John MacQuarrie was particularly interested in analogy applied to God himself:

analogical language – and all symbolic language – has a paradoxical character. Simply to affirm an analogue or symbol is to fall into that over-literalness which, if we are applying the image to God, leads into an attitude of idolatry. Whatever symbol or analogue is affirmed must be at the same time denied; or, better still, whenever one symbol is affirmed, others that will modify or correct it must be affirmed at the same time.[75]

As an illustration of the need for modifying symbols in theology, Mac-Quarrie cited what was at the time a recent and controversial argument, in John Robinson's *Honest to God* (1963), that symbols of depth are more helpful than symbols of height in relation to God and his nature. For MacQuarrie, Robinson had simply replaced one set of limiting ideas with another, and a 'big advance' toward a 'more adequate thought of God' would be made if these two symbols were 'held in tension'.

Not unlike Coleridge, MacQuarrie distinguishes between religious symbols, analogues, and images, which call from us a 'response of commitment', and metaphor, which is 'used mostly in literary contexts' and which elicits an aesthetic response.[76] Although limiting in its sharp separation of the credal from the aesthetic, and of the religious from the literary, this distinction is helpful with reference to language which attempts to describe God's nature. F. W. Dillistone, in his study on *Christianity and Symbolism* (1955), distinguishes between analogy, which has links with the simile, and metaphor, which has links with the contrast. Metaphor, he observes, is the favourite tool of the great poets:

Through it the prophet leaps outside the circle of present experience, the realm of the factual and the commonsense, the typical and the regular. He parts company with those who are travelling the surer and steadier road of analogical comparison. By one act of daring he brings into creative relationship the apparently opposite and contrary and, if his metaphorical adventure proves successful, gains new treasure both for language and for life.[77]

Sallie McFague, who cites Dillistone in her *Metaphorical Theology* (1982), offers an 'amalgam' of the views of writers such as I. A.

Richards, Max Black, Paul Ricoeur, and Nelson Goodman on metaphor, and particularly its 'tensive' character:

By retaining the interaction of *two* thoughts active in the mind, one recalls, as
one does not with a simile, that the two are dissimilar as well as similar . . .
A metaphor that works is sufficiently unconventional and shocking so that we
instinctively say no as well as yes to it, thus avoiding absolutism . . . Religious
metaphors, because of their preservation in a tradition and repetition in ritual,
are especially prone to becoming idols.[78]

But we have seen that MacQuarrie makes very similar comments on
symbols and analogues. Dillistone, who observes that when a metaphor
is first presented we are 'surprised, even shocked, by the fact that this
word does not really belong to the situation in which it is being used',
adds that the same could be claimed to be true of the analogy, although
in this case 'the transition is so gentle and so natural that we are not
shocked: we are only conscious of a feeling of general approval and
satisfaction'.[79]

Modern linguistic theory has, of course, shifted the whole ground of
the discussion, and metaphor is now treated not only as a specific figure
of speech but also, in its broader sense, as the foundation of language
itself. Whereas nineteenth-century Evangelicals such as Bickersteth
thought in terms of a 'heavenly' figurative language which was as
immutable as the Word, Sallie McFague characterizes a metaphorical
theology as 'open-ended, tentative, indirect, tensive, iconoclastic, *trans-
formative*' (my emphasis),[80] and we saw earlier that in Matthew
Arnold's view, Jesus's new language 'transformed' the materialist Jewish
notions concerning the resurrection of the body. It is in similar terms
and in a similar context that Michael Edwards begins his study on the
language of literature and religion, entitled *Towards a Christian Poetics*
(1984). Basing his theory on what he calls the 'cosmology of Christianity', namely 'creation, fall and re-creation', Edwards cites St Paul's
teaching in 1 Corinthians 15 that the 'natural body' will be raised at the
end as a 'spiritual body', and argues that 'the function of language and
literature is to strain towards that spiritualising of the body'.[81] What
follows is a late-twentieth-century reworking of materials (drawn from
Bishop Butler) that were very familiar to the eighteenth and nineteenth
centuries.[82]

It seems, then, that the theology of a future life is still fertile ground
for the student of religious language. As we move towards understand-

ing the Christian poetics of death, we will find that the boundaries between 'literary' and 'non-literary' writing, and between the metaphoric and the analogical, are far from clear. We need working definitions, however, and perhaps the best way to distinguish between metaphor and analogy for the purposes of this study is to see analogy as a parallel relation based upon similarity, whereas metaphor, being contrastive, functions through substitution. Thus the Christian analogy of 'sleep' is based upon the parallel relation, or analogue, sleep: awakening / death:resurrection. The breakdown of communication associated with this analogy in the kind of Victorian consolatory discourse relating to the deathbed and the grave to be examined in Chapter 1 is uncannily anticipated in a prototypical New Testament narrative: the story of the raising of Lazarus in John 11.

'OUR FRIEND LAZARUS SLEEPETH': A TEST CASE

The eleventh chapter of the fourth gospel, a crucial passage in a New Testament which contains little specific teaching on the nature of resurrection, provided a fascinating test case in relation to the questions of biblical authority and language in the nineteenth century. Matthew Arnold noted in *God and the Bible* (1875) that every detail of the account of the raising of Lazarus had been 'canvassed with elaborate minuteness'.[83] No part of the narrative had received closer attention than verses 11–14:

he saith unto them, Our friend Lazarus sleepeth [*kekoimētai*]; but I go, that I may awake him out of sleep. Then said his disciples, Lord, if he sleep, he shall do well.

Howbeit Jesus spake of his death [*thanatou*]: but they thought that he had spoken of taking of rest in sleep [*koimēseōs tou hupnou*].

Then said Jesus unto them plainly, Lazarus is dead [*apethanen*].

(John 11.11–14)

This is one of several examples in the fourth gospel of the disciples' failure immediately to comprehend or rightly interpret Jesus's sayings. One question posed by the passage touches upon the issues of the gospel's authorship and its relationship to the synoptic gospels: Why did the disciples fail to recognize a figure of speech which they might reasonably have been expected to remember from earlier usages, and particularly from the other two recorded miracles in which Jesus recalled the dead to life – the raising of Jairus's daughter (Mark 5, Luke 8, and

Matthew 9, where the father is not named) and of the son of the widow
of Nain (Luke 7)? E. H. Bickersteth addressed the question in *The
Shadowed Home* (1875), where he explained the biblical context of the
opening sentence of the burial service – 'I am the Resurrection and the
Life, saith the Lord: he that believeth in Me, though he were dead, yet
shall he live: and whosoever liveth and believeth in Me shall never die':

when His hour was come, Jesus arose to go into Judaea again . . . And as
they were going, He said, Our friend Lazarus sleepeth, but I go that I may
awake him out of sleep. In heaven's language the death of saints is sleep; but
this language was not here understood by the disciples. The lofty freedom of
the Divine style is excellent beyond compare; but man's dull apprehension
makes Scripture often stoop to our more sombre way of speaking. Christ, on
an earlier occasion, had interpreted this celestial dialect, when, ere He raised
Jairus' daughter, He said, The maiden is not dead, but sleepeth [*katheudei*].
But, probably, from misunderstanding His words, This sickness is not unto
death, but for the glory of God [John 11.4], the disciples were persuaded that
Lazarus would not actually die; and therefore when He afterwards said, Our
friend sleepeth, they thought that the Lord had given His beloved sleep, – that
at His command Lazarus had fallen into that long, refreshing, peaceful sleep,
which so often marks a favourable crisis in dangerous illness. Jesus therefore
drops heaven's figurative language, and speaks in that of men: Lazarus is dead
. . .[84]

The casualness with which Bickersteth equates the terms 'dialect' and
'style' betrays a lack of precision in his treatment of religious language,
although this is hardly surprising in a popular book of meditations on
the burial service. More significantly, he considers Christ's 'heavenly'
language to be a mark of his divinity, and thus ignores the critical
question of how this language was mediated to us in the *writing* of the
gospel.[85] Like his use of the language of the Victorian sick-bed, however
('that long, refreshing, peaceful sleep, which so often marks a favourable
crisis in dangerous illness'), Bickersteth's references to heaven's language
provide a clue to his method in his own writing on death. At the end
of the section headed 'I am the Resurrection and the Life', for example,
he refers to the corpse as 'the sacred tabernacle' and the burial-ground
as 'God's acre',[86] and we will see that in the deathbed scene in his epic
poem, *Yesterday, To-Day, and For Ever*, his favourite figure is that of
euphemism.

Interestingly, the first example in the OED of euphemism in the sense
of 'an instance of this figure' is from the second volume of James Beattie's *Elements of Moral Science* (1793), where he quotes Acts 7.60:

'When it is said of the martyr St Stephen, that "he fell asleep,"
[*ekoimēthē*] instead of – he died, the euphemism partakes of the nature
of metaphor, intimating a resemblance between sleep and the death of
such a person.'[87] A hundred years after Beattie, John Hutchison, DD,
writing on the disciples' 'slowness of apprehension' in the Lazarus narrative, explained that 'the figure of sleep, – the blessed euphemism for
death, – though not unknown to Jewish and Gentile modes of thought,
was far from being then in common use, as it is now', and describes
the words 'Lazarus is dead' as a translation into 'plain, direct, prosaic
words'.[88] Like Bickersteth, then, Hutchison thought of Jesus as an interpreter or translator, although unlike Bickersteth he acknowledged that
the 'figure of sleep' was generated in a this-worldly rather than an other-
worldly plane.

F. D. Maurice, in his discourses on John, passed over the problem of
the provenance and currency of the word 'sleep' as applied to death in
the New Testament, and, in much sharper contrast to Bickersteth, wrote
of Jesus as a teacher of a new language:

Our Lord is evidently teaching His disciples a new language; a language drawn
from nature and experience; one which had mixed itself with other forms of
speech in the dialect of all nations; but yet which was not easy for them to
learn, and which we understand very imperfectly yet.[89]

Maurice had developed this last point more fully two years previously,
in 1855, when he explained his reservations about some of the
euphemisms in common currency at mid-century. His text in *Death and
Life*, a sermon delivered at a memorial service for C. B. Mansfield at
Lincoln's Inn, where he was chaplain, was I Thessalonians 4.14: 'For
if we believe that Jesus died and rose again, even so them also which
sleep [*koimēthentas*] in Jesus will God bring with Him.' Maurice argued
here that the death and resurrection of Jesus Christ caused a change in
Paul's 'mode of speech', and he asked the congregation to recollect

the synonyms which we have adopted for the words – 'That man is dead.' All
point to some aspects of death; all are felt, at some point or other, to fail. We
say, sometimes, 'He sleeps in the grave,' – 'After life's fitful fever he sleeps
well!' There is something in such language which harmonizes with our feelings;
there is something which jars with them. You remember the bodily pain, the
restlessness of mind, you have seen in some one you have known well. The
thought that he is in repose is the one you fly to most eagerly. But oh, that
dreary, earthly repose! can it ever accord with the activity and energy which

you knew were in him, which were expressed in his words, which you saw in his countenance? Was this all to end in a dull stagnation? You task yourself to discover some better form of thought than that: – 'He has departed this life.' . . . 'He has yielded to the inevitable destiny of man.' . . .

Now compare these expressions with St. Paul's; 'He sleeps in Jesus.' There is the rest which you were longing to claim for him, the termination of uneasy struggles, of doubts, of sufferings. But it is rest in Him from whom all his energies and activities were derived, in Him who was the secret spring of his soul's life and his body's life.[90]

Although Maurice's use of the word 'synonym' glosses over the question of the difference between death and sleep, his subsequent comments directly address the problem that confronted not only preachers and theologians, but also poets and novelists: namely, working with the analogy of sleep without falling into literalism. Maurice's own comments on the aptness of St Paul's 'He sleeps in Jesus' flow from his uneasiness with the material associations evoked by such language, and are reminiscent of Schleiermacher's observation that the only 'essential thing in every conception [the Christian] may form of existence after death' is the 'persistent union of believers with the Redeemer'.

Returning to the passage from John 11, we have so far considered a number of interpretations which are in one sense uncritical: that is, they comment upon the exchange between Jesus and his disciples as if it were a verbatim record of an actual conversation. D. F. Strauss, whose *Life of Jesus* was first published in England in 1846, in Marian Evans's translation, takes a quite different approach:

The alleged conduct of the disciples . . . is such as to excite surprise. If Jesus had represented to them, or at least to the three principal among them, the death of the daughter of Jairus as a mere sleep, how could they, when he said of Lazarus, *he sleeps, I will awake him,* . . . think that he referred to a natural sleep? One would not awake a patient out of a healthy sleep; hence it must have immediately occurred to the disciples that here sleep (*koimēsis*) was spoken of in the same sense as in the case of the maiden. That, instead of this, the disciples understand the deep expressions of Jesus quite superficially, is entirely in the fourth evangelist's favourite manner, which we have learned to recognise by many examples. If tradition had in any way made known to him, that to speak of death as a sleep was part of the customary phraseology of Jesus, there would immediately spring up in his imagination, so fertile in this kind of antithesis, a misunderstanding corresponding to that figure of speech.[91]

Comparisons between the 'resuscitations of the dead' in the Old Testament and that of Lazarus had, in Strauss's view, long ago persuaded theologians of more 'enlarged' views that 'the resurrections in the New Testament are nothing more than mythi, which had their origin in the tendency of the early Christian church, to make her Messiah agree with the type of the prophets, and with the messianic ideal'.[92]

Within the boundaries of his historicist approach, Strauss seems to ignore the fact that memories are unreliable. More significantly, the words of misunderstanding in verse 12 – 'if he sleep, he shall do well' (*ei kekoimētai sōthēsetai*) – reveal, when read figuratively, the very secret of salvation itself, and the possibility of dying into life.[93] One modern commentator argues that sleep in the passage from John 11 is not simply a euphemism for death, and that the ambiguous word *kekoimētai* in verse 11 'points us to the deeper background of actual death': 'The theological statement which relativises the power of death by the reality of salvation moves on from the Old Testament and apocalyptic basis beyond the assertions of Hellenistic religion . . . proclaiming the basic powerlessness of death in the light of the resurrection.'[94]

This piece of commentary might have appealed to Matthew Arnold, who considered that Strauss's explanation of the miracles in the New Testament as a reiteration of the miracles of the Old was too systematic. For Arnold, 'every miracle has its own mode of growth and its own history, and the key to one is not the key to others'.[95] Arnold also disagreed with Strauss about the relative importance of the authorship of the fourth gospel: 'Not whether or no John wrote it, is for us the grand point, but whether or no Jesus said it.'[96] When he himself turns to John 11, therefore, he argues that the miracle story probably grew out of the *logion* (or saying), 'I am the resurrection and the life', and effaced the very truth which Jesus wished to convey.[97] In questioning the authenticity of the miracle story, Arnold ignores the misunderstanding under discussion and concentrates instead upon Jesus's initial statement in verse 11:

To the eye of Jesus, the kingdom of God, the reign of the saints, the introduction and triumph of everlasting righteousness, – that triumph in which re-live all the saints who are dead, and the saints who are yet alive live for evermore, – was at this moment beginning.[98]

Arnold's idealist interpretation of the *logion* can be compared with 'inaugurated eschatology',[99] and is based upon a suspicion of literalism that is reminiscent of his contemporary F. W. Farrar. We have seen that F. D. Maurice was also concerned about the possible materialist associations of the analogy of sleep, as in the idea of sleeping in the grave, for example, but that he laid special emphasis upon the raising of Lazarus because it specifically addresses the very issue of the physical (or material) reality of death.

The physical and the spiritual, the this-worldly and the other-worldly, the literal and the figurative: each category becomes problematic when applied to a miracle story that also contains a crucial *logion*, as we have seen in the work of nineteenth-century commentators. At one extreme Bickersteth blithely invokes 'the lofty freedom of the Divine style', while at the other Strauss and Arnold question the authenticity of the miracle. Only Maurice, in his uneasiness concerning the danger of misapplying Jesus's 'new language' in the clichés of the Victorian epitaph, comes close to acknowledging what is central to an understanding of nineteenth-century religious language associated with death and the future life: namely that it is at the very point of stress or fracture in the language of consolation that both the provisional nature of language and communication *and* the very grounds of Christian faith are laid bare. It is to that language of Christian consolation in Victorian literature and theology that we now turn.

CHAPTER I

🌾🌾

Death

Death and its two-fold aspect! wintry – one,
Cold, sullen, blank, from hope and joy shut out;
The other, which the ray divine hath touched,
Replete with vivid promise, bright as spring.
(Wordsworth, *The Excursion*, v.554–7) [1]

Evidence of the Victorians' obsessive interest in death is as widely available in the imaginative literature of the period as it is in the theology. The deathbed scene, for example, was a familiar literary convention not only in prose fiction but also in narrative poetry and biography;[2] and a remarkably high proportion of the lyric poetry of the period, particularly by women writers, addressed the themes of death and dying, bereavement and mourning.[3] Deathbed scenes and anthologies of poems for mourners are features of the 'Victorian cult of death', together with mourning costume and jewellery, the elaborate plumes and other trappings of the Victorian funeral, black-edged mourning paper and envelopes, the gravestone and the pious epitaph, and 'God's acre', whether small country churchyard or vast urban necropolis.[4]

The existence of a Victorian cult of death implies a measure of social and intellectual homogeneity. So too does the fact that a cluster of key ideas and symbols associated with death and the future life provided writers with a shared vocabulary which can be described as characteristically Victorian. The variety, however, of images of death itself in nineteenth-century literature reflects the wide range of responses to the subject that one would expect to find in any period. The traditional figure of death the Reaper, for example, plies his scythe in Bailey's *Festus*.[5] Charlotte Brontë describes death as 'that dread visitant before whose coming every household trembles', and Newman's Gerontius announces that a 'visitant / Is knocking his dire summons'.[6] But death is also often described as a friend. Death calls to Tennyson's Elaine 'like a friend's voice from a distant field / Approaching through the darkness' ('Lancelot and Elaine', 992–3).[7] Elizabeth Stone observes in *God's Acre; or, Historical Notices Relating to Churchyards* (1858) that

The much-suffering look on Death not as the destroying angel on the pale horse, not as the ghastly spectre whose unerring dart bears on its point the annihilation of all their joys and pleasures, but as the friend who is to give them release and repose, as the guide who is to lead them home.[8]

More grimly, in a Punch cartoon of the Hungry Forties entitled *The Poor Man's Friend*, the skeletal figure of death stands over the bed of a pauper who is praying for his release from a life of hardship and squalor (illustration 2). Through the window of his hovel can be seen the 'Union' or workhouse to which he would have been taken if his prayer had remained unanswered.[9] (The idea of death as the leveller, incidentally, familiar to readers of eighteenth-century graveyard poetry, was rather less prominent in the nineteenth century, when the elaborate funeral and mourning customs of the middle classes reinforced in death the subtle gradations of social hierarchy established in life.)

Our main concern in this study is with a hope which was popularized in the consolatory euphemism, 'Not lost, but gone before', and in such conventions as calling the earthly death-day of the departed his or her heavenly birthday.[10] Again, however, examples of a quite different perspective can be cited, such as the sense of death as a terminus (a fitting analogy in the railway age), which is reflected in the frequent references in the nineteenth century to Hamlet's 'undiscovered country, from whose bourn / No traveller returns'.[11] Whereas E. H. Bickersteth sees death as a new beginning, and writes of a 'veil' between mortals and departed spirits sometimes being lifted by God, who separates time from eternity,[12] Pater's Marius reflects that death 'must be for every one nothing less than the fifth or last act of a drama' (*Marius the Epicurean*, 1885; 28). A. O. J. Cockshut adopts the same analogy as Pater when he argues that Victorian biographers seldom distinguished clearly between two ideas of the moment of death: 'the curtain line, and the adumbration of the future'.[13]

What Wordsworth called 'death and its *two-fold* aspect' in *The Excursion* (1814) was, however, directly addressed by many theologians and preachers, poets, novelists, and painters in the nineteenth century. Frederick W. Robertson, for example, the famous Brighton preacher, argued that our difficulty in coming to terms with death results from the fact that our lives are dedicated to being, and surviving in order to be:

Talk as we will of immortality, there is an obstinate feeling that we cannot master, that we end in death; and *that* may be felt together with the firmest belief of a resurrection. Brethren, our faith tells us one thing, and our sensations tell us another. When we die, we are surrendering in truth all that with which we have associated existence. [14]

The double consciousness of faith, which holds the this-worldly and the other-worldly in tension, finds in death and the future life a subject which is at once fitting and problematic.

Like Frederick Robertson, F. D. Maurice acknowledged that the most devout of men and women know the anguish of doubt, and he valued greatly his friend Tennyson's treatment of 'honest doubt' in *In Memoriam* (1850). Maurice also argued in his discourses on the fourth gospel (1857) that the raising of Lazarus, in John 11, provides comfort to the bereaved because it meets the very question which they ask when a loved one dies: 'Can light ever penetrate into that darkness?'[15] He confessed in the second edition of his *Theological Essays* (1853) that he did not dare lose faith in an 'abyss of love'. The words that followed – 'I sink into death, eternal death, if I do so' – almost proved to be prophetic, as he suffered doubts and 'nervous fears' on his own deathbed, before affirming: 'I am not going to *Death* . . . I am going into *Life!*'[16]

These conflicting ideas and emotions associated with death in its two-fold aspect or paradoxical nature – as the first of the four last things, as terminus and point of departure, or as loss and gain – often focused upon two sites in the nineteenth century: the deathbed and the grave. Social and literary conventions relating to the deathbed included the visit from a doctor or priest, the presence of a loving attendant to whom a dying confession could be made or of a family on whom a dying blessing could be bestowed, the laying out of a corpse in a darkened room, the 'last visit' of the bereaved, and the closing of the coffin. Those associated with the grave included the funeral procession, the funeral itself, the burial, the erection of a memorial stone, and subsequent visits to the grave made by the bereaved.[17] These conventions formalized the different stages of death and bereavement, giving shape and thus possibly some meaning to a transitional phase between one state and another.[18]

Such transitions, whether physical (from living body to corpse) or spiritual ('from this world to the next'), are characteristically difficult and ambiguous. Victorian writing on death is frequently ambiguous, and in deathbed scenes and graveyard scenes – key sites of communication and interpretation – alternative meanings are often either conflated or confused, as in the Lazarus story. The function of analogy, for example, is often problematic in these contexts. By examining the naming of death as sleep, and, by extension, of the grave as a bed, as crucial examples of ambiguity in Victorian writing on death, we can approach the nineteenth-century debates concerning judgment and the future life (the subject of Chapters 2–4) via the problems of language associated with the subject.

THE DEATHBED: CONSOLATION AND COMMUNICATION

To sum up . . . in a few words the circumstances in which most people seem to think a happy death consists . . . ; – if a man has had distinct notice some considerable time before hand that his end was approaching, and has thus been enabled to occupy that interval in what is usually termed, preparation for death; – if he has been attended by a minister, and has received the sacrament of the Lord's Supper a little before his departure; – if, though he may have suffered considerably in the course of the disease, he at last dies calm and easy both in body and mind, in full possession of his faculties, and professing the most perfect confidence of his acceptance with God; and finally, if his body receives what is called christian burial in consecrated ground, and especially if a handsome monument is erected over it; – this person's death is thought to combine all the circumstances which are usually reckoned the most desirable, important, and satisfactory.

Now if such opinions, such cases, and such feelings as I have been describing, are rational and christian, we may expect to find them agreeable to the christian *Scriptures*; if otherwise, they cannot be unattended with danger . . .[19]

Richard Whateley, Professor of Political Economy at Oxford and later Archbishop of Dublin, was perhaps the best known of the group of Fellows known as the Oriel 'Noetics'. In contrast to the Evangelical who anxiously looked for signs of grace in a departing brother or sister in Christ, or the Roman Catholic who hurriedly arranged for the last rites to be administered to the dying, Whateley took a rational approach to what he called 'A Christian Departure' in his study entitled *A View of the Scripture Revelations Concerning a Future State* (1829). Conventions associated with the *ars moriendi* (art of dying), familiar to the educated English reader from Jeremy Taylor's *Holy Dying* (1651), were deeply rooted in the corporate memory of the faithful, and provided nineteenth-century novelists with excellent material on which to work. Like Whateley, however, although not always on such strictly scriptural grounds, writers of many different persuasions questioned both the validity and the efficacy of these conventions.

Take, for example, the desire to be 'attended by a minister'. Whereas Charles Reade assumed that the visit to the deathbed was the essential priestly function,[20] the 'spirit' who records a recent visit to earth 'to see and assist the passing away of a young girl' in the Spiritualist *Glimpses of a Brighter Land* (1871) holds different views. Although the visitant from the other side reports that she successfully 'unwound the threads of life that bound [the girl's spirit] to the earthly husk or covering', her efforts are not made easier by the presence of a clergyman, whose 'cold ignorant attempts at comfort' are ineffective, both for the dying child and her mother:

Yet the man was sincere, he preached that which he had learnt, and knew no more. Oh how I longed to flood his brain with truth divine, celestial truth, to open and expand the narrow portals of his mind, to let him see and feel the Father's love, to enable him to progress and teach others while yet on earth![21]

The inadequacy of the clergyman as a comforter of the dying was also the subject of Samuel Butler's black humour in his treatment of Christina Pontifex's death in *The Way of all Flesh*, which was begun in the early 1870s, but remained unpublished until 1903.[22] F. W. Farrar, who considered that the common Protestant view of judgment and damnation was abhorrent, and might therefore have agreed with Butler, was equally sceptical about deathbed conversions. In *Mercy and Judgment* (1881), the sequel to his sermons on *Eternal Hope*, he stated that in recent years he had been called to many deathbeds:

Those scenes have left on my mind the deep conviction that a death-bed very rarely makes any observable difference in the general habit of mind of the dying . . . very frequently I find the strongest possible disinclination to speak of religious subjects, or the habit of fencing off all approach to anything like a heart-searching intercourse . . . And, so far as I have seen, they die, in nine cases out of ten, exactly as they have lived.[23]

H. N. Oxenham, who wrote against Farrar during the controversy which followed the publication of *Eternal Hope*, shared his doubts about dying conversions, but saw the issue from the quite different perspective of Catholic eschatology:

Take . . . the case of what are called death-bed conversions. I am far from denying that such cases are possible, and may be not uncommon, though there is not, perhaps, much evidence to show for it . . . But the habits and associations of a lifetime are not so easily unlearnt, and the work of sanctification has still to be accomplished. The soul . . . must be cleansed, and braced, and perfected in the fires of God's righteous correction, before it can bear the unclouded sunshine of His love.[24]

The last words of the dying, however, had a special significance for the Victorians, and became something of a literary convention in their own right. Kingsley's *Alton Locke* (1850) ends with a poem entitled 'My Last Words', and Owen Meredith's poem, 'Last Words', appeared in an early volume of the *Cornhill*.[25] Thomas Hardy, whose use of place in his fiction and poetry reflects an agnostic's reverence for sites of painful human emotion, wrote of the 'sacredness of last words' in *The Mayor of Casterbridge* (1886; 45). When a large number of such words are brought together, as in the American F. R. Marvin's *The Last Words (Real and Traditional) of Distinguished Men and Women* (1900), a high degree of cultural shaping is revealed. The poet Mrs Hemans, for example, is reported to have said: 'I feel as if I were sitting with Mary at the feet of my Redeemer, hearing the music of his voice, and learning of Him to be meek and lowly.'[26] After that it is tempting to focus on more mundane, but also, ironically, more moving examples, such as Dickens's last words: because he was losing his balance and was afraid of falling, he said, 'On the ground'. But last words which convey spiritual experiences, including deathbed visions of some kind, also deserve serious attention. Elizabeth Barrett Browning's last words – 'It is beautiful' – typify the numberless beatific visions which have been recorded down the centuries, and which in the nineteenth century were often associated with the 'smile of death' which suggested a glimpse of future glory.

Nineteenth-century physiology was aware that contractions of the facial muscles sometimes follow death,[27] but a more interesting challenge to the sentimental tradition of the smile of death was Emily Brontë's, in *Wuthering Heights* (1847). When Cathy dies, Nelly Dean tells Heathcliff that she 'lies with a sweet smile on her face; and her latest ideas wandered back to pleasant early days' (16). Heathcliff's response is extremely violent, and he curses Cathy as a 'liar to the end', who would certainly not go to some conventional heaven. When Nelly later finds Heathcliff himself lying dead in the coffin-like bed at the Heights, the smile on his face is unnerving:

Mr. Heathcliff was there – laid on his back. His eyes met mine so keen and fierce, I started; and then, he seemed to smile.

I could not think him dead – but his face and throat were washed with rain; the bed-clothes dripped, and he was perfectly still.

. . .

I tried to close his eyes . . . They would not shut – they seemed to sneer at my attempts, and his parted lips, and sharp, white teeth sneered too! Taken with another fit of cowardice, I cried for Joseph.   (34)

Nelly's repeated 'seemed' indicates that this is one of the many problems of interpretation that she encounters as a narrator. *Wuthering Heights*, a profoundly elusive novel, thus provides a suitable context for a Gothic critique of the interpretation of the dying process.

Another convention associated with the Victorian deathbed was the presence of a comforter, usually a woman, who ministered to the dying. Priscilla Maurice, editor of *Sacred Poems for Mourners* and the author of manuals for sick-visitors, also published *Prayers for the Sick and Dying* (1853), the second part of which includes 'Texts Suited to be Read to Dying Persons', to be read '*very* slowly, *very* distinctly, and with pauses between; longer or shorter, according to the state of the person'.[28] The patient comforter who looked to the spiritual as well as the physical needs of the dying was often described as 'angelic'. Thackeray, for example, uses this stock epithet in *Vanity Fair* (1847–8): 'When women are brooding over their children, or busied in a sick-room, who has not seen in their faces those sweet angelic beams of love and pity?' (61). Levels of meaning can be confused, with unintended comic effect, however, where religious language is used in a realistic novel. In Dinah Craik's *John Halifax, Gentleman* (1856), for example, Phineas Fletcher, the narrator, describes the moment when the hero breaks the news to his future wife, Ursula March, that her father is dying:

One thing I can tell, for she said it to me herself afterwards, that he seemed to look down upon her like a strong, pitiful, comforting angel; a messenger sent by God.

Then she broke away, and flew up-stairs.   (13)

A word like 'angel', of course, has considerable potential for ambiguity. When Elizabeth Stone asserts in *God's Acre* that angels 'do most especially minister' at a deathbed, it is not immediately clear whether the signified is other-worldly or this-worldly, a guardian angel or an 'angelic' human being.[29] E. H. Bickersteth exploits this kind of ambiguity in a different way in his epic poem *Yesterday, To-Day, and For Ever* (1866), when the Seer describes the period in which he seemed to be hovering (a favourite word in deathbed scenes) between life and death:

> Six days I lay
> In that strange borderland, so she, who watch'd
> Unwearied as an angel day and night
> Beside my pillow, told me when I woke
> From the function of celestial love
> To drink in, like a thirsty traveller,
> The sweetness of her human love once more: –
> Never so sweet as now. They sin who deem
> There can be discord betwixt love and love.   (1.100–8)[30]

During this transitional phase, the Seer found in love the continuity between his experience on earth and the existence that was promised him, and that he is now enjoying, in heaven. His wife's angel-like 'watching' was an earnest both of his guardian angel's watching of his 'footsteps from the wicket gate of life' (1.464–5), and of the couple's reunion in paradise. Characteristically, Bickersteth idealizes where he might have attempted a negotiation between the real and the ideal. There is no hint here of the physical realities of the comforter's role beside a sick-bed, and no awareness of the potential irony in references to 'human love' where a man is dying with his sexual partner beside him.'[31] Rather, it is as if the pair were already in heaven, where there is no marriage or giving in marriage.

Philippe Ariès, a leading authority on the history and sociology of death, characterizes the post-Romantic deathbed as being charged with emotion and sexuality, and death as an event that is witnessed by a family who are now active participants in the drama.[32] In his sweep through the history of the West, Ariès draws other equally significant conclusions from a mass of data. He finds in the nineteenth-century cult of death, for example, a sense that death was unacceptable, and argues that it came to be thought of as 'Thy death'. (This tendency is reflected in the emphasis upon the bereaved person in Romantic English elegy.)[33] Many aspects of Victorian culture cry out for Ariès's psycho-sexual analysis. In everyday life, as well as in religious epic poems, the bed in which a woman died might well have been that in which she had conceived and given birth to her children. In a less mobile society than our own, this same bed might even have been a family heirloom, in which she herself had been conceived and born. The apogee of the public deathbed scene in the period is probably W. I. Walton's *The Last Moments of HRH The Prince Consort,* in which doctors and statesmen, as well as the grieving royal family, are gathered in the state bedchamber (illustration 3). John Morley contrasts this formal, establishment picture with a crude 'cut out' version of the event, in which Albert's children hurry to his embrace.[34] Walton's picture, however, not only suppresses emotion, but also conceals a potential for sexual irony, with the children of a fruitful marriage gathered near the bed. The overt analysis of the relationship between *eros* and *thanatos,* however, was largely the preserve of the Gothic in the nineteenth century, where the 'normal' (and safe) compartmentalizing of birth, marriage, and death was disrupted. The marriage-bed is shown to be a deathbed, for example, in *Wuthering Heights,* and in Sheridan Le Fanu's terrifying story, 'Schalken the Painter'.

Of more immediate relevance to our central theme, however, are the less sensational but equally important associations with the bed, to which Ariès pays little attention: namely, the bed as a place of rest, and of sleep from which we rise again each day to new life. When applied analogically to death and resurrection, in the novel, for example, the idea that the dead person 'sleeps' is fraught with technical difficulties. Bickersteth's poem, quoted above, is narrated by a Seer who has passed through death, and who views the earth and the universe, past, present, and future, from the 'other side'. Thus his description of waking from sleep to find his wife ('as an angel') beside him, is, from heaven's perspective, a type of that waking to new life (with a guardian angel) that is death. As such a privileged narrative perspective, however, was not normally adopted by the Victorian novelist or poet, the deathbed was generally viewed from a limited, this-worldly perspective in which the question of a future state was a matter of faith and hope. Set firmly in a temporal context, but perceived within the larger horizon of the eternal, the deathbed scene was the perfect site for an investigation through language of the problems of interpretation associated with death and its two-fold aspect.

The most basic problem of interpretation in Victorian death scenes is diagnostic: is the dying person alive or dead? In Browning's dramatic monologue, 'The Bishop Orders his Tomb at Saint Praxed's Church' (1845), the dying person himself is not always sure about this:

> As here I lie
> In this state-chamber, dying by degrees,
> Hours and long hours in the dead night, I ask
> 'Do I live, am I dead?' Peace, peace seems all.[35]

Many of Browning's most successful monologues work on what his Bishop Blougram calls 'the dangerous edge of things', where the paradoxes of human nature are most vividly displayed: 'the honest thief, the tender murderer, / The superstitious atheist'.[36] The worldly Bishop at Saint Praxed's does not anticipate transcendence through death, but rather perpetuity in the peaceful church that represents the nearest he has come to a glimpse of heaven:

> And up into the aery dome where live
> The angels, and a sunbeam's sure to lurk . . .

Newman, preaching on 'Holiness Necessary for Future Blessedness', argued that heaven would not be like this world, but much more like a church. Thus heaven, where every man must do *God's* pleasure, would be 'hell to an irreligious man'.[37] Browning's Bishop, whose eye stops at the dome of the church, reverses the simile (his church is like heaven), and thus puts off the question of judgment, heaven, and hell. Through the workings of his imagination, his deathbed becomes his tomb. Shaping himself into his own effigy ('I fold my arms as if they clasped a crook') he prepares for the sleep of death. Eternity, however, is understood from the this-worldly viewpoint of the monumental mason:

> And 'neath my tabernacle take my rest,
> With those nine columns round me, two and two . . .

The word 'tabernacle' (for Bickersteth a euphemism for the corpse) is here an architectural feature, and the effigy reposing beneath it – the Bishop's idealized self – substitutes for the immortal soul as the antithesis of and emotional defence against the corruption of the flesh:

> Gritstone, a-crumble! Clammy squares which sweat
> As if the corpse they keep were oozing through . . .

In 'The Bishop Orders his Tomb', the nature of the confusion of death with life reveals the spirituality of the dying person. In Thomas Hood's poem 'The Death-Bed' (1831) the confusion is of the more familiar kind – that shared by attendants at the bedside, who are interpreters:

> We watch'd her breathing thro' the night,
> Her breathing soft and low,
> As in her breast the wave of life
> Kept heaving to and fro!
>
> So silently we seem'd to speak –
> So slowly moved about,
> As we had lent her half our powers
> To eke her living out!
>
> Our very hopes belied our fears,
> Our fears our hopes belied –
> We thought her dying when she slept,
> And sleeping when she died!
>
> For when the morn came dim and sad –
> And chill with early showers,
> Her quiet eyelids closed – she had
> Another morn than ours![38]

The chiasmus at the heart of the poem, and of my present theme – 'We thought her dying when she slept, / And sleeping when she died' – is worked for from the opening line of the poem, where a gentle pressure is first applied to the simple but ambiguous words associated with the deathbed. 'Watch'd her breathing' suggests more than 'observed her respiration'. Other senses of 'watch' are present – to be vigilant or careful, and to stay awake – and 'breathing' also means, metonymically, living. As so often in nineteenth-century writing on death, the wave metaphor that follows, and that Tennyson used in *In Memoriam* (lyrics 11 and 19), barely suppresses the more familiar associations with death that it contains: life is said to 'ebb away', for example, and a dying person 'goes out with the tide'. In the second stanza, the emphasis shifts to those who 'watch'. They are no longer tensely passive, but, through an act of will, attempt the impossible: a transfusion of energy to the dying woman. Whereas the antithesis we/she cannot be resolved, the reversal of the antitheses in the third stanza (hope/fear, die/sleep) prepares for the collapse of this-worldly categories in the unwilled transcendence of the final stanza, when eyes that, against nature, close at daybreak, open to that other morn which is beyond the horizon of those who watch but cannot see. A problem of interpretation (is she asleep or dead?) has given way to an affirmation of transcendence through the analogy between sleep:awakening and death:resurrection.

To put this another way, the last two stanzas of 'The Death-Bed' bring together two kinds of interpretation: reading signs and making sense. Both are particularly challenging to the children who figure in many deathbed scenes. Bickersteth introduces the theme in *Yesterday, To-Day, and For Ever*, and shows how the questions of frightened children can be answered by referring them to the Bible. The Seer's children are summoned to his deathbed:

> They were but learners in the infant school
> Of sorrow, and were scarcely able yet
> To spell its simplest signs. But when they caught
> The meaning of their mother's words, and knew
> That I was going to leave them, one low sob
> Broke from them, like the sighing of the wind
> That frets the bosom of a silver lake
> Before a tempest.
> . . .
> I raised my head upon the pillow, saying,
>
> 'Weep not, my children, that your father's work
> Is over, and his travelling days are done.
> For I am going to our happy home,
> Jerusalem the golden, of which we
> On Sabbath evenings have so often sung,
> And wish'd the weary interval away
> That lay betwixt us and its pearly gates.'   (1.190–210)

The Seer's reference to family hymns supplies the children with a firm point of reference from which they can make sense of what is going on. It provides the key not only to Bickersteth's favourite methods in his writing on death, but also to the most characteristic Victorian response to bereavement. For the Seer's use of biblical language when he reminds his children of what they have been taught concerning death and the future life – 'The Bridegroom cometh quickly/', 'Let your loins / Be girded', 'the sleep of death', 'Your Father's house', and so on (1.220–9) is taken up by the children themselves as they read, one by one, 'in a low voice most musical / Some fragments of the book of life' (1.306–7). Publishing his epic poem shortly after Newman's *Dream of Gerontius,* Bickersteth substitutes the family of a married clergyman for Gerontius's 'Attendants', and portions of scripture for the last rites in the *Rituale Romanum.*

Whereas the grief of the Seer's children's parting from their father (1.374–85) is absorbed into a consolatory religious language, George Eliot's handling of a similar episode in 'Amos Barton', one of her *Scenes of Clerical Life* (1857), is stark and uncompromising. The Revd Amos Barton's wife, Milly, is dying. When she sends for her children, each responds according to his or her age – the eldest, Patty, bursting into sobs, while little Walter stretches out his arms and smiles (8). The children are led away before their mother dies, and they do not witness their father shrieking 'She isn't *dead?*' and being 'dragged out of the room'. Even at the beginning of her career as a novelist, George Eliot overtly treats the children's bemused sense of loss as a problem of interpretation, which she takes up in a reprise of the deathbed scene, with the children this time gathered around the grave:

Patty alone of all the children felt that mamma was in that coffin, and that a new and sadder life had begun for papa and herself . . . Fred and Sophy, though they were only two and three years younger, and though they had seen mamma in her coffin, seemed to themselves to be looking at some strange show. They had not learned to decipher that terrible handwriting of human destiny, illness and death. Dickey . . . stood close to his father, with great rosy cheeks, and wide open blue eyes, looking first up at Mr Cleves and then down at the coffin, and thinking he and Chubby would play at that when they got home.

(9)

The only continuity between the deathbed and the grave in 'Amos Barton' is that of sustained grief and an inability to make sense of events. Amos's consolation is limited to 'outward solace', in the form of acts of human kindness from a formerly hostile congregation, and these cannot 'counteract the bitterness of this inward woe'. Whereas Bickersteth bathes the wounds of bereavement in a warm solution of consolatory texts, the bleakness of George Eliot's treatment of the subject is relieved only by a solitary, and thus highly charged use of religious language:

There were men and women standing in that churchyard who had bandied vulgar jests about their pastor, and who had lightly charged him with sin; but now, when they saw him following the coffin, pale and haggard, he was consecrated anew by his great sorrow,' and they looked at him with respectful pity.

The ordinal is emptied of sacramental mystery in the humanist consecration of the sufferer through sympathy. Two years earlier George Eliot had fiercely attacked Revd Edward Young, author of *Night Thoughts* (1744–5), whose description of the Last Judgment she described as 'a compound of vulgar pomp, crawling adulation, and hard selfishness, presented under the guise of piety'. In the same essay she referred, in contrast, to an ideal that was to be her own as a writer: 'the widening and strengthening of our sympathetic nature'.[39]

Returning, however, to the theme of the child's failure fully to grasp the meaning of death, I wish briefly to consider the death of Helen Burns in *Jane Eyre* (1847), a *locus classicus* of its kind, and too well known to require detailed description. It begins with an exchange in which Jane is precipitated into knowledge of a reality which she attempts to efface:

'Why are you come here, Jane? It is past eleven o'clock: I heard it strike some minutes since.'

'I came to see you, Helen: I heard you were very ill, and I could not sleep till I had spoken to you.'

'You came to bid me good-bye, then: you are just in time probably.'

'Are you going somewhere, Helen? Are you going home?'

'Yes; to my long home – my last home.'

'No, no, Helen:' I stopped, distressed.   (9)

Earlier, Jane has defeated Mr Brocklehurst by refusing to engage with him in the formal religious language of the catechism, answering his questioning on the avoidance of hell with the famous response: 'I must keep in good health, and not die' (4). Now, her down-to-earth interpretation of the word 'good-bye', which is uncannily reminiscent of the disciples misunderstanding Jesus's reference to Lazarus falling asleep, defers her recognition of the most common contemporary ideas of death and heaven: namely, parting, or departure, and the long, or last home. The two girls discuss the question of a 'future state', with Jane, as usual, questioning Helen at every point, until they fall asleep. They are discovered in one another's arms in the morning: 'I was asleep, and

Helen was – dead.' The pause gives added weight to the contrast between their states, or, more accurately, that antithesis which Strauss located in John 11. Within this pause, however, there is also a trace of the word 'asleep', perhaps from Helen's description in an earlier chapter of eternity as 'a *rest* – a mighty home' (6), or from the words that are almost her last: 'I feel as if I could sleep' (9). By a kind of unconscious association, the words 'dead' and 'asleep' are superimposed. Thus the reality revealed in the cold light of day, and conveyed through antithesis, contains the germ of a hope of a future life through a potential synonymy of the kind F. D. Maurice discussed in the funeral sermon quoted earlier. Fifteen years after Helen's death, the adult Jane has a gravestone made for her. It is inscribed with her name, and the word 'Resurgam' (9).[40]

Jane meditates upon Helen's ideas on death later in the novel, and her youthful rejection of her friend's total denial of the world in favour of a heavenly reward is tempered in adulthood by her respect for her universalist creed. Jane's thoughts go back to Helen when she is called to her Aunt Reed's deathbed at Gateshead-hall. The deathbed scenes contrast sharply in their emotional content:

In pondering the great mystery, I thought of Helen Burns: recalled her dying words – her faith – her doctrine of the equality of disembodied souls. I was still listening in thought to her well-remembered tones – still picturing her pale and spiritual aspect, her wasted face and sublime gaze, as she lay on her placid death-bed, and whispered her longing to be restored to her divine Father's bosom – when a feeble voice murmured from the couch behind: 'Who is that?'   (21)

This is one of several moments in the novel when Jane is brought back from a dream-like state to a present reality, and here she has to re-establish her identity with her aunt, who has summoned her so that she can 'ease her mind' before she dies – a familiar desire among the dying. Aunt Reed veers alarmingly between levels of meaning:

'Well: I must get it over. Eternity is before me: I had better tell her. Go to my dressing-case, open it, and take out a letter you will see there.'

The awkward contiguity of the lofty private thought about eternity and the prosaic instruction concerning a letter in a dressing-case reflects not only the tension in *Jane Eyre* between the demands of the novel and those of romance, but also that between the other-worldly and the this-worldly in all Victorian writing on death.

When Jane returns to Thornfield from Gateshead-hall, quietly, and in the evening, Rochester plays with the very sentiments which, if Jane had loved her aunt, would have been sacrosanct:

'Yes – just one of your tricks: not to send for a carriage . . . but to steal into the vicinage of your home along with twilight, just as if you were a dream or a shade. What the deuce have you done with yourself this last month?'
'I have been with my aunt, sir, who is dead.'
'A true Janian reply! Good angels be my guard! She comes from the other world – from the abode of people who are dead; and tells me so when she meets me alone here in the gloaming!' (22)

Rochester's characteristically irreverent use of the language of the death-bed, and the touch of Gothic which he adds for effect, disperse any minimal emotion which had been attached to the cold, inflexible Aunt Reed in her dying.[41]

Although adult responses to death and bereavement are, of course, just as harrowing as those of children, they are often held in tension with a mature faith in some kind of life after death. As a result, a blurring effect is frequently to be detected in the language of consolation. The correspondence of the Hares, a prominent Broad Church family, provides several interesting and characteristic examples. Like many other works of its kind, Augustus Hare's pious family record entitled *Memorials of a Quiet Life* (1872–6) is littered with references to the deaths of friends and relations. The context in which these are described is captured in Hare's thumb-nail sketch of his adoptive mother, Maria, the inspiration of and main correspondent in the Memorials. The writer's loving memory, Maria's own fervent religious beliefs, and, possibly, the influence of Baron Bunsen (a family friend), combine to create an idealized vision:

During the early years of her life at Lime my dearest mother seemed to live so completely in heaven that all outward times and seasons were so many additional links between it and her. Spring came to her as the especial season of the Resurrection, and in the up-springing of each leaf and flower she rejoiced as typical of the rising again of all her loved and lost ones.[42]

Closer to the complexity of reality than this prose version of *The Christian Year* are the mourning letters that Hare reproduces in the *Memorials*. Here, for example, Lucy Hare (née Stanley), wife of Marcus Hare, writes to Maria Hare, her sister-in-law, on 28 March 1842:

Our beloved Mary Grey has entered into her Rest, on the evening of yesterday, Easter Sunday, the same day *our* mother entered into hers; at six o'clock she fell asleep. All she had so dreaded of the struggle between soul and body was spared her; there was no struggle, she slept most of the day, all pulsation seemed to cease at four, and she breathed her last sigh two hours after, so peacefully, they scarcely knew when she was gone . . . We had heard on Saturday she was so much better, we did not think how near she was – that the gate of Everlasting Life was opening for her, and that in a few hours she was to be with the Lord.[43]

The juxtaposition of the mundane and the supramundane is similar to the Aunt Reed deathbed scene in *Jane Eyre*. In the first sentence, 'fell asleep' has a religious meaning, and reinforces the words, 'entered into her Rest' (Hebrews 4). Yet in the next sentence, which describes the last hours of the dying person, the word 'sleep' is used in the purely secular and commonplace sense: 'she slept most of the day'. It seems, then, that like the disciples in John 11, the writer of the letter can separate the two senses to the extent of forgetting the existence of the other. When the two meanings are brought together, however, in the third sentence, the effect is one that is becoming familiar. The prosaic 'she was so much better' prepares for the plain 'how near she was [to death]', which is elided into the euphemistic 'the gate of Everlasting Life was opening for her'.

In private correspondence of this kind, rational thought tends to be subordinated to the emotional needs of the writer and the recipient, and, even in a learned clerical family such as the Hares, the profound theological implications of affirming that the dead person is meeting the Lord in a few hours are silently passed over in order to draw consolation from familiar pieties. Indeed, it is for the same reason that precisely the opposite of this separation of two senses of 'sleep' occurs in a letter of 1845 from Maria Hare, where she describes the death of her brother-in-law, Marcus: 'At five o'clock, on Wednesday morning, our beloved Marcus gave up his spirit into his Father's hands, and literally 'fell asleep' without a struggle.'[44] The quotation marks around the familiar biblical phrase contradict the word 'literally'. Under the pressure of emotion, the writer conflates an actual physical death which looked like falling asleep, and the spiritual transcendence of death promised in the New Testament.

Returning to prose fiction, we can examine the effect of emotion attached to death on the treatment of the subject in *John Halifax*,

Gentleman, quoted earlier. Mr March's transition from sleep to death, at the aptly named Enderley, is concisely and conventionally marked:

We both ran through the empty kitchen to the foot of the stairs that led to Mr. March's room.

Mr. March's room! Alas, he owned nothing now on this fleeting, perishable earth of ours. He had gone from it: the spirit stealing quietly away in sleep. He belonged now to the world everlasting. (13)

It is concern for the dead man's daughter, Ursula, that proves to be the controlling emotion in this episode, and the word 'sleep' is made to do no work here. Later in the novel, John Halifax's own daughter, Muriel, who is blind, dies in the same house. Phineas Fletcher records that the night seemed very like that on which Mr March had died. In the morning, long before it is light, Phineas is greeted by Guy, one of Muriel's young brothers, who plans to go out and gather beech-nuts and fir-cones for her:

'It's her birth-day to-day, you know.'

It was, for her. But for us – Oh, Muriel, our darling – darling child!

Let me hasten over the story of that morning, for my old heart quails before it still.

John went early to the room up-stairs. It was very still. Ursula lay calmly asleep, with baby Maud in her bosom; on her other side, with eyes wide open to the daylight, lay, – that which for more than ten years we had been used to call 'blind Muriel.' She saw, now. (28)

Again we find the use of dashes to indicate elisions: 'But for us [it was her death-day]'; 'lay, [Muriel's dead body].' The sense that Muriel has passed into a new life (it is her heavenly as well as her earthly birthday), and into a light which for her is indeed new and glorious, is heightened by the presence of the quietly sleeping figures of her mother and baby sister, in a way that is reminiscent of Helen Burns's death in *Jane Eyre*. When the adults of the family later gather around her bed, Phineas Fletcher reports: 'One could almost fancy the little maid had just been said "good-night" to, and left to dream childish dreams on her nursery pillow, where the small head rested so peacefully.' By a clumsy plot device the narrator is left to witness the grief-stricken John Halifax 'alone' with his daughter and imploring her to return to him. The chapter ends with a plaintive comment from Phineas, itself like an echoing call: 'But thou wert with the angels, Muriel – Muriel!' This part of the narrative is rounded off in the opening sentence of the following chapter, which carries the metaphor of sleep over from the deathbed to the bed that is the grave: 'We went home, leaving all that was mortal of our darling sleeping at Enderley underneath the snows' (29). The snow loses none of its chill through the association with the white sheets of the child's nursery bed, but its whiteness reinforces the sense of her innocence which had been established in the preceding chapter.

In contrast, then, to the death of Mr March, Muriel's is described with intense emotion, and her passing from this world to the next is softened, or blurred, through the use of terms that slip between literal and metaphorical meanings: birthday, lay . . . asleep, eyes . . . saw, daylight, good night, dreams, rested . . . peacefully, sleeping. Phineas Fletcher, as a retrospective narrator, controls this ironic slippage from the beginning of the passage quoted, where the elided 'death-day' is antithetical to two senses of 'birthday', which are themselves mutually antithetical in a different plane. It is often through such misunderstandings and ambiguities that the pain of bereavement is accommodated in consolatory language in Victorian writing on death.

Victorian deathbed scenes involving children have been the subject of much adverse criticism. In a letter of 1881, Gerard Manley Hopkins commented in detail on Robert Bridges's poem 'On a Dead Child', which Bridges himself considered to be the best he had written. Hopkins argues that although it is a 'fine poem', neither the rhythm nor the thought is 'flowing enough', and the diction is 'not exquisite', but belongs to

a familiar commonplace about 'Reader, have you never hung over the pillow of . . . pallid cheek, clammy brow . . . long, long night-watches . . . surely, Sir Josiah Bickerstaff, there is *some* hope! O say not all is over. It cannot be.' You know. [Hopkins's ellipses.][45]

By this date the 'death of the child' has become so conventionalized and sentimentalized that Hopkins's amusing parody is aimed at a large target. Early in Bridges's poem, an uncanny moment of recognition reverses the usual sequence from life to death:

> To me, as I move thee now in the last duty
> Dost thou with a turn or gesture anon respond;
> Startling my fancy fond
> With a chance attitude of the head, a freak of beauty.

Here is a subject fit for Thomas Hardy, who would have drawn out the irony of this 'freak of beauty'. Bridges, however, maintains the idealizing tone:

> So I lay thee there, thy sunken eyelids closing, –
> Go lie then there in thy coffin, thy last little bed! –
> Propping thy wise, sad head,
> Thy firm, pale hands across thy chest disposing.[46]

Much twentieth-century criticism on the treatment of the death of children in Victorian fiction – little Paul in *Dombey and Son* (1846–8), for example, or Eric in F. W. Farrar's *Eric; or, Little by Little* (1858), or William in Mrs Henry Wood's *East Lynne* (1861) – is hostile. Peter Coveney discusses the deathbed scenes in *East Lynne* in a chapter entitled 'Reduction to Absurdity', arguing that 'William's death is the one last, careful, twist of the knife of the sadist masquerading as moralist': 'It is part . . . of what might be called the 'death-wish' of the whole work.'[47] It is certainly true that the punishment of Lady Isabel for her adultery, and for her abandonment of her husband and family, borders on the sadistic. The infuriated Coveney, however, passes over interesting features of the episode, such as the confusion of meanings that I have noted elsewhere. The dying William's question, 'Papa . . . is the trial over?', at first elicits no reply from his father, who does not know whether the boy refers to his last illness or to the current trial of a murderer (III.20). William's sister, Lucy, mistakes his 'Good-bye' in the same way that Jane mistakes Helen's in *Jane Eyre*. The most significant example of misinterpretation, however, and the most ambitious, is that on which the whole episode is based: Madame Vine, the governess who weeps at the bed side, is in fact Lady Isabel, the boy's disguised and disfigured mother. Left alone with her dying son, she flings up her arms 'in a storm of sobs':

'Oh, William, darling! in this dying moment let me be to you as your mother!'
Again he unclosed his weary eyelids. It is probable that he only partially understood.
'Papa's gone for her.'
'Not *her*! I – I – ' Lady Isabel checked herself, and fell sobbing on the bed.

Her self-disclosure to her son, who cannot take it in, prepares for her deathbed confession to her husband, which soon follows (III.21). In both cases the hope of reunion where they neither marry, nor are given in marriage, and where the bond between the mother and her children can in some way be renewed, underpins both deathbed scenes.

Coveney, however, is particularly incensed by the opening paragraph of the chapter, which is somewhat gruesomely entitled 'The Death Chamber':

> By the side of William Carlyle's dying bed knelt the Lady Isabel. The time was at hand, and the boy was quite reconciled to his fate. Merciful indeed is God to dying children! It is astonishing how very readily, where the right means are taken, they may be brought to look with pleasure rather than fear, upon their unknown journey.

Coveney exaggerates when he states that 'one might excusably feel more kinship with the mutterings of savagery', and that the word "pleasure' gives the whole emotional facade away'.[48] Mrs Henry Wood has, in Coveney's view, 'perhaps said too much'. Perhaps Coveney would prefer the child to die in fear? We have seen that in *Yesterday, To-Day, and For Ever* the Seer's children are buoyed up in their grief by consolatory hymns and Bible readings that affirm the resurrection of the body and the life everlasting. William Carlyle and his parents discuss the description of heaven in the Revelation, and John Martin's famous painting, *The Plains of Heaven* (illustration 8). The boy is certain that he will be fetched in a boat, as in the picture, and is only concerned to know whether Jesus can be in all the boats. Mrs Wood, like E. H. Bickersteth, draws on a shared cultural resource in her treatment of William's consolation which cannot be brushed lightly aside.

Perhaps the most moving and painful example of this kind of consolation in the nineteenth century is recorded in Mrs Catharine Tait's narrative of the death through scarlet fever of five daughters, aged between one and ten years, between 6 March and 10 April 1856, in the Deanery at Carlisle. Catharine Tait, the youngest daughter of Archdeacon Spooner, and her husband Archibald, who later became Archbishop of Canterbury, survived this ordeal only through faith, and in the knowledge of the widespread sympathy aroused by their bereavements, including that of the Queen herself. Both they and their children drew upon hymns and Bible passages to sustain them at this time. Three weeks after the birth of baby Lucy, who survived (together with a son, Crauford), 'Chatty', aged five, died. The eldest daughter, 'Catty', chose a hymn for the remaining children to sing in the schoolroom:

> Here we suffer grief and pain,
> Here we meet to part again,
> In heaven we part no more.
>   Oh! that will be joyful,
>   Joyful, joyful, joyful!
>   Oh! that will be joyful,
>   When we meet to part no more.[49]

This children's hymn, which Catharine Tait quotes in full, was one of many of its type sung in Victorian homes, as well as in Sunday Schools.[50] So the language of these hymns, and the themes to which they repeatedly return – Jerusalem the Golden, families meeting in heaven, Jesus the good shepherd – were not reserved for Sundays and church, but were part of everyday life, particularly for clerical families like the Bickersteths or the Taits. They therefore provided a genuinely consolatory discourse at such times of crisis.

Like the story of the raising of Lazarus, the death of a child is a stern test of faith, and the two are brought together in Mrs Tait's narrative after the third death, that of Frances, aged three. The parents did not tell their firstborn child, 'Catty', who was already ill, that her sister had died:

We had not dared to tell you, but I believe that God Himself had revealed to you the tidings of joy. She slept, but as the coffin which contained the form of her beloved Frances crossed the threshold of our door, she raised herself in her bed, and with a loud voice said, 'Jesus cried, Lazarus, come forth. And he that was dead came forth, bound hand and foot with grave-clothes; and Jesus said, Loose him, and let him go.' When she had said this, she lay quite still in a deep sleep.[51]

When Catty herself is dying she looks 'upward towards heaven' and points there 'distinctly with her finger':

While pointing upward I said, 'She sees in heaven her Chatty, her Susan and Frances.' When I mentioned the name of the latter, of whom before we had not spoken to her as taken from us, a brighter light came upon her, and again she pointed clearly and distinctly, and then with an earnestness no words can convey, stretched forth both her hands to be taken also.[52]

Two acts of interpretation are going on here: the daughter's and the mother's. Both are informed by faith that is grounded in scripture. Significantly, however, Catharine Tait does not, like Bickersteth, pass over the terrible reality of a painful death. She writes of the death of little Susan:

The little body was quite stiff, the arms and legs twitching . . . It was a sight full of agony; the conflict with death was long. Between six and seven more hours we kept our sad watch, expecting every moment that all would be over. It was between one and two when our darling little Susan left our poor home on earth to join her Chatty in the Fold above . . . I never saw my little lamb again.[53]

As in the correspondence of the Hare family, death itself is marked by a transition from a descriptive to a consolatory religious language, in this case the language of children's hymns: 'Fold above', 'little lamb'. Even in the earlier, descriptive sentence, however, the words 'agony' and 'conflict' place the child's suffering in the context of Christ's passion, through which the hope of resurrection was won.

Coveney's critique of *East Lynne* takes no account of the fact that for a girl like Mary, aged eight, the last of the five Tait daughters to die, death had from her earliest babyhood seemed 'a great and blessed reality, the way by which she was to attain her real life'.[54] Dean Tait wrote in his diary, five months after these tragic weeks of illness and death: 'May the memory of these afflictions help to sanctify my heart.'[55] He also recorded at this time that he had been reading Trench's introduction to *Sacred Poems for Mourners*, and found his analysis of the burial service 'very striking'.[56] A culture which throws up volumes such as Priscilla Maurice's may seem quaint, morbid, or even sinister to late-twentieth-century eyes. To Archibald Tait or to Edward Henry Bickersteth (who himself published memorials of a daughter who died at the age of nineteen),[57] such volumes were aids to understanding death and its two-fold aspect within the horizon of eternal life.

THE GRAVE, AND THE ANALOGY OF NATURE

Whereas Richard Whateley's critique of people's idea of a 'happy death' and a good burial was grounded in scripture,[58] Wordsworth's critique of early-nineteenth-century customs and attitudes in his 'Essay upon Epitaphs' (1810) was based upon the authority of nature. The poet's description of the traditional 'parish-church, in the stillness of the country', as a 'visible centre of a community of the living and the dead', and his comments on 'the soothing influences of nature', could be cited as examples of the 'Victorian Wordsworth' – the Wordsworth of John Keble and of Matthew Arnold.[59] Earlier in the essay he contrasts the burial grounds in modern towns and cities with the Greek and Roman practice of interment by the wayside, asking the reader to imagine the impact of the 'lively and affecting analogies' such as 'death as a sleep overcoming the tired wayfarer' on ancient monuments:

These, and similar suggestions, must have given, formerly, to the language of the senseless stone a voice enforced and endeared by the benignity of that nature with which it was in unison. – We, in modern times, have lost much of these advantages; and they are but in a small degree counterbalanced to the inhabitants of large towns and cities, by the custom of depositing the dead within, or contiguous to, their places of worship . . .

In moving the site of burial – and thus the memorial stone – from the wayside to the interior of a church, the immediacy of certain analogies is lost. The Victorian cult of the rural or semi-rural burial site, in the country churchyard or tree-lined suburban cemetery, represents an attempt to restore something of that immediacy by placing the memorial stone in a context which is redolent of the 'soothing influences of nature'. The aim of this section is to demonstrate that, as in Victorian deathbed scenes, language comes under great pressure in what can broadly be described as graveyard scenes, when analogies drawn from different scriptural and secular sources conflict or collide with each other. And Wordsworth provides a fitting starting point, as some of the contradictions and difficulties encountered by Victorian writers are at least partly attributable to him.

Wordsworth's 'Essay upon Epitaphs' was later reprinted as an appendix to Books v–vii of *The Excursion* (1814), a work which has been described as 'almost the Bible' of the early-Victorian poetry-reading public.[60] His description in Book v of Grasmere church, 'screened by tufted trees' (81) and with rafters like 'leafless underboughs, in some thick wood' (148), and of its incumbent, who loves his 'native soil' (116), emphasizes their naturalness. Stephen Prickett has argued that Wordsworth's organicist aesthetic profoundly influenced Keble, Newman, and F. D. Maurice, among others, in their thinking on the nature of the Church of England.[61] The portrayal of the Anglican clergyman in *The Excursion* suggests that these churchmen were indebted to Wordsworth for his treatment of feeling and moral truth rather than of theology, for the Pastor is notoriously vague on

matters of doctrine. Of special interest here is Wordsworth's avoidance
of the problems associated with death and the future life which Victorian writers were later to address.

As in Gray's 'Elegy', the grander monuments within Grasmere church
('all / Ending in dust', 174–5) are briefly described and then left in favour
of the graves in the 'green churchyard' (229). The latter, however, proves
to be the site of conflicting interpretations. For the sceptical Solitary it is
a 'subterraneous magazine of bones' (345). For the Poet this 'pregnant
spot of ground' (371) gives rise to mixed emotions and thoughts. The most
significant interpretation, however, and the most surprising, is that of the
Pastor himself, for although he refers to Christ as Saviour (and
Wordsworth made various 'Christianizing' additions to the poem in later
years), he says nothing about judgment, and emphasizes human solidarity
rather than resurrection in his references to the dead:

> To a mysteriously-united pair
> This place is consecrate; to Death and Life,
> And to the best affections that proceed
> From their conjunction; consecrate to faith
> In Him who bled for man upon the cross;
> Hallowed to revelation; and no less
> To reason's mandates; and the hopes divine
> Of pure imagination; – above all,
> To charity, and love, that have provided,
> Within these precincts, a capacious bed
> And receptacle, open to the good
> And evil, to the just and the unjust;
> In which they find an equal resting-place:
> Even as the multitude of kindred brooks
> And streams, whose murmur fills this hollow vale,
> Whether their course be turbulent or smooth,
> Their waters clear or sullied, all are lost
> Within the bosom of yon crystal Lake,
> And end their journey in the same repose!
>
> And blest are they who sleep; and we that know,
> While in a spot like this we breathe and walk,
> That all beneath us by the wings are covered
> Of motherly humanity, outspread
> And gathering all within their tender shade,
> Though loth and slow to come!   (v.903–27)

The Pastor's subtext is from the Sermon on the Mount: 'Thou shalt love thy neighbour, and hate thine enemy . . . for he maketh his sun to rise on the evil and on the good, and sendeth rain on the just and on the unjust' (Matthew 5.43, 45). His speech, however, draws more heavily upon 'reason' and 'imagination' than upon the revealed Word in scripture. Consciously or unconsciously he takes the rain in the gospel passage into the natural simile of the streams which debouch into the adjacent lake. The Poet, the Wanderer and the Solitary have followed the same track as both a funeral procession (down from the fells to the church), and a stream (down to the lake).

For the Pastor, then, the graveyard by the lake is a 'capacious bed', a communal resting-place rather than the orthodox 'God's acre' of individual 'narrow beds'. The absence of discussion on the subject of judgment and a future life partly explains why Evangelicals attacked the laxity of the representation of faith in *The Excursion*.[62] Death and life are 'mysteriously-united' in the Pastor's existential interpretation of the churchyard because death defines the finished shape of the lives of those whose 'authentic epitaphs' or epitomes (650–1) he is about to narrate. Those lives are characterized by obscure suffering and resignation, and it has been suggested that the 'primacy of mind over faith' makes the poem a meditative rather than a devotional work.[63]

Evidence of this is supplied by the epigraph to this chapter, in which the Pastor speaks of 'death and its two-fold aspect', and by a passage that precedes it, where he affirms that human life is 'either fair and tempting' or 'a forbidding tract of cheerless view', depending on how it is 'looked at, or approached' (526–30). The 'contrast' he draws is, however, on his own account even more appropriate to death than to life:

> Thus, when in changeful April fields are white
> With new-fallen snow, if from the sullen north
> Your walk conduct you hither, ere the sun
> Hath gained his noontide height, this churchyard, filled
> From east to west, before you will appear
> An unillumined, blank, and dreary plain,
> With more than wintry cheerlessness and gloom
> Saddening the heart. Go forward, and look back;
> Look, from the quarter whence the lord of light,
> Of life, of love, and gladness doth dispense
> His beams; which, unexcluded in their fall,

> Upon the southern side of every grave
> Have gently exercised a melting power;
> *Then* will a vernal prospect greet your eye,
> All fresh and beautiful, and green and bright,
> Hopeful and cheerful: – vanished is the pall
> That overspread and chilled the sacred turf,
> Vanished or hidden; and the whole domain
> To some, too lightly minded, might appear
> A meadow carpet for the dancing hours.   (v.531–51)

The 'lord of light' is the beneficent God who works through his creation rather than the incarnate Son of John 1 (conflated with the forces of nature and thus erased in a submerged pun on sun/Son). Although Wordsworth's use of place and of natural analogy in *The Excursion* provided a model for Victorian writers (and the passage quoted above was particularly well known),[64] he did not address the specific problem of accommodating the 'lively hope' of the gospel within his scheme of resignation in life and memorializing through epitaphs in death. Rather, the Solitary's 'slighted Hope' (III.459) and the Wanderer's 'Admiration, Hope, and Love' (IV.763) are left in opposition in the poem, as the Pastor, whose title emphasizes his role as ministering shepherd rather than administering priest, recounts the lives of the flock who lie in his green churchyard.

The relationship between the Wordsworth of *The Excursion* and his Victorian successors is complex. Certainly his powerful influence can be traced in the emphasis upon natural process in Victorian graveyard scenes. Unlike in Book v of *The Excursion*, however, the grave is often portrayed in these later scenes as the site of a transition from the death-bed to a future state, and of a hope of resurrection. I have suggested that the contradictions and difficulties encountered by Victorian writers are partly attributable to Wordsworth, but we have also seen already that contradictions and difficulties associated with death and burial abound in New Testament theology itself. Similarly, the burial service in the Book of Common Prayer, far from reinforcing the manageable stages of separation enshrined in Victorian mourning customs, consoled the bereaved through affirmations of faith which are based upon some of the most challenging paradoxes and contraries in the New Testament. The priests and clerks 'meeting the Corpse at the entrance of the Church-yard, and going before it, either into the Church, or towards the Grave, shall say, or sing',

I am the resurrection and the life, saith the Lord: he that believeth in me, though he were dead, yet shall he live: and whosoever liveth and believeth in me shall never die.   (*St. John* xi.25, 26)

The lesson, from 1 Corinthians 15, teaches that the resurrection of the dead is sown in corruption, dishonour, and weakness, and is raised in incorruption, glory, and power. It is sown a natural body, and raised a spiritual body, in St Paul's natural analogy. And in the supremely earthly and earthy rite of committal itself, when the body is lowered into the ground, earth to earth, ashes to ashes, dust to dust, the priest shall say:

in sure and certain hope of the Resurrection to eternal life, through our Lord Jesus Christ; who shall change our vile body, that it may be like unto his glorious body, according to the mighty working, whereby he is able to subdue all things to himself.

The scriptural language of the burial service speaks of a resurrection that is as miraculous as the *hidden and mysterious* workings of nature: of life in death, of incorruption in corruption, of rising in descending. Joseph Butler, in the *Analogy of Religion*, cites not only the dramatic transformations which occur in the chrysalis, but also the scarcely discernible changes which are continually taking place in trees and in human body tissue. Similarly, graveyard scenes in Victorian literature seek to draw consolation not only from St Paul's description of the miraculous transformation of the spiritual body 'in the twinkling of an eye', but also, and simultaneously, from natural analogies such as diurnal and seasonal cycles which speak of an organicist gradualism that is also available to secular forms of consolation.

Like the deathbed, then, the grave is a site of conflicting ideas. It is also a site of strong and often confused emotions, not least because the mourner will naturally meditate on his or her own 'end' as well as that of the 'departed'. Tennyson shaped his 'Supposed Confessions of a Second-Rate Sensitive Mind', written before the death of Arthur Hallam, around lugubrious meditations which are not dissimilar to those of the mid-eighteenth-century 'graveyard' tradition. In Tennyson's poem, however, the separation of the speaker from the community of the faithful is registered in the subjunctive mode:

> How sweet to have a common faith!
> To hold a common scorn of death!
>   And at a burial to hear
>   The creaking cords which wound and eat

> Into my human heart, whene'er
>   Earth goes to earth, with grief, not fear,
> With hopeful grief, were passing sweet!   (33–9)

The alienation of the sensitive mind anticipates that of the narrator of
Maud (1855), Tennyson's 'little *Hamlet*'. From the effect of the
'creaking cords' on 'my heart', the poem moves finally to an imaginative
projection to 'my' grave and the inevitable decay of 'my' body:

>   Oh teach me yet
>   Somewhat before the heavy clod
> Weighs on me, and the busy fret
> Of that sharp-headed worm begins
> In the gross blackness underneath.
> O weary life! O weary death!
> O spirit and heart made desolate!
> O damned vacillating state!   (183–90)

The weight of the 'heavy clod' seems to betray a fear of burial as the
final, irreversible separation of the dead from the world of the living,
although it could also be argued that because only a living and conscious
being could register such a weight, the passage also reveals an unconscious fear of premature interment, a phenomenon which occurred frequently enough in the nineteenth century to encourage the more nervous
to ask for alarm systems to be rigged up in their graves.[65] The 'sharp-
headed worm' has more complex associations. Most obviously the work
of the worm on the corpse reminds us of the corruption of the body. It
also, however, recalls the worm that 'dieth not' (Mark 9.44), and thus
reinforces the association of the grave with hell (or Hades), as in the
burial and descent 'into hell' of Christ, affirmed in the creeds. Swinburne's poem, 'After Death', which begins with the ambiguous lines
'The four boards of the coffin lid / Heard all the dead man did', ends
with the dead man asking the boards,

> 'What good gift shall God give us?'

> The boards answered him anon:
> 'Flesh to feed hell's worm upon.'[66]

Swinburne gleefully plays with the biblical idea, often discussed in
the nineteenth century, of death as Adam's curse (Romans 5.12), and
of the corruption of the body after death as a mark of man's fallen

state, and of his utter reliance upon God's mercy. Thus fears associated with death and burial were closely linked with the fear of judgment and hell. This complex of anxieties was exploited by preachers and teachers of many different persuasions, as we shall see in Chapter 4. In his notorious series of 'Books for Children', for example, Father Furniss described for his young readers the bloated and stinking state of the exhumed corpse of a drunkard, and recommended that they said the Hail Mary for their drunken parents every day, lest they themselves were taken to hell with their parents.[67] At the other extreme, however, secularists boasted that with the shedding of fears of hell and judgment it was possible to lose the fear of death. Austin Holyoake, for example, published a burial service in 1870 which contained a statement to be read at the grave side of a male secularist who had 'long been free from the fears and misgivings of superstitious belief'.[68] Whereas the Burial Service in the Book of Common Prayer emphasizes the hope of a future resurrection, Holyoake's somewhat laboured order of service ends with this wooden dismissal: 'Peace and respect be with his memory. Farewell, a long farewell!'

Holyoake is buried in the same grave as his intimate friend, James Thomson, who wrote of death as release from a world without hope:

> The certitude of Death, which no reprieve
> Can put off long; and which, divinely tender,
> But waits the outstretched hand to promptly render
> That draught whose slumber nothing can bereave.[69]

Later in *The City of Dreadful Night* (1874) a funeral oration, reminiscent of Holyoake's, modifies the Christian perspective on death as sleep:

> This little life is all we must endure,
> The grave's most holy peace is ever sure,
>   We fall asleep and never wake again;
> Nothing is of us but the mouldering flesh,
> Whose elements dissolve and merge afresh
>   In earth, air, water, plants, and other men.   (XIV)

Because of the corruption of the flesh, the grave requires some kind of purification or cleansing, and here the agent is nature, through the absorption of the body into the earth. The corruption of the body is confronted directly in the New Testament, of course. The raising of Lazarus initiates the sequence of events which leads to Christ's own

death and burial, and his victory over death in John 11 anticipates his
own resurrection:

> Jesus said, Take ye away the stone. Martha, the sister of him that was dead,
> saith unto him, Lord, by this time he stinketh: for he hath been dead four days.
> Jesus saith unto her, Said I not unto thee, that, if thou wouldest believe, thou
> shouldest see the glory of God?   (John 11.39–40)

Martha's blunt reference to the corruption of the body reinforces the
connection (John 11.2) between the raising of Lazarus and Mary's
anointing of Jesus with spices (John 12.3), which itself looks forward
to his death and burial. The raising of Lazarus is one of the lessons
used in Christian burial services. In the Roman Catholic Church the
ritual cleansing of the body and the grave by the priest re-enacts the
sanctifying act of Jesus Christ who, in the words of one of the prayers
in the ancient order of Compline, 'didst rest in the sepulchre, and didst
sanctify the grave to be a bed of hope'. This theme is taken up in an
aphorism in Coleridge's *Aids to Reflection*, where the grave is described
as 'thy bed of rest': 'thy Saviour has warmed it, and made it fragrant'.[70]
  These ideas were reinforced and popularized in the thousands of
tracts, sermons, and hymns which poured from the religious presses
during the Victorian Age. Elizabeth Stone in *God's Acre* reminded her
readers that the first Christians called their places of burial '*coemeteria*,
"dormitories" or "sleeping places," because they looked on death as a
sleep merely, and the departed only as it were laid to rest until the
resurrection should awaken them'.[71] Although many popular treatments
of 'God's Acre' tended towards sentimentality, some religious writers
saw that the claims of Christianity with respect to the dead who peopled
the graveyard were in fact unsentimental and uncompromising. Mrs
Alexander, author of 'Once in royal David's city' and 'All things bright
and beautiful', uses words from the Apostles' Creed – 'descended into
hell; The third day he rose again from the dead' – as the epigraph to
another of her popular *Hymns for Little Children* (1848) entitled 'The
rich man did of Pilate crave', in which the reality of death is sharply
conveyed:

> There are short graves in churchyard, round,
>   Where little children buried lie,
> Each underneath his narrow mound,
>   With stiff cold hand, and close shut eye;
> Bright morning sunbeams kiss the spot,
> Yet day by day, they open not.

But surely as our SAVIOUR rose
  On Easter morn from Joseph's cave,
Shall all those mounds at last unclose,
  And Christian people leave the grave.
He died, He slept, He rose to be
An earnest of our victory.

Lord, Who for us so cold and deep
  Down in that garden grave hast lain,
When we like Thee must fall asleep,
  Be with us in our hour of pain,
That strengthened by Thy Grace Divine,
Alive or dead we may be Thine.[72]

Late-twentieth-century sensibilities may be shocked by the first verse quoted here. The image of the dead infant lying in the grave, however, is identical to one which many children who first sang the hymn would actually have seen: namely, that of a child lying (or 'sleeping') in its coffin (or 'bed') in the days immediately following its death, and before the physical corruption to which the hymns cannot, perforce, refer, sets in. The body of Christ, perfect and incorruptible, was raised from 'sleep' on the third day, an earnest of the resurrection of the 'Christian people' of the hymn, and Mrs Alexander's description of the dead children in their graves implies that their bodies will be raised incorruptible (I Corinthians 15.52). Thus the grave is treated as the site of a transition from the deathbed, which it resembles, to the heaven to which it points.

This idea is also hinted at in the exchange between the fading William Carlyle and his mother, Lady Isabel (disguised as 'Madame Vine'), in *East Lynne*:

'When you are very, very tired, William, does it not seem a luxury, a sweet happiness, to lie down at night in your little bed, waiting for sleep?'

'Yes. And I am often tired; as tired as that.'

'Then, just so do we, who are tired out with the world's cares, long for the grave in which we shall lie down to rest. We *covet* it, William; long for it; almost pray for it: but you cannot understand that.'

'*We* don't lie in the grave, Madame Vine.'

'No, no, child. Our bodies lie there, to be raised again in beauty at the last day. We go into a blessed place of rest, where sorrow and pain cannot come. I wish – I wish,' she added with a bursting heart, 'that you and I were both there!'

'Who says the world is so sorrowful, Madame Vine? I think it is lovely . . .'

(III.10)

Mercifully, Lady Isabel's death-wish is not understood by William, but his correction – '*We* don't lie in the grave' – elicits from her a description of a place which sounds like a familiar Victorian euphemism for the grave: 'a blessed place of rest'.

Such conflations of the deathbed, the grave, and heaven (the place of eternal rest) are the literary equivalent of the work of the monumental masons whose angels and cherubic effigies of children were designed to make the Victorian graveyard a heaven upon earth. But Lady Isabel's emphasis upon a place of *rest* is a product of the context in which she speaks: she holds out the hope of an end to sickness and fever while also suggesting a continuity between this world (William lies in bed) and the next (he will enter into his rest). Keble's *The Christian Year* (1827), the most popular volume of verse in the nineteenth century, also adapts the idea of rest to the homiletic context in this way. 'Morning', the first poem in the series, includes lines that are familiar from the popular hymn:

> New every morning is the love
> Our wakening and uprising prove;
> Through sleep and darkness safely brought,
> Restored to life, and power, and thought.
>
> New mercies, each returning day,
> Hover around us while we pray;
> New perils past, new sins forgiven,
> New thoughts of God, new hopes of Heaven.[73]

In 'Morning' Keble emphasizes the call to work to the glory of God which each day brings. He therefore describes heaven, in the final stanza, as 'perfect Rest above', a fitting reward after the long day that is our mortal life. In 'Burial of the Dead', however, heaven is the 'new heaven' of the *parousia*, in contrast to the place of rest (or sleep) which follows death:

> Far better they should sleep awhile
>   Within the church's shade,
> Nor wake, until new heaven, new earth,
> Meet for their new immortal birth
>   For their abiding place be made,
>
> Than wander back to life, and lean
>   On our frail love once more.[74]

This idea of the grave as a place of sleep 'within the church's shade' combines a sense of place (in the shade of a church) and a sense of membership (in the Catholic and Apostolic Church). Both literally and metaphorically, the emphasis is upon peace: the dead sleep undisturbed in God's acre. We have seen, however, that F. D. Maurice was troubled by the familiar euphemism, 'He sleeps in the grave', because although it is comforting in the context of former pain and illness, the thought of a long, dreary sleep in the grave is disturbing. Again, the problem with figurative language is that although it may suit a specific context or spiritual need, other extraneous and purely physical associations can be evoked. This is a particularly frequent occurrence in writing on death and burial, where the other-worldly perspective of a bereaved person is all too likely to be interrupted by the physical reality of this world. Consider, for example, the first verse of Edward Caswall's hymn:

> Days and moments quickly flying
> Blend the living with the dead;
> Soon will you and I be lying
> Each within our narrow bed.[75]

As in Gray's 'Elegy' ('Each in his narrow cell'), the grave contains and limits what in life had freedom of movement in space. 'Narrow bed', however, also suggests a chaste solitariness. What, then, of graves in which husbands and wives are buried together? Interestingly, Elizabeth Stone in God's Acre cites Edmund Burke's reflections on Westminster Abbey, and his preference, like Gray's, for a country churchyard: 'The good old expression, 'family burying-ground,' has something pleasing in it, at least to me.'[76] She continues:

When in earlier times it was forbidden to inter two bodies in one grave, exception was always made in the case of husband and wife – the most touching and most reverent acknowledgment of the sanctity of the marriage tie that it is possible to conceive.

Macabre alternatives, however, to Mrs Stone's sentimental view of the subject are suggested by one of the most appropriate biblical texts in this context: Adam's description of Eve as 'bone of my bones, and flesh of my flesh' (Genesis 2.23). Eros and thanatos are brought into grotesque juxtaposition in Heathcliff's account in Wuthering Heights of his arrangement with the sexton to prepare Cathy's grave as a kind of double bed for him, from which Edgar, her lawful husband, is to be excluded (29). Nelly Dean is shocked that Heathcliff should have 'disturbed' the dead, but he claims that he 'disturbed nobody'. Like Cathy's substitution of the heath for an orthodox Christian heaven which, in her dream, did not seem to be her 'home' (9), Heathcliff's idea of bodies dissolving into each other displaces a 'vertical' spiritual transcendence in favour of a consolation which is rooted in natural process. Following Nelly's account of local reports that the spirits of Cathy and Heathcliff 'walk', and Lockwood's reference to the disintegration of the kirk, the pieties of Lockwood's final sentence are profoundly ironic: 'I . . . wondered how anyone could imagine unquiet slumbers, for the sleepers in that quiet earth' (34).

The churchyard in which Edgar Linton, Cathy, and Heathcliff are buried ('next the moor') is the site of word-play ('heath and hare-bells') rather than Christian analogy: the moths that flutter are merely moths. Indeed, Emily Brontë's rejection of analogy is an aspect of her radicalism. For whereas *Wuthering Heights* seeks for explanations in nature alone, much mainstream Victorian literature and art drew upon the analogical tradition which came down from Bishop Butler and his *Analogy of Religion* (1736), and which drew parallels between nature and the revealed truths of scripture. James Buchanan, whose treatise on *Analogy* (1864) was quoted earlier, believed that 'the future resurrection of the body has its natural analogue in the annual resurrection of Nature from the death-like torpor of winter'.[77] St Paul's analogy of the body as a seed which is buried in the ground (1 Corinthians 15) was often cited in this context. Similarly, the tree was a favourite organic analogy in the religious writings of Coleridge and Newman, both of whom drew upon Butler. These analogies were used in Bowler's *The Doubt*: '*Can These Dry Bones Live?*' (illustration 1), the painting discussed at the beginning of this book. In adapting for Victorian tastes the familiar meditative figure leaning on a gravestone from eighteenth-century engravings, Bowler explored the tension between the feeling that all life ends in death and the hope of a future life that haunted the nineteenth century.

Richard Whateley's caricature of a 'happy death' in his *View of the Scripture Revelations Concerning a Future State* included 'christian burial in consecrated ground, and especially if a handsome monument is erected over it'. Such ideas were not 'agreeable to the christian *Scriptures*'. The nineteenth-century ideal of a quiet death in one's own bed, followed by interment in the charming 'natural' setting of a country churchyard, was certainly far from the experience of the early church. Bultmann has argued that nowhere in the New Testament is the attempt made to 'interpret death as a natural occurrence and thus to neutralise it':

Even where its abolition through resurrection is thought of and dying and rising again are described according to the analogy of a natural process (1 Cor.xv.36; John xii.24), it is not conceived of as a natural occurrence any more than the resurrection. That event, used as an analogy, is not in the biblical sense to be understood as a natural process in the Greek scientific sense.[78]

At first sight, Bowler's placing of Faithful's grave in the proximity of a church and beneath a spreading chestnut tree would seem to be 'unscriptural' in emphasis. Yet the analogical tradition within which he works is more effective in its presentation of Christian truth claims than such an interpretation would allow. *The Analogy of Religion* opens with a chapter entitled 'Of a Future Life', in which Butler argues the 'presumption or probability' of a future existence for man in the light of the 'analogy of nature, and the several changes which we have undergone', and other examples of *transformation* such as that of the worm turning into the fly.[79] Like St Paul's analogy of the grain of wheat, that of the worm (or larva) and the fly, while 'natural', does not soften death or domesticate resurrection. Rather, it challenges the faithful in the way that the Burial Service does in the Book of Common Prayer: these things are mysteries. *The Doubt* confronts the reality of physical decay, and the exhumed bones exposed to public view remind us of the radical *opposition* between the deep grave below ground (corruption, darkness, and death) and the gravestone inscription above ground (incorruption, light, and new life). The mysterious transformation of the small chestnut into the tree, the dimensions of which can only be guessed at, is an adequate if limited analogy to the mysterious transformation that is the resurrection of the body. But then the transformation of chestnuts into trees, like that of worms into flies, is, after all, no more than an analogy, and human souls are neither worms nor chestnuts. Indeed, the interest of Bowler's *The Doubt* as a 'problem picture' lies in the way in which its analogical parallelism is presented to the viewer in such a way that the stark reality of the exhumed bones is not erased, or explained away, but rather held in tension with the hope of resurrection offered by the text from John 11 on the gravestone (a *logion* that exercised the biblical critics, as we have seen). Thus the viewer is driven back to the ultimate question of *faith* that confronts the mourner, such as Lazarus's sister, and the lady in Bowler's picture. Natural analogies are not proofs, but aids to reflection for those who already believe.

Whereas Faithful is buried in a green English churchyard, Lazarus's tomb (Gk. *mnēmeion*) was made in rocky terrain: it is described as a 'cave' (*spēlaion*) with a stone covering the entrance. Although Christ's tomb was also cut out of rock, it was situated in a 'garden' (*kēpos*) which, to an English ear, has helpful organic associations. Mrs Alexander's hymn for children refers to Christ's rising 'from Joseph's cave'. In contrast, the little children of the hymn are buried in 'churchyard ground'. In a later verse, however, the two forms of burial are conflated in the lines 'Lord, Who for us so cold and *deep* / *Down* in that garden grave has lain'. In the nineteenth century, God's acre was thought of as a garden in which each body was sown in its own 'plot'. Millais's paintings provide a particularly interesting example of such associations. *Autumn Leaves* (1856; illustration 4), which, unusually for Millais, he intended to 'awaken by its solemnity the deepest religious reflection', is set in the garden of Annat Lodge in Perth, where he and his wife Effie had settled after their marriage in 1855.[80] Meanwhile he was planning to paint 'a picture with nuns in it', and two years later he completed *The Vale of Rest* (1858; illustration 5), which was to be his favourite among his own works.[81] The background to this picture was taken from the walled garden at Effie's family home in Perth, and the graveyard portion in the foreground from an old churchyard in Perth. In the painting, however, the burial ground is simply part of a convent garden. Other symbols in the picture, such as the bell, the ivy, the death's head on the rosary, and the ring-like wreaths that remind us of the spiritual marriage of a nun, encourage an analogical interpretation of the garden/ graveyard. This is supported by the fact that the poplars silhouetted against the sunset clearly refer to the garden scene of *Autumn Leaves*. Like the Bowler, however, Millais's picture with its open grave presents the viewer with a challenging question: it is mute, or unstated, but is to be found in the steady gaze of the sister on the right, who has dedicated her life (and death) to Christ.

Apart from parallels between burial in a plot of consecrated ground and the planting of seeds in a garden, God's acre is also a place where both wild and cultivated flowers grow, and Mrs Stone devotes a whole chapter of her book to 'Flowers on Graves'. Tennyson writes in *In Memoriam* of Hallam's burial:

'Tis well; 'tis something; we may stand
Where he in English earth is laid,
And from his ashes may be made
The violet of his native land. (18)

Tennyson himself compared the stanza with these lines from *Hamlet:*

Lay her i' th' earth,
And from her fair and unpolluted flesh
May violets spring! (V.1.232–4)[82]

Flowers growing on graves are a familiar convention in classical as well as Christian elegy, and they figure in Shelley's 'Adonais': 'The leprous corpse, touched by this spirit tender, / Exhales itself in flowers of gentle breath.' The butterfly in God's acre, however, is a specifically Christian analogy, which we have seen in Bowler's painting. It is used on the illustrated cover of E. H. Bickersteth's *The Shadowed Home*, which epitomizes the popular treatment of such ideas in the Victorian period (illustration 6). The butterfly above the grave and the rays of the morning sun (associated with the resurrection hour) are embossed in gilt on purple cloth. The epitaph on the grave board is from the *Pilgrim's Progress*:

THE PILGRIM THEY LAID IN A CHAMBER
WHOSE WINDOW OPENED TOWARD THE SUN RISING
THE NAME OF THE CHAMBER WAS PEACE
WHERE HE SLEPT TILL BREAK OF DAY.

The idea of the churchyard as a garden also has comforting domestic associations, and thus strengthens the link between the grave and heaven as a place of rest or peace, or as our last home. Great efforts were often made in the nineteenth century to bring those who died abroad home to their 'native soil', as in the case of Arthur Hallam. In Charlotte Yonge's best-selling novel, *The Heir of Redclyffe* (1853), however, the hero, Sir Guy Morville, dies in Roman Catholic Italy and is buried there, at sunrise, in the 'stranger's corner' of a graveyard: 'for of course the church did not open to a member of another communion of the visible church' (36). An English clergyman, however, reads the English rite over his grave:

The blessing of peace came in the precious English burial-service, as they laid him to rest in the earth, beneath the spreading chestnut-tree, rendered a home by those words of his Mother Church – the mother who had guided each of his steps in his orphaned life. It was a distant grave, far from his home and kindred, but in a hallowed spot, and a most fair one; and there might his mortal frame meetly rest till the day when he should rise, while from their ancestral tombs should likewise awaken the forefathers whose sins were indeed visited on him in his early death; but, thanks to Him who giveth the victory, in death without the sting.   (36)

Displaced from the garden of home (an English churchyard), by the sins of the fathers, Guy finds a true spiritual home in the indivisible one Catholic and Apostolic Church, via the liturgy of the Church of England to which he has always remained true.[83] The 'spreading chestnut-tree', reminiscent of Bowler's painting of an English churchyard exhibited two years later, domesticates the promise of resurrection.

Anxieties concerning the 'natural' resting place of the dead are reflected in similar strategies in the poetry of Matthew Arnold, who fell into a necessary error in his elegy on Charlotte Brontë when he wrote of the sisters who had died before her:

> Round thee they lie – the grass
> Blows from their graves to thy own![84]

Arnold wrote 'Haworth Churchyard' shortly after Charlotte Brontë's death on 31 March 1855. Although he had been in Haworth three years earlier, he had evidently not discovered that the Brontë graves were in a vault in the church, and not in the churchyard 'next the moors'. When Elizabeth Gaskell informed him of this in a congratulatory letter, he replied:

I am almost sorry you told me about the place of their burial. It really seems to me to put the finishing touch to the strange cross-grained character of the fortunes of that ill-fated family that they should even be placed after death in the wrong, uncongenial spot.[85]

Revealing as this comment is about Arnold's idea of a congenial spot for burial, he might also have added that he needed a more congenial site for his 'pindarics'.

In 'Rugby Chapel: November, 1857', however, which is written in the same form as 'Haworth Churchyard', Arnold's negative emotional response to his father's burial within the walls of a church is worked out and transcended within the poem itself:

> Coldly, sadly descends
> The autumn-evening. The field

Strewn with its dank yellow drifts
Of withered leaves, and the elms,
Fade into dimness apace,
Silent; hardly a shout
From a few boys late at their play!
The lights come out in the street,
In the school-room windows; but cold,
Solemn, unlighted, austere,
Through the gathering darkness, arise
The chapel-walls, in whose bound
Thou, my father! art laid.

Although his father's body is pent in the grave within the unlit chapel, the poet stands in what both he and Wordsworth would have considered a more congenial site of mourning: an autumnal scene of withered leaves and elm trees that one might find in a country churchyard. The lights in the school-room windows and in the street prepare for later stanzas in which compensation for loss is achieved through the poet's memory and the recognition that those whom Dr Arnold influenced for good in the school are now working in the 'sounding labour-house vast / Of being'. Unlike the hero of Thomas Hughes's *Tom Brown's Schooldays* (also 1857), who finds inspiration at the end of the novel by praying at the chapel altar under which Dr Arnold was buried, Matthew Arnold's meditations spring from standing in the autumnal evening scene and thinking of 'bygone autumns' with his father.

Eighteen years later, in *God and the Bible* (1875), Arnold was to claim that Jesus's words to Martha – 'I am the resurrection and the life' – were intended to 'transform' the materialist Jewish concept of the resurrection of the body, but that his words provided the basis for the evolution of a miracle story 'exactly effacing the truth which [he] wished to convey'.[86] Our 'hope of immortality', he wrote, our 'common materialistic notions about the resurrection of the body and the world to come', are 'in direct conflict with the new and loftier conceptions of life and death which Jesus himself strove to establish'. The position of Arnold (the critical spirit incarnate) in the grounds outside the chapel in which his father is buried allows him to avoid the question which, in F. D. Maurice's view, the story of the raising of Lazarus answered for mourners with a will to believe: 'Can light ever penetrate into that darkness?' Or as the Lord said to Ezekiel: 'Can these dry bones live?'

CHAPTER 2

✳

Judgment

Day of Wrath! O day of mourning!
See fulfill'd the prophets' warning!
Heav'n and earth in ashes burning!
Oh, what fear man's bosom rendeth
When from Heav'n the Judge descendeth,
On Whose sentence all dependeth!

(Dies Irae)

We saw in the last chapter that Victorian conventions and practices associated with death and bereavement formalized different stages of separation and loss, giving shape and thus possibly some meaning to a transitional phase between one state and another. We also saw, however, that these transitional phases were difficult, painful, and, in terms of language and symbolism, often profoundly ambiguous. As we now turn from earthly 'rites of passage' to the subject of the judgment of the dead, and the question of an intermediate or transitional state between death and either heaven or hell, a similar pattern emerges.

The anthropologist Victor Turner cites Van Gennep's original definition of *rites de passage* as 'rites which accompany every change of place, state, social position and age', and then explains the three phases that Van Gennep identified in these rites:

The first phase (of separation) comprises symbolic behavior signifying the detachment of the individual or group either from an earlier fixed point in the social structure, from a set of cultural conditions (a 'state'), or from both. During the intervening 'liminal' period, the characteristics of the ritual subject (the 'passenger') are ambiguous; he passes through a cultural realm that has few or none of the attributes of the past or coming state. In the third phase (reaggregation or reincorporation), the passage is consummated.[1]

Turner's interest is in rites of passage which involve a withdrawal from and a subsequent return to society, such as fertility rituals in primitive African tribes or pilgrimages in Roman Catholic countries. Interpreted broadly, these ideas also have a useful application to the subjects of death and bereavement, and of post-mortem divine judgment.

In figure 1, the concept of liminality is applied to the deathbed as the passenger's site of transition, seen from a this-worldly perspective:

Fixed state *Liminal phase* *Fixed state*

Life → Recognition: death is anticipated → Dying process → Moment of death → Death

Figure 1

But for the bereaved person who attends to the body after death, the diagram can be drawn like this:

Deathbed → Moment of death → Period of transition → Burial → Grave

Figure 2

The concept of liminality can also help us to relate Victorian ideas concerning death and dying to the theology of the period which focused upon judgment. For in both the transition from the deathbed to the 'bed' that is the grave, and the 'intermediate state' between the moment of death and the last judgment, the characteristics of the passenger and the language applied to him or her are often ambiguous. Christ's death and resurrection conforms to Turner's model in this way:

Life on earth → Death → Three days in the tomb → Resurrection → Life in heaven

Figure 3

The passive humility which Turner associates with liminality is epitomized in the passion and burial of Christ: humbled for a season, he ceases to act after the arrest and is simply acted upon. During the three days after the crucifixion his body lies in the tomb. Meanwhile, according to tradition, his spirit 'descends into hell', or Hades, to save the saints of ancient Israel.[2]

The three days in the tomb have inspired various traditional Christian rituals, particularly as a subject of penitential meditation and practice. St Patrick's Purgatory, for example, the three-day pilgrimage at Lough Derg in Ireland, is organized as a ritual 'death' to the world, a descent into a 'purgatory', and a final rising to new life in the spirit on the third day.[3] In the nineteenth century, the three days in the tomb provided writers with a model on which to base teaching on death and the future life. In *The Blessed Dead*, for example, first read as a paper before a private 'prophetical society' in 1862, E. H. Bickersteth addressed the question of 'those now sleeping in Jesus': 'What . . . says the Scripture regarding the intermediate state of departed saints, who are absent from the body and present with the Lord?'[4] In Bickersteth's view the Bible says that the intermediate state is the period between the death of the 'saint' and the second coming. He argues that it is a state of rest, and comments on the word 'sleep',

which is so frequently used of death, relating perhaps first to the body, which is laid in the grave as in a bed, but also, when used of the saints, to the calm rest of the spirit when the day's work is over.[5]

Although a state of rest, it is also a state of 'consciously living to God', and here he draws an important parallel with Christ, whose body rested in the tomb until the resurrection, but whose spirit 'gained new powers of motion, and travelled . . . on a blessed mission to the region of departed spirits'.[6] We can therefore gather that our spirit shall acquire new life in losing the burden of the flesh.

From Bickersteth's other-worldly perspective, lying in the grave does not represent the final state of the body. Rather, the earthly or 'natural' body lies in the grave (another kind of bed) only for a season, and is raised a 'spiritual' body (1 Corinthians 15.44) when it is reunited with the soul at the general resurrection. Meanwhile the soul exists in a (diminished) 'intermediate state':

Earthly state → Death → Intermediate state → Resurrection → Final state

Figure 4

As a 'premillennialist', who believed that the second coming (or *parousia*) would precede the thousand years of Christ's reign upon earth, Bickersteth argued that there was a further transitional period between the intermediate state and the last judgment – the 'Millennial sabbath':

Intermediate state → Resurrection → Millennial sabbath → Last judgment → Final state

Figure 5

As we will see later, in Bickersteth's epic poem, *Yesterday, To-Day, and For Ever,* the *parousia*, the inauguration of the millennial sabbath, and the last judgment are the most significant events in a complex scheme of repetitions and deferrals which create a sense of steadily increasing anticipation.

This combination of anticipation and *deferral* will figure prominently in this chapter, where the relationship between judgment (whether 'particular', 'private' and immediate, at the moment of death, or 'general' and final, at the last judgment) and the 'intermediate state' in nineteenth-century theology, and the relevance of this to Victorian literature, are to be discussed. The 'lively hope' of the New Testament is affirmed in the context of eschatological expectation and the delayed *parousia*. In the midst of persecution and injustice the early Christians looked forward in confidence to the coming of the kingdom. Christ's death and resurrection as the 'first fruits', or as an 'earnest' of a 'lively hope'; the looked-for *parousia*; the anticipated inauguration of Christ's kingdom on earth: all are part of a scheme in which those who wait and hope in the here-and-now look forward in lively expectation to that which is to be revealed. As St Gregory of Nyssa taught, 'all holy desires grow by delays'.[7] On Bultmann's analysis, however, the apostles also lived in the end-time, as Christ had already been raised, and, paradoxically, the 'lively hope' is already an 'eschatological blessing'. Another way of expressing this is in the terms *chronos* and *kairos*, adopted by Frank Kermode in *The Sense of an Ending* (1966). Although not always contrasting in New Testament Greek, these words can be said to maintain 'a certain polarity'. While waiting in consecutive time (*chronos*) which passed without bringing the anticipated *parousia*, the apostles saw their own time or season (*kairos*) as 'filled with significance, charged with a meaning derived from its relation to the end'.[8]

The kind of apocalyptic thinking that Kermode traces from the Middle Ages to Lawrence is associated with both hope and fear, and reflects Christ's paradoxical nature as both saviour and judge. New Testament teaching on judgment, upon which both the intermediate (or 'pareschatological')[9] and final (or eschatological) states of the soul turn, also has a temporal dimension. Kermode writes:

Already in St. Paul and St. John there is a tendency to conceive of the End as happening at every moment; this is the moment when the modern concept of *crisis* was born – St. John puns on the Greek word, which means both 'judgment' and 'separation.' Increasingly the present as 'time-between' came to mean not the time between one's moment and the *parousia*, but between one's moment and one's death.[10]

This change in the concept of the present as 'time-between' also threw into strong relief other aspects of the four last things, and particularly that future and *post-mortem* 'time-between' which begins with one's death and ends with the last judgment. Anticipation of the *parousia* in the earthly life was thus taken up into doctrines relating to a future state in which the faithful wait or are prepared for God's final judgment upon all mankind.

Eschatology is grounded in concepts of judgment, and perhaps the clearest modern account of this aspect of Christian tradition is S. G. F. Brandon's in *The Judgment of the Dead* (1967), where he discusses the attempts made in the early church to harmonize what appeared to be conflicting beliefs: Christ as both saviour and judge, his message being for Jew and for Gentile, and his judgment being of a group (or nation) and an individual. Brandon argues that with the continuing delay of the *parousia* the church went through a process of eschatological re-interpretation, and that this was already evident in the Lucan and Johan-nine gospels: 'From that of the essentially eschatological figure who was about to intervene catastrophically in the cosmic process, and gather to their eternal reward his Elect, they being already incorporated into him, Christ now began to be imagined as dwelling in heaven as the mediator between God and men.'[11]

A number of difficulties arose, however, in the process of accommod-ating these developments in a scheme that preserved the primitive eschatology inherited from Jewish apocalyptic (the last day, the general resurrection, and the last judgment): Where were the dead until the last day? In what condition? Were they conscious or unconscious? A further complication originates in the parable of Dives and Lazarus (Luke 16.22) and Jesus's promise to the penitent thief on the cross (Luke 23.43), both of which imply some kind of immediate post-mortem judgment and entry into paradise.[12] These issues were central to the development of doctrine concerned with the four last things in the early church; they were still live and, indeed, highly contentious issues in the nineteenth century, which drew heavily upon patristic theology. In order, then, to gain some purchase on these doctrinal questions and their treatment in our period, we can turn to F. W. Farrar (in 1878 Rector of St Margaret's, Westminster and Canon of Westminster) and his summary in the preface to the first edition of *Eternal Hope* of the four main views of eschatology prevalent in the 1870s, and then consider both the doctrine of an intermediate state and millenarianism in the nineteenth century. For it is in the context of these doctrines and forms that the theme of judgment in Victorian poetry and fiction is to be discussed.

JUDGMENT, THE INTERMEDIATE STATE, AND THE MILLENNIUM

Farrar's analysis of what he calls the 'common view' of eschatology is similar to that of his mentor and former tutor, F. D. Maurice, who believed that the main weakness of Protestantism was its assumption that the saved were the exception to a rule:[13]

The *Common view*, which, to the utter detriment of all noble thoughts of God, and to all joy and peace in believing, except in the case of many who shut their eyes hard to what it really implies – declares (i.) that at death there is passed upon every impenitent sinner an irreversible doom to endless tortures, either material or mental, of the most awful and unspeakable intensity; and (ii.) that this doom awaits the vast majority of mankind.[14]

Farrar wanted his own Church of England to remove 'the greatest of all stumbling-blocks from the path of faith' by, among other things, restoring 'the ancient belief in an intermediate state' and emphasizing God's love and mercy.[15] Although the main thrust of his argument was against a literalist view of hell as a place of everlasting physical torment, the concept of an 'irreversible doom' (or judgment) at death also troubled him profoundly.

An alternative to the common view was annihilationism, or 'conditional immortality': 'the opinion that after a retributive punishment the wicked will be destroyed'.[16] Drawing on a handful of proof texts such as Romans 6.23 ('For the wages of sin is death') and 2 Timothy 1.10 ('Our Saviour Jesus Christ, who hath abolished death'), conditionalists held that a sentence of death passed on man at the fall had been mercifully withheld, that those who believed in Christ were saved and thus immortal, and that those who did not were annihilated. Exponents of such views were mainly Congregationalists and Anglican Evangelicals, and included in the second half of the nineteenth century adventists and millenarians.[17] Geoffrey Rowell discerns two varieties of conditionalists: those who emphasized the biblical language of the 'second death' (Revelation 20.14, 21.8) and argued that annihilation occurred after the wicked had been punished, and those who, influenced by Darwinism, believed in annihilation at death, while the saved (or fittest) survived. Henry Constable, one of the latter group, quoted Tennyson's lyric 56 in *In Memoriam* (' "So careful of the type?" but no') in drawing an analogy between the 'whole races of living things', which, as the fossil record showed, God had destroyed, and God's purpose for sinners.[18] Although the idea of annihilation, at death or after a period of punishment, was for many preferable to the common belief in everlasting punishment for sinners, it seemed to challenge New Testament teaching on our sharing Christ's risen life (e.g. 1 Corinthians 15). Schleiermacher wrote in *The Christian Faith*: 'if the soul of the Redeemer were imperishable, but our souls perishable, it could not justly be said that as man He was like us in all points, except sin'.[19]

Thirdly, there is purgatory:

the view that besides Heaven, the final state of the blessed, and Hell, the final doom of the accursed, there is a state wherein those souls are detained and punished which are capable of being purified, – an intermediate purification between death and judgment.[20]

The maturation from the fourth century of doctrine relating to some kind of trial after death to the general acceptance of belief in purgatory in the late twelfth century and beyond has been traced by Jacques Le Goff, who shows how purgatory is an 'intermediate place' in two senses:

the souls there are neither as happy as the souls in Paradise nor as unhappy as the souls in Hell, and Purgatory comes to an end at the time of the Last Judgment. All that remained to make it truly intermediary was to assign it a location between Paradise and Hell.[21]

Temporally and spatially 'in-between', purgatory is hope.[22] With purgatory, however, the state of the soul at death is crucial. Indeed, Le Goff argues that purgatory was one of the main reasons for the 'dramatization of the moment of death' in the thirteenth century,[23] as purgatory, like the 'intermediate state', can be explained only in terms of an immediate 'private' or 'particular' judgment at death. Moreover, as purgatory comes to an end at the last judgment it is both delimited and defined by acts of divine judgment. It thus retains the sense of a (catastrophist) ending within a (gradualist) scheme of purification. The obvious attraction of such an accommodation to nineteenth-century thinkers should be noted, as catastrophist and gradualist (or 'uniformitarian') models conflicted in many spheres, including political theory, historiography, and biology, as well as theology.[24]

Belief in some kind of purgation in a future state was not restricted to Roman Catholics in the nineteenth century. The views of Anne Brontë's heroine in *The Tenant of Wildfell Hall* (1848), for example, have been related to Patrick Brontë's reticence about hell: 'through whatever purging fires the erring spirit may be doomed to pass – whatever fate awaits it, still it is not lost, and God, who hateth nothing that He hath made, will bless it in the end!'[25] Like Helen Burns's views in *Jane Eyre*, Helen Huntingdon's reflect the Brontë sisters' leanings towards the fourth view of eschatology defined by Farrar: '*Universalism*, or, as it is now sometimes termed Restorationism: the opinion that all men will be ultimately saved.'[26] Although Origen's universalist eschatology of 'restoration' (*apocatastasis*) was rejected as unorthodox in the Eastern Church in the third century, his influence and that of other early Hellenistic Fathers survived down the ages, offering an alternative to the doom-laden Augustinian tradition of mainstream western theology. The dominant view of the fall, for example, was questioned by Schleiermacher in the early nineteenth century, when, following Irenaeus, he emphasized man's development towards a future perfection, rather than man's falling away from a pre-lapsarian ideal state in the past.[27] Some liberal Victorian theologians, such as F. D. Maurice, may at first appear to be broadly universalist in their views, and the sympathies of many poets and novelists of the period, including Tennyson, Philip Bailey (author of *Festus*), Browning, George MacDonald, and Olive Schreiner, also tended in this direction. Considerable care must be exercised here, however. Although a dividing line was drawn by F. W. Farrar, for example, between universalism and his own theology of hope, he was accused by his critics of

having used universalist arguments while repudiating universalist conclusions in *Eternal Hope*, and had to write *Mercy and Judgment* (1881)
in order to clarify his position.[28]

The minutiae of the doctrinal issues involved in this debate are discussed by Rowell, and do not concern us here.[29] It is worth noting, however, that one of Farrar's major objections to universalism is its potential
impact on moral behaviour. For in many debates in the nineteenth century on the range of views that he outlines – the common view, condi-
tionalism, purgatory, and universalism – there is a tension between a
longing for a more hopeful and less dark eschatology, and a fear lest
the weakening of belief in judgment and some kind of punishment
should have a damaging effect on the morals both of believers and
unbelievers. Gladstone, for example, writing at the end of the century,
expressed his anxiety lest the moral efficacy of the 'terrors of the Lord'
be lost.[30] More positively, however, belief in God's judgment was also
sustained in the nineteenth century by an acute sense both of man's
fallen condition and of the injustices of this world. The doctrine of a
'Judge and Judgment to come' was in Newman's view a 'development
of the phenomenon of conscience',[31] and the belief that God's judgment
would finally correct injustice is summed up in the words of Edmund
Gurney: if 'the present iniquitous distribution of good and evil was . . .
final, I should . . . desire the immediate extinction of the race'.[32]

We have seen, then, that all four views referred to by Farrar are based
upon the interpretation of doctrine relating to God as judge. Farrar is
less concerned in *Eternal Hope* with the temporal significance of the
Greek word *krisis*, discussed by Kermode, than with what he considered
to be its mistranslation and doctrinal application as 'damnation'.[33] He
never denied what he called the 'doctrine of a retribution',[34] but directed
his argument against those who accepted the 'common view' of damnation and who appeared to gloat over the idea of the wrath of God,
expressed, for example, in the Dies Irae on which the epigraph to this
chapter is based. He regretted that the Reformers, in rejecting the
'Romish doctrine' of purgatory which had become over-systematized
and associated with such corruptions as indulgences, did not preserve
the ancient and perhaps necessary belief in some kind of intermediate
state. 'There is hope for you', he declared in one of his sermons, 'though
you . . . may have to be purified in that Gehenna of aeonian fire beyond
the grave'.[35] Belief in some kind of spiritual *progress* in an intermediate
state was remarkably widespread among nineteenth-century Protestants

of widely differing theological positions. H. B. Wilson, for example, whose liberal views on hell were challenged in the ecclesiastical courts, suggested an organicist model of post-mortem development in his article in *Essays and Reviews* (1860):

we must . . . entertain a hope that there shall be found, after the great adjudication, receptacles suitable for those who shall be infants, not as to years of terrestrial life, but as to spiritual development – nurseries as it were and seed-grounds, where the undeveloped may grow up under new conditions – the stunted may become strong, and the perverted be restored.[36]

For H. M. Luckock, a Tractarian and Canon of Ely, progress after death is a corollary (by analogy) of the consciousness of the soul in the intermediate state:

If it be admitted that the soul exists after death, and is conscious, it seems almost impossible to believe that it remains altogether unchanged.

Conscious life by all analogy involves progress or retrogression, growth or decay . . .

. . . is not progress, steadily advancing progress, a very law of God's kingdom?[37]

Gladstone also believed in what he called the 'progressive state' of the 'Christian dead', but argued that, as pain is one of God's instruments of restoration in the earthly life, by analogy we have no right to assume that the progressive state after death will not involve 'an admixture of salutary and accepted pain'.[38]

These commentators wrestled with difficulties that nineteenth-century Protestantism had inherited from the Reformation, when, as Brandon shows, the Reformers found that in abandoning purgatory they were faced with the problems which that doctrine had been designed to solve. Calvin, unlike Luther, rejected the idea that souls sleep until the last judgment (*psychopannychia*) and stated that they are 'gathered into rest, where they await with joy the fruition of their promised glory; and thus all things remain in suspense until Jesus Christ appears as the Redeemer'.[39] Such a view assumes an immediate judgment but is unspecific about the paradisal intermediate state, emphasizing instead the deferral of 'glory' until after the *parousia*. In the nineteenth century, paradise was often distinguished from heaven (the final state of the saved) by those who believed in some kind of intermediate state. Meanwhile the damned also know their eternal doom from the time of their death. H. P. Liddon, a conservative High Churchman, and Canon and Chancellor of St Paul's, wrote in a Passiontide sermon of 1887:

We know that those who die in a state of grace enter not heaven as yet, but Paradise – an intermediate state in which they are gradually becoming more and more ready for the fully unveiled Beauty of the Most Holy. We know that just as the lost enter upon a fearful looking for of judgment and fiery indignation [Hebrews 10.27], which is not yet the place of punishment: so the saved are in an antechamber of heaven, the door of which will open for them at the last great day. Of this truth the supreme Revelation was made by our Lord upon the cross.[40]

Similarly, the Evangelical E. H. Bickersteth thought of paradise as one division of Hades, separated from the prison of the lost by the 'great gulf fixed' between Dives and Lazarus (Luke 16.26).[41] Unlike Liddon, however, Stewart Salmond, Professor of Theology at the Free Church College, Aberdeen, argued that there is too little evidence in the gospels to give us grounds for saying that Christ taught any doctrine of an intermediate state.[42]

Nevertheless, Geoffrey Rowell can argue at the end of *Hell and the Victorians* that the growing importance of the doctrine of the intermediate state in the nineteenth century was the one notable common feature which contrasted with the eschatology of earlier generations. The term 'intermediate state' itself, he believes,

was characteristic of the nineteenth century, and, whether it took the form of a tentative reappraisal of purgatory, or of a fore-shortened hell, or as a place of moral progress and expansion of the mind, it represented a move away from a predominantly Calvinist eschatology . . . It fitted better with a dynamic, evolutionary picture of the universe, than the conception of fixed and unalterable states into which men entered at death.[43]

Unlike what Farrar calls the 'common view' of eschatology, any scheme which includes an intermediate state, however defined, also offers some degree of *deferral* of God's final judgment upon mankind. In the case of progressive models the idea of an intermediate state also holds out the hope either of salutary purgation or of spiritual growth in preparation for the deferred final state that is heaven.

When we look back, however, to early-nineteenth-century schemes that most late-Victorian thinkers rejected, we find that different kinds of anticipation and deferral also characterize millenarianism, to which Rowell devotes comparatively little attention, incidentally. 'Premillennial' thinking, which commanded serious attention in the 1820s and 1830s, and enjoyed a revival as late as *c.* 1867–73, places great emphasis on the time between death (or the *parousia* in the case of those who are still alive when that event occurs) and the last judgment. The second coming of Christ represents a 'glorious hope' because it will inaugurate the millennium, when Christ will reign upon earth, and is therefore anticipated with joy and fervent expectation.

Narrower and more exclusive than most late-nineteenth-century schemes, millenarianism has deep historical roots. The sub-title to Norman Cohn's study, *The Pursuit of the Millennium* (1957), also reflects another kind of radicalism: 'Revolutionary millenarians and mystical anarchists of the Middle Ages'. According to Revelation 20 it was the Christian martyrs who were to 'live and reign with Christ a thousand years', although early sects soon interpreted this as including themselves as the suffering faithful who could anticipate the second coming in their lifetime. Cohn, like most modern commentators, interprets the word 'millenarianism' in the still broader sense of a particular type of salvationism, which he describes as collective, terrestrial, imminent, total, and miraculous.[44] Although Augustine had taught that the millennium was not a physical state, but a spiritual state accessible to believers through the sacraments and other means of grace, outbreaks of apocalyptic millenarianism recurred in the Middle Ages, when Joachite prophecy added a further dimension to the movement's history.[45] Interestingly, Victor Turner draws parallels between the properties of liminality in tribal rituals and in millenarian movements, including homogeneity, equality, anonymity, absence of property, abolition of rank, and acceptance of pain and suffering.[46]

J. F. C. Harrison's study on popular millenarianism 1780–1850 focuses upon the prophecies of Richard Brothers in the 1790s and of Joanna Southcott in subsequent decades until the 'virgin birth' fiasco and her death in 1814.[47] During this post-revolutionary period of war between England and France, many 'believers' became convinced that they were living in the last days, and English poets who were of millenarian persuasion later looked back on the French Revolution and the rise of Napoleon as critical 'signs of the times'.[48] Unlike 'postmillennialists', whose world-view was gradualist, progressive, and reformist in orientation, as for them the second coming was to *follow* the millennium, 'premillennialist' ideas were revolutionary and catastrophist, seeing Christ's second coming as the sudden inauguration of his kingdom on earth. (Some believed that the second coming had already occurred and that the millennium had begun.) The attractiveness of premillennialism to working-class radicals of the time is obvious.[49] Unusually, however, in both England and America in the early nineteenth century, and particularly *c.* 1820–35, it also drew support from well-off and even wealthy believers.[50] In England the years preceding the First Reform Act of 1832 were fraught with anxiety for the Evangelicals and nonconformists who dominated the millenarian movements of the day. The repeal of the old Test and Corporation Acts in 1828 and the introduction of the Catholic Emancipation Act in 1829 led to fears of disestablishment among Churchmen.[51] Ernest R. Sandeen cites a summary of the beliefs of millenarians at this time in the form of a six-point statement published in 1829 as the conclusion of a series of conferences held under the auspices of Henry Drummond, an Irvingite millenarian and a Member of Parliament:

1 The 'dispensation' or age will not end 'insensibly' but cataclysmically in judgment and destruction of the church in the same manner in which the Jewish dispensation ended.

2 The Jews will be restored to Palestine during the time of judgment.

3 The judgment to come will fall principally upon Christendom.

4 When the judgment is past, the millennium will begin.

5 The second advent of Christ will occur before the millennium.

6 The 1,260 years of Daniel 7 and Revelation 13 ought to be measured from the reign of Justinian to the French Revolution. The vials of wrath (Revelation 16) are now being poured out and the second advent is imminent.[52]

It was generally believed in English millenarian circles that the next important events would occur between 1843 and 1848, and that the end of time would occur between 1866 and 1873.[53] E. H. Bickersteth specifically referred to his treatment of the second coming, the 'millennial sabbath' and the last judgment when he wrote in the preface to the first edition of *Yesterday, To-Day, and For Ever* (1866),

The design of the following poem has been laid up in my heart for more than twenty years. Other claims, however, prevented me from seriously undertaking the work until little more than two years ago. But then the deep conviction that those solemn events, to which the latter books of my poem relate, were already beginning to cast their prophetic lights and shadows on the world, constrained me to make the attempt.[54]

This sense of urgency was shared by preachers such as William Ker, Vicar of Tipton, Staffordshire, whose discourses on '*The Things which must Shortly come to Pass*' (1868) included two entitled 'The Advent of "The Avenger"' with a text from Revelation 16.15: 'Behold, I come as a thief.'[55]

Bickersteth's epic poem and Ker's sermons are only two examples of a kind of writing which characterized the period of social and political crisis in which the Second Reform Act was introduced and George Eliot wrote *Middlemarch*, a 'novel of crisis' set in that earlier period of apocalyptic expectation, the late 1820s and early 1830s.[56] Like the idealists of George Eliot's novel whose ambitions are thwarted by the realities of provincialism in an unheroic century, those who looked for the imminent return of Christ to earth, there to reign with his saints for a thousand years, had to come to terms with various degrees of disappointment, especially when what appeared to be the last days brought no *parousia*. Edmund Gosse sardonically describes a stronger response than this particular kind of disappointment in his father, Philip, a member of the Plymouth Brethren and a fervent Adventist:

He waited, with anxious hope, 'the coming of the Lord,' an event which he still frequently believed to be imminent. He would calculate, by reference to prophecies in the Old and New Testament, the exact date of this event; the date would pass, without the expected Advent, and he would be more than disappointed, – he would be incensed. Then he would understand that he must have made some slight error in calculation, and the pleasures of anticipation would recommence.[57]

Edmund Gosse's strong antipathy to the more extreme beliefs which his father forced upon him in his youth made mature reflection upon the potential spiritual value of such 'pleasures of anticipation' impossible. In his view, to turn to miscalculation as an explanation was to rationalize an absurdity. On this argument it could be claimed that the 'millennial sabbath', a paradisal but earthly time-between which defers the last judgment and entry into the full joys of heaven (and thus sustains a sense of expectation and of hope deferred), is simply an idealized projection from the time-between that is the present life of one who looks to the second coming and the inauguration of that sabbath. A more sympathetic but critical approach to prophecies in the Revelation such as the millennium would, on the other hand, emphasize that the Revelation was written specifically for Christians suffering under Roman persecution; that the book's author drew heavily upon Jewish apocalyptic; and that the enduring value of the Revelation lies in its spiritual content and the message that Christians should live as if Christ's second advent were imminent, their lamps trimmed, awaiting the Bridegroom. Christina Rossetti discusses these traditional types and symbols at length in her devotional commentary on the Apocalypse, *The Face of the Deep* (1890),[58] and uses them extensively in her own poetry. A particularly striking example is the opening of 'Advent', written in 1858, later read at her own funeral, and regarded by Swinburne as 'perhaps the noblest of all her poems'.[59] Here, however, the sense of 'hope deferred' refers to a lack of 'signs' rather than to disappointment that signs have failed to bear fruit:

> This Advent moon shines cold and clear,
>   These Advent nights are long;
> Our lamps have burned year after year
>   And still their flame is strong.
> 'Watchman, what of the night?' we cry
>   Heart-sick with hope deferred:
> 'No speaking signs are in the sky,'
>   Is still the watchman's word. [60]

What, then, is the relationship between adventist and millenarian 'hope deferred' and judgment? Whereas the doctrine of an intermediate state takes a number of different forms which reflect a variety of beliefs, the theology of the 'millennial sabbath' tends to conform quite closely to that of Farrar's deprecated 'common view' of eschatology: the separation of saints from sinners during the millennium anticipates the division of the sheep and goats at the last judgment. Whereas the 'saints' who are alive at the inauguration of the millennium never experience death, the damned are imprisoned and await the 'second death' in store for them at the last judgment. As we turn to the poetry and fiction of the period, however, and consider the ways in which writers treat the subject of judgment and the last things in the epic, or the dramatic monologue, or the novel, we must attend not only to such broad questions as God's nature as judge and the extent of his ultimate forgiveness, but also to the ways in which models of judgment can be related to literary form. For whereas the religious epic, an extended form, can attempt a cosmological explanation in and through time, shorter poetic forms accommodate a more this-worldly and experiential treatment of the subject. Meanwhile the development of the Victorian novel is marked by a decline in the use of the judgmental ending, that secularized last assize.

POETIC FORMS AND APOCALYPTIC VISIONS

Having first paid homage to the great Turner collection in the Tate Gallery, London, many modern visitors move on to three massive paintings, each measuring about six and a half feet by ten feet: the famous 'judgment paintings' of John Martin, executed between 1851 and 1854. Perhaps it is the thought of the labour which went into these canvases that attracts viewers; or the lurid colours; or the sensational effects which influenced the historical epics of early Hollywood. Martin's subjects – *The Last Judgment, The Great Day of His Wrath* (originally named *The End of the World*), and *The Plains of Heaven* – also appeal to the contemporary taste for the apocalyptic, reflected in postmodernist versions of the sublime, for example, and in one of the cinema's most popular forms, the disaster movie. An interest, however, in the subject of death and the future life, is perennial.

John Martin was never accepted into membership of the Royal Academy. Ruskin attacked his work on several occasions, contrasting it unfavourably with Turner's.[61] Martin's judgment paintings, however, caused a sensation when they went on tour in Britain and America after his death in 1854: engravings of his work hung in the Parsonage at Haworth; and Mrs Henry Wood referred to *The Plains of Heaven* in *East Lynne* (1861), one of the most popular novels of the century. The sharp separation of the saved from the damned in the paintings also invites comparison with popular millenarianism in the mid-nineteenth century, a period in which both the hell-fire sermon and the pious volume on the recognition of friends in heaven flourished. Significantly, however, Martin's attempt to portray the saved, the damned, and the heavenly host in one painting, *The Last Judgment*, failed (illustration 7). The eye cannot take in both the picture's design, with its complex perspectives and disturbing vertical hierarchy, and the mass of details which clamour for close attention. Similar problems confronted those nineteenth-century writers who emulated Dante and Milton in epic poems on the subject of the 'four last things', while liberal Protestant theologians challenged the common view of hell and the idea that the vast majority of mankind would suffer everlasting physical torments, and be viewed by the elect in heaven from the other side of a 'great gulf fixed'.

Martin's paintings epitomize the 'apocalyptic sublime'[62] which became fashionable in English painting and poetry in the 1820s and 1830s, depicting biblical and historical subjects which combine what Tennyson described in 'Armageddon' as 'vast sights' and 'inconceivable visions' with a sense of imminent ending, or of God's sudden and dramatic intervention as judge in the course of time. Martin's *The Fall of Babylon* and *Belshazzar's Feast* were exhibited in 1819 and 1821 respectively. *The Destruction of Pompeii and Herculaneum* (1822) was the subject of a poem of the previous year by his friend Edwin Atherstone, with whom he enjoyed a friendly rivalry, as well as of Edward Bulwer's more famous novel, *The Last Days of Pompeii* (1834). Similarly, Martin's *The Fall of Nineveh* (1828) appeared in the same year as the first six books of a poem by Atherstone which was to grow to thirty books by 1868, and *The Last Man* (1833) was preceded by literary works on the same subject by Thomas Campbell and Mary Shelley.

The best known literary treatment of judgment itself in this pre-Victorian era, however, is Byron's *The Vision of Judgment* (1822), a brilliantly playful satiric riposte to Southey's *A Vision of Judgment* (1821), in the preface to which the laureate had scored some cheap points against him. Neither poet treats the last judgment, of course, but rather the coming to ('immediate') judgment of old King George, who had died in 1820. Southey, however, in the opening passage of his poem, adopts the convention, often also followed by those who wrote on the second coming and the last judgment, of introducing his portrayal of last things with a description of an evening scene:

'Twas at that sober hour when the light of day is receding,
And from surrounding things the hues wherewith day has adorn'd them
Fade, like the hopes of youth, till the beauty of earth is departed:
Pensive, though not in thought, I stood at the window, beholding
Mountain and lake and vale; the valley disrobed of its verdure . . .

Earth was hush'd and still; all motion and sound were suspended . . .

Pensive I stood and alone, the hour and the scene had subdued me,
And as I gazed in the west, where Infinity seem'd to be open,
Yearn'd to be free from time, and felt that this life is a thraldom. [63]

A passing bell for the late king then induces in the poet a longing for release from the 'thraldom' of this life.

In describing the vision that follows, Southey uses prophetic language associated with the Holy Spirit ('a sound like the rushing of winds, or the roaring of waters') and invokes Dante as his precursor: 'to thy mortal sight shall the Grave unshadow its secrets; / Such as of yore the Florentine saw'. The overweening ambition of *A Vision of Judgment* that so infuriated Byron, and the vast vagueness of such phrases as 'where Infinity seem'd to be open', were also characteristic of the eighteenth-century tradition of meditative-descriptive poetry to which the opening of the work is indebted. Edward Young's *Night Thoughts* (1742–5), together with Blair's *The Grave* (1743) and Thomson's *The Seasons* (1726–30), was still one of the most widely read poems in the late eighteenth century.[64] George Eliot's description of Young's treatment of the last judgment as 'a compound of vulgar pomp, crawling adulation, and hard selfishness, presented under the guise of piety' was quoted earlier.[65] During the hundred years that separate Young and Eliot, however, many other ambitious religious poets had invoked the Holy Spirit as their spiritual muse and described the last things in all their awesome glory. Macaulay, whose comparative analysis of Dante and Milton (1825) was a significant contribution to critical discussion on religious symbolism in poetry, attacked the work of his contemporary, Robert Montgomery, on grounds that were similar to George Eliot's in her critique of Young:

The Day of Judgment is to be described, and a roaring cataract of nonsense is poured forth upon this tremendous subject. Earth, we are told, is dashed into Eternity. Furnace blazes wheel round the horizon, and burst into bright wizard phantoms . . . The red and raging eye of Imagination is then forbidden to pry further. But further Mr Robert Montgomery persists in prying . . .

And this is fine poetry! . . . This is what has been described, over and over again, in terms which would require some qualification if used respecting Paradise Lost! [66]

Macaulay's distaste for the 'puffing' of Montgomery's *The Omnipresence of the Deity* (1828) is matched by his abhorrence of the poetaster's vaunting ambition. Montgomery's 'prying' into the mysteries of the four last things certainly contrasts with Macaulay's own more humble approach in a poem of 1826, written four years before his review. 'Dies Irae' includes these lines:

Jesus, hast *thou* borne the pain,
And hath all been borne in vain?
Shall thy vengeance smite the head
For whose ransom thou hast bled? . . .

Mercy, mercy, save, forgive,
Oh, who shall look on thee and live? [67]

'Dies Irae', however, is a short meditative poem which avoids the
problems that confronted those who were inspired to write on the grand
scale, like Montgomery. Robert Pollok's hugely ambitious epic, *The
Course of Time* (1827), is perhaps the most interesting of many attempts
in this period to narrate the unnarratable, and to tread where the writers
of the Revelation, the *Divine Comedy*, and *Paradise Lost* had already
trodden. The publishers paid Pollok the huge sum of £2,500 for the
poem, much more than was given for the poems of Scott or Campbell.
Its continued popularity in the mid-Victorian period is reflected not only
in the number of editions published – the twenty-fifth edition appeared
in 1867 and the 'seventy-eighth thousand' in 1868, when millenarian
expectations were again intense – but also in Blackwood's publication
of an attractive illustrated edition in 1857, for which Birket Foster and
John Tenniel provided designs. This edition is prefaced by an anonymous Memoir in which the genesis of the poem is described. While training for the Secessionist ministry in Scotland, Pollok was inspired by the
thought that no previous poet had done justice to the subject of the
general resurrection. He thereupon took up his pen and wrote part of
what he originally intended to be the first book of a long poem on the
subject. As time went on, however, other subjects presented themselves,
and he began to reorder his materials until finally, in another moment
of inspiration, 'the idea of the poem struck him, and the plan of it, as
it now stands, stretched out before him; so that, at one glance, he saw
through it from end to end like an avenue, with the Resurrection as
only part of the scene'.[68] The general resurrection of the dead thus
became the subject of Book VII in a poem of ten books, roughly equivalent in its placing to Milton's climactic Book IX (the description of the
fall) in his epic of twelve books. In other respects, however, Pollok's
narrative strategies are very different from Milton's. They are principally those of deferral and suspense combined with repetition, allowing
the poet to dwell on the sinfulness of man at great length, and thus to

justify the sharp separation of the sheep from the goats at the last judgment, which is delayed until the final books.

The poem opens in paradise after the last judgment, and therefore after the end of time when the earth was destroyed. Two 'youthful sons of Paradise' (here not distinguished from heaven) welcome a newly arrived stranger from another world who has seen hell on his journey, and who asks them for an explanation. They take him to an 'ancient bard of Earth' who answers his questions by narrating the history of man from the creation. The bard's lengthy description of man's fallen state on earth continues to the beginning of Book v, where he takes stock of the course of time:

> The span of Time was short, indeed; and now
> Three-fourths were past, the last begun, and on
> Careering to its close, which soon we sing.
> But first our promise we redeem, to tell
> The joys of Time, her joys of native growth;
> And briefly must, what longer tale deserves.[69]

The celebration of the innocent joys of life on earth which follows has the double function of balancing the gloomy account of man's wretchedness which has preceded it and deferring the promised description of time's 'close'. After thirty pages there follows a description of the 'evil state of society that preceded the Millennium'. This catalogue of signs of the times includes the inevitable attack on the Roman Catholic Church, the 'scarlet-coloured Whore, / Who on the breast of civil power reposed / Her harlot head'.[70] The great battle of three days, however, comes suddenly and with devastating effect, as 'the Lord, clad like a man / Of war', presides over the fall of Babylon, the divorce of Church and State, the binding of Satan, and the inauguration of the millennium, when 'Messiah reigned; / And Earth kept jubilee a thousand years'.[71]

Significantly, the millennium itself is described in only a few pages at the end of Book v, for Pollok's true subject is the depravity of sinners, and it is to this that he returns in the following book, where Satan is unbound and, in the words of the Argument, 'violence and crime prevail over all the earth, now ripe for final doom'.[72] This doom is not to be described until much later in the poem, however, and what follows is a repetition of the great battle before the millennium, as 'God in his car of vengeance comes', and the last night begins – 'the long, dark, dark,

dark night'.[73] The bard falters as he approaches the subject of the damned:

> What harp of boundless, deep, exhaustless woe,
> Shall utter forth the groanings of the damned,
> And sing the obsequies of wicked souls,
> And wail their plunge in the eternal fire? –
> Hold, hold your hands! hold, angels! – God laments,
> And draws a cloud of mourning round his throne:
> The organ of Eternity is mute,
> And there is silence in the heaven of heavens.[74]

This cosmic pause (cf. Revelation 8.1), of which there are several in the poem, is reflected in the narrative itself, which pauses in order to recapitulate:

> But we have overleaped our theme: behind,
> A little season waits a verse or two –
> The years that followed the Millenial [sic] rest.[75]

So another opportunity is provided to describe the sinful nature of man and to anticipate God's judgment, thus extending, in narrative terms, the suffering of those sinners in the liminal state which precedes the last judgment. Then the end of the world seems to have come:

> O earth! thy hour was come: the last elect
> Was born, complete the number of the good,
> And the last sand fell from the glass of time.[76]

But the narrative is again interrupted, this time by the call to the heavenly equivalent of Evensong.

This established pattern of deferral and repetition is continued in Book VII, where the bard returns to the last day (when 'suddenly, alas, fair Earth! the sun / Was wrapped in darkness'), and there is another cosmic pause:

> and beasts of every kind stood still.
> A deep and dreadful silence reigned alone . . .

> In horrible suspense all mortals stood;
> And, as they stood and listened, chariots were heard
> Rolling in heaven . . .

> Earth, arrested in her wonted path,
> As ox struck by the lifted axe, when nought
> Was feared, in all her entrails deeply groaned.[77]

What Pollok in his Argument calls the 'universal pause of Nature' precedes the trumpet call which heralds the resurrection: 'Awake ye dead!' The twenty pages that follow were presumably the first that Pollok wrote, and they represent the first major summit towards which the poem has been labouring. When the dead are raised, old men regain their prime, a mummy comes to life as the 'brown son of Egypt' who stands beside the 'European, his last purchaser', and there is much busy sorting out of 'essential organs' and 'fellow particles', particularly in the graveyards:

> The doors of death were opened; and in the dark
> And loathsome vault, and silent charnel-house,
> Moving, were heard the mouldered bones that sought
> Their proper place.[78]

Meanwhile the damned are also raised in order to suffer 'the second death'.

Although one might have expected the last judgment to follow immediately, the whole of the lengthy subsequent book (VIII) is devoted to the 'last pause of expectation' as every member of the human race dwells on his or her follies and sins, again allowing the poet to make *his* judgments upon mankind and to warn the reader against the temptations of the world. For the third time in the poem, God's sudden (and almost identical) intervention follows a long period of anticipation and delay:

> and suddenly
> In heaven appeared a host of angels strong,
> With chariots and with steeds of burning fire . . .[79]

Like the millennium earlier in the poem, the last judgment itself is described briefly: as in Matthew 25, the sheep are separated from the goats, and families are divided, never to meet again. Significantly, however, whereas the saved are described in only half a page, six pages are devoted to Satan, and at the end of the book the heavens are divided by a bow on which are written words that might have served as Pollok's epigraph to *The Course of Time*: 'As ye have sown, so shall ye reap this day!'[80]

The final book (x), as the Argument reveals, amounts to a rewriting of Book IX, following a crisis of narrative confidence:

Prayer and thanksgiving of the Author. – Solemn dedication of his labours. – Supplication for the Divine Influence. – The Bard resumes. – The Judgment-day – what it really was. – The redeemed and the reprobate still standing as described in Book IX. – Universal calm of Earth waiting her doom. – The trumpet sounded by Michael. – Gathering of the heavenly hosts . . .[81]

The poem ends with Christ the Judge passing sentence on the damned ('Depart from me, ye cursed, into the fire, / Prepared eternal in the gulf of hell'),[82] destroying the 'guilty earth' with fire, and inviting the blessed to join him at God's right hand.[83] The bard's last lines are those of a celestial (and thus omniscient) narrator who has gone the second mile with the new arrival from earth:

> Thus have I sung beyond thy first request,
> Rolling my numbers o'er the track of man,
> The world at dawn, at mid-day, and decline:
> Time gone, the righteous saved, the wicked damned,
> And God's eternal government approved.[84]

The order and closure celebrated here, however, mask the unsatisfactory nature of Pollok's vision of judgment, which fails not least because the earlier descriptions of divine intervention in the poem make the last judgment itself virtually redundant in narrative terms.

The problem, then, for the writer of this kind of Christian epic is to sustain a sense of anticipation within a providential scheme of repetition and reinforcement that can easily become static and closed. This problem confronted Edward Henry Bickersteth in *Yesterday, To-Day, and For Ever* (1866), probably the last poem of its kind in English letters. Published during the last major period of heightened millenarian expectation in the nineteenth century, the work went through seventeen editions by 1885, and had sold 27,000 copies in England and 50,000 in the United States by 1907.[85] (Bickersteth's biographer, Aglionby, however, commented in 1907 that in future the poem was more likely to be studied than read.) The poem is of greater significance and interest than Pollok's, largely because Bickersteth emphasizes personal spirituality rather than corporate guilt in his treatment of death and the future life. Beginning with the Seer describing his own death, surrounded by his family,[86] the poem goes on to develop the relationship between the Seer and his guardian angel, Oriel, the life, death, and final judgment of the damned Theodore, and the inner torment and self-abasement of Satan, in ways that are closer to Milton than to Pollok and his more generalized treatment of human types. Bickersteth's interpretation of scripture, explained in detail in his end-notes, also differs from Pollok's, as, for example, in his belief that the earth is not to be destroyed by fire on the last day, but will be purged and renewed to become the site of God's 'many mansions' – the final state that is heaven itself.[87] Like Pollok, however, Bickersteth was a premillennialist, and at least one contemporary reviewer believed that it was in the last four books of the twelve-book poem, where he described 'The Bridal of the Lamb', 'The Millennial Sabbath', 'The Last Judgment', and 'The Many Mansions', that Bickersteth was most impressive, as this was 'more untrodden' ground.[88] The circumspect Aglionby, on the other hand, writing forty years later, emphasized that millenarianism represented a minority view.[89]

Like Pollok's, Bickersteth's title emphasizes the temporal, while also providing a clue to the poem's structure. Hebrews 13.8 was a favourite and often quoted text in the nineteenth century: 'Jesus Christ the same yesterday, and to day, and for ever'.[90] In the central books of the poem the Seer's guardian angel, Oriel, tells him 'the story of the great To-day of Time' (v.956), and explains God's providential scheme since the 'yesterday' that was before the creation. The later books convey their teleological argument by representing the lot of the 'Risen Saints' as a preparation for, and a series of ascents towards the 'Many Mansions' of heaven (Book XII). Thus as God's 'Last Judgment' (Book XI) brings the saved to the highest heaven, the distance between them and the damned in the lowest deeps of hell is infinitely great.

A sense of ascent and separation later in the poem is heightened by its beginning with a 'Descent to Hades' (Book I), following the Seer's death. In the nether 'Paradise of the Blessed Dead' the Seer meets Oriel, who explains that he shall see 'greater things than these' (1.872). The presence of Enoch and Elijah in this intermediate state of paradise, rather than the final state of heaven, which Bickersteth justifies in an end-note, provides a focus for the anticipation which is generated at the end of Book II:

> their presence here
> Is pledge and earnest to the Blessed Dead
> Of that great resurrection day, whose dawn
> Already gilds the Easter of the world:

> They with the saints who rose when Jesus rose
> Are wave-sheafs of the harvest.
>
> (II.1011–16)

Like Pollok, Bickersteth tries to convey a feeling of adventist expectation through narrative suspense, as in Oriel's closing words:

> But of these
> And other mysteries in earth and heaven
> Conversing, on the range of yonder hills,
> Whose summits bound these beatific fields,
> And look far off into the waste beyond,
> If such thy pleasure, let us wait the end.
>
> (II.1016–21)

The plot of the 'blessed dead' in paradise – the subject of Bickersteth's tractate of 1862, cited earlier – is left in suspense while Oriel shows the Seer 'The Prison of the Lost' (Book III) and relates the story of Theodore, one of the 'lost souls' in hell who 'wait their sentence' at the judgment which is 'beyond' (III.594). The first three books of the poem are thus anticipatory, like the intermediate states in Hades that they describe, and that are explained by Oriel later in the poem in terms of God's foreknowledge of the fall:

> He, foreseeing all this ruin, had form'd,
> Deep in the unfathomable depth that lies
> Beneath the ocean veiling things unseen,
> Two vast receptacles *sunder'd though near*;
> One luminous, one dark: the first He named
> After this lovely Eden, Paradise,
> Henceforth the outer court of heaven itself;
> The other, precinct to the fiery lake
> Of dread Gehenna, Hell: and, ever as death
> Touch'd with his icy spear the sons of men,
> Thither their spirits dismantled should descend,
> And there await His judgment-bar, when they
> And rebel angels should receive their doom.
>
> (V.669–81; my emphasis)

The central books of the poem are devoted to Oriel's account of 'The Creation of Angels and of Men' (IV), 'The Fall of Angels and of Men' (V), 'The Empire of Darkness' (VI) – Satan's council after the flood – and 'Redemption' (VII), which describes Christ's life, death, descent into

Hades, and resurrection. Book VIII, 'The Church Militant', is reminiscent of Pollok's *The Course of Time* in its anti-Roman Catholic excesses.
Oriel then invites the Seer to recount 'spirit's life' (VIII.982–3). With
the end of their colloquy and a sudden trumpet call – 'the first / Of the
three trumpet signals fore-announced, / That usher in the long-expected
close' (VIII.1016–18) – the narrative enters a new phase in which Oriel
and the Seer together witness the unfolding of God's final purpose for
man and the earth. That purpose is enacted through judgment and the
infinitely wide separation of those who in Hades were 'sunder'd though
near'.

As in Pollok's poem, the resurrection of the dead (in Book IX, 'The
Bridal of the Lamb'), is the fulcrum on which Bickersteth's epic turns.
The Seer's 'sainted wife', who is now rapturously greeted by him, is
both antitype and type: as one of the blessed dead she is 'Not consort,
but what consort typifies' (IX.68), but her reunion with her earthly
husband in paradise is only a 'precious foretaste of the feast at hand'
(49). Oriel announces that 'The time is short' (92) and the blessed dead
rise to the earth, where the resurrection occurs in the twinkling of an
eye (321). Avoiding the pitfalls of *The Course of Time*, where the resurrection is described in too much literalist detail, Bickersteth follows
Pollok in making the resurrection the occasion of another preliminary
judgment. Joined by the 'thousand times ten thousand living saints, /
Changed and transfigured, from all lands and seas' (335–6) (with
whom, incidentally, all Adventists wished to be numbered), the 'soaring
multitudes' witness the 'Bridal of the Lamb' with his church. Babylon
falls (372), Elijah completes the restoration of the Jews (411), and Christ
inaugurates 'The Millennial Sabbath', the subject of the subsequent
book (X). Here again the typology of the sabbath – 'The memory of a
bygone Paradise, / The earnest of a Paradise to come' (X.29–30) – underlines the transitional nature of this part of God's providential plan,
where the end of the millennium is seen as 'the golden eve of everlasting
day' (X.594).)Characteristically, the sense of fulfilment in the inauguration of the millennium at the beginning of Book X – 'It dawn'd at last'
(45) – has been displaced by a sense of continued anticipation by the
end, for all has now been prepared for the final transitional phase which
separates the damned and the risen saints from their final states: 'The
Last Judgment' (Book XI).

While the risen saints have enjoyed the first fruits of the millennium
on earth, the damned in hell have broken an 'oppressive silence' only

to bemoan and confess past sins (XI.19). As in earlier books, there are several pauses in Book XI – narrative lacunae that suggest the awesomeness and the unnarratability of the separation of the damned from the Logos, and that, unnervingly, make it possible to hear the slightest murmur of the damned. During Satan's confession, for example, he acknowledges that he and the 'lost' are 'damn'd for evermore':

> Again was silence for a space in hell,
> So terrible, that only the quick breath
> Of spirits in pain was heard like tongues of flame
> Sibilant in the sultry atmosphere.   (XI.123–6)

Released from their bondage, the fallen angels return to the 'renovated earth' (209), where Satan's envy prompts him to comment that 'this is worse than hell' (256). A final rebellion is planned as the millennium draws to its close and 'fiendish malice' is loosed upon the earth. Again a sense of anticipation is expressed in the language of adventism:

> Watchman, what of the night? Night is far spent:
> Morn is at hand, the morn of endless day.
> Broods yet a tempest? Yet the last, hell's last
> Expiring struggle, heaven's last victory:
> Beyond is cloudless light and perfect peace.   (353–7)

A sense of heightened anticipation is justified here, as the last battle between God and Satan, and the last judgment itself, are the final narratable events of the epic: the final state of 'cloudless light and perfect peace' is ineffable, and cannot be written.

Narratable events therefore serve as types of that which will follow. When the conspiracy of 'devils and men' is put down, for example, the Lord himself lays on Satan the 'right hand of Omnipotence':

> The touch
> Alone was foretaste of the second death,
> Such death as damned spirits for ever die.   (482–4)

His hosts, now manacled, wait 'in speechless horror' for the last judgment, while the prison of the damned is emptied and destroyed. Like Pollok, Bickersteth gives much more space to the damned than to the risen saints here, emphasizing 'the terrors of the wrath to come' (511) rather than the hope of heaven. The description of the judgment itself follows Matthew 25, with Christ calling his own to inherit 'the royalties and realms' prepared and destined for them before 'the foundations of the world were laid' (637–40):

> So saying, He drew us nearer to His side,
> And placed us on his glorious right. O scene
> Of solemn unimaginable awe!   (646–8)

This 'unimaginable' spectacle is of the Messiah on his judgment-throne, surrounded by the thrones of the saved who are to witness the judgment of the damned:

> Each in its order'd place, tier above tier,
> Rank above rank, so marvellously set,
> Or such the virtue here of sight and sound,
> We saw the shades that pass'd on every brow,
> We heard the whisper of the faintest sigh.   (658–62)

'Face to face' with the elect, the 'apostate spirits' acknowledge the right-eousness of a Lord whose 'tones of wrath' are 'so strangely blent with grief':

> And, as the awful sentence fell on each
> Of chains and everlasting banishment
> To his own portion in the lake of fire,
> As by the Spirit of holiness compell'd
> We and the blessed angels said, Amen.   (701–5)

Satan is then crushed under the 'burning heel' of his 'Conqueror', the 'crystal empyrean' opens beneath him, and he and his rebel armies fall into a 'yawning gulf':

> Standing upon its rugged edge we gazed
> Intently' [sic] and long down after them; and there
> They sank and sank, the forms more indistinct,
> The cries more faint, the echoes feebler, till
> The firmamental pavement closed again:
> And silence was in heaven.   (740–5)

The 'millions of the dead', the lost, are then also judged, beginning with Cain and including Theodore, and are finally dismissed to everlasting fire 'Beneath Gehenna's burning sulphurous waves / In the abyss of ever-during woe' (879–80).

Bickersteth in his consolatory writings used euphemisms which exclude the this-worldly: the dead body is a 'tabernacle' but not also a corpse; the graveyard is 'God's acre' but not also a burial ground. In order to continue with a text of this kind the reader must suspend his or her knowledge of the tension between the this-worldly and the other-worldly which is the ground of incarnation theology and the subject of more complex imaginative literature on death and the future life. In his description of the last judgment in *Yesterday, To-Day, and For Ever*, Bickersteth implicates the reader in a sense of exclusive Calvinist solidarity through the Seer's narrative in the first-person plural. With the benefit of a perfect view and perfect acoustics, the spectators at the last assize miss not a single detail. The privileged perspective of the Seer from his vantage point among the company of the saved at God's right hand is validated by the acquiescence in the faces of the damned which his gaze meets, and by their reinforcement of his sense of Christ as 'Almighty Love'. Indeed, this climactic justification of the ways of God to men dramatizes what has been present in the text from the beginning. For whereas the damned in hell (the 'Prison of the Lost') are truly in a liminal phase – humble, ground down, vulnerable, passengers uncertain of their destination after the '*unknown* wrath to come' (III.982; my emphasis) – the blessed dead in paradise (Book II) are assured of God's purpose for them, and the Seer himself is provided with Oriel as a divine interpreter and guide on a safe journey which leads ever upwards towards unspeakable glory.

This imbalance in Bickersteth's depiction of the damned and the saved is maintained in his portrayal of the last judgment when he applies a favourite Victorian text (Revelation 7.17, 21.4) in an unusual way. The elect see that Christ weeps 'tears / Of grief and pity inexpressible' over the damned (890–1):

> And straightway we remember'd who had wept
> Over Jerusalem, and is the same
> For ever as to-day and yesterday;
> And in full sympathy of grief the springs
> Gush'd forth within us; and the angels wept:
> Till stooping from the throne with His own hand
> He wiped the tears from every eye, and said,
> 'My Father's will be done; His will is Mine;
> And Mine is yours: but mercy' [*sic*] is His delight,
> And judgment is His strange and dreadful work.
> Now it is done for ever. Come with me,
> Ye blessed children of my Father, come;

> And in the many mansions of His love
> Enjoy the beams of His unclouded smile.'   (892–905)

The familiar prophetic utterance, 'And God shall wipe away all tears from their eyes', normally taken to refer to the consoling of those who have come out of 'great tribulation', is here used to underline the continuity between 'us' and 'him', and between our will, his will, and the will of his Father in the unpleasant duty of dispatching the lost to everlasting torments. As time collapses ('the same / For ever as to-day and yesterday') so too do the defining (earthly) polarities of man and God. 'We' weep not for 'them', but for him whose will is also 'ours'. The reader is allowed no imaginative freedom within a closed scheme of salvation and damnation.

Christ then rises majestically towards the heaven of heavens, and the torments of a contrite Satan and the damned are described, again with reference to the power of the divine eyesight: 'His Eye, who is consuming fire, / Unintermittently abode on them' (XI.923–4). Book XI ends with a hymn of praise to God from the depths of hell: 'Glory to God who sitteth on the throne, / And to the Lamb for ever and for ever' (XI.1019–20). For the damned, God is 'there'. For the elect, in the words of the last line of the poem, 'God is here' (XII.653). The last book tells of 'our' final ascent, with Christ, to the 'Many Mansions' of the Father, where God is 'all in all' (XII.292). Interestingly, Bickersteth emphasizes that heaven is not static, and that not all its delights are revealed at once:

> Hence they err'd, who taught
> That in His presence faith and hope are lost
> Who is the God of patience and of hope.
> Things once invisible were visible;
> Things hoped for present: but beyond them all
> Illimitable fields untravelled lay ... (393–8)

Thus even in the final state of the saved there is a sense of anticipation of further bliss.

Although unorthodox in its millenarianism, Bickersteth's eschatology typifies in most other respects what Farrar called the 'common view': the 'vast majority of mankind' is condemned to everlasting punishment, and God is ultimately 'all in all' only to the saved. Whereas Pollok deploys narrative techniques such as suspense and repetition in order to sharpen his own judgments on sinful man, Bickersteth uses the same techniques to emphasize the widening of the great gulf fixed between the saved and the damned under the providence of a loving God. Much of the intellectual energy of liberal theologians who wrote on eschatological subjects in the nineteenth century, such as F. D. Maurice and F. W. Farrar, was directed against this common view. In dedicating *Mercy and Judgment* to Tennyson, Farrar described him as the 'poet of "the larger hope"'. Hallam Tennyson's gloss on the famous phrase from *In Memoriam* (55) also describes the hopes of many other writers who, if not strictly universalist in their views, were at least sympathetic to that position: 'he means by "the larger hope" that the whole human race would through, perhaps, ages of suffering, be at length purified and saved'.[91]

Philip James Bailey's *Festus* (1839), the best known work by the 'Spasmodic School' of poets, was frankly universalist in its otherwise confused theology. The poem was admired, albeit with reservations, by several eminent contemporaries, including Tennyson, particularly after the appearance of the second edition in 1845.[92] The first, anonymous edition of Bailey's eccentric reworking of the Faust legend contained a little over 8,000 lines; the second, which was attributed, nearly 13,000; and the last – the eleventh (1901) – just under 40,000.[93] Although the numerous and increasingly redundant additions to the poem reflect changes in Bailey's conception, his theological position is always liberal:

> *Festus.*
> We dare to ask for all things in Thy name;
> We dare to pray for all that live or die.
> Man dies to man; but all to Thee, God, live.
> We pray Thee, therefore, for the general dead. . .[94]

In *Festus*, God is not 'all in all' only for the elect. Indeed, the kind of position taken by Pollok and Bickersteth is parodied by Bailey in the 'Market-place' scene, where Lucifer, assuming the role of a ranting Evangelical, preaches a sermon. 'Beginnings are alike', he declares, 'it is ends which differ', and he goes on (in a passage marked by Tennyson in his copy of the second edition)[95] to warn his listeners that they shall 'perish sudden and unsaved':

> The counsellor, wise fool!
> Drop down amid his quirks and sacred lies.
> The judge, while dooming unto death some wretch,
> Shall meet at once his own death, doom, and judge.

> The doctor, watch in hand and patient's pulse,
> Shall feel his own heart cease its beats – and fall.[96]

This reference to the judge prepares for Bailey's judgment scene at the end of the poem, as does Festus's lengthy public prayer which follows Lucifer's sermon, and which Bailey added in the second edition:

> for all,
> Quick, dead, we ask Thy boundless mercy, more
> Than all sin, all defect, as infinite
> O'erlaps all finites. But by us be none
> Condemned. Shall culprits take the Judge's seat?
> Christ's lesson of forgiveness mote not we
> Forget . . .
>
> To whom shall mercy hope deny?[97]

If Pollok's key word is 'sin', Bailey's is 'hope'.[98]

Whereas Pollok's and Bickersteth's epic poems are narrated from an other-worldly and post-mortem perspective, Bailey's poetic drama adopts a Goethean model in which earthly scenes ('A Mountain', 'A Metropolis', and so on) are interspersed with visits to other worlds ('A Better World', 'Heaven', 'Hell'). Significantly, however, the last scenes of *Festus*, which follow the death of the hero, conform to a pattern which is similar to those of the Evangelical epic writers. In the first of these final scenes, which is very brief and is set in 'The Skies', God dismisses Lucifer to Hades, 'there / To wait my will while the world's Sabbath lasts'.[99] Typically, Bailey devotes much more space (over forty pages in later editions) to the 'Angel World', in which the angels and saints praise God. This worship continues in 'The Millennial Earth', where Hope exclaims,

> How sweet, how sacred now, this earth of man's,
> The prelude of a yet sublimer bliss![100]

and the Archangel explains to Festus the nature of the intermediate state:

> God works by means. Between the two extremes
> Of earth and Heaven there lies a mediate state, –
> A pause between the lightning lapse of life
> And following thunders of eternity; –
> Between eternity and time a lapse,

> To soul unconscious, though agelasting, where
> Spirit is tempered to its final fate . . .[101]

This interpretation of the intermediate state would have met with the approval of Tennyson, F. D. Maurice, and F. W. Farrar, although they would have queried the soul's *unconscious* state. In the following scene, however, entitled 'Hades', Death's announcement that 'the end's at hand', his removal of Lucifer, the resurrection of the dead, and the Archangel's announcement that the 'general judgment is at hand' would seem to prepare for an orthodox ending.[102] Similarly, in 'Earth' the Angel reports the last battle against Lucifer.[103] It is in the Son of God's speech in 'The Judgment of Earth' that Bailey subverts the Evangelical position by substituting Matthew 7 ('Judge not, that ye be not judged') for Matthew 25 ('Depart from me, ye cursed, into everlasting fire'):

> *Son of God.* I come to repay sin with holiness,
> And death with immortality; man's soul
> With God's Spirit; all evil with all good.
> All men have sinned: and as for all I died,
> All men are saved. Oh! Not a single soul
> Less than the countless all can satisfy
> The infinite triumph which to me belongs,
> Who infinitely suffered. Ye elect!
> And all ye angels, with God's love informed,
> Who reign with me o'er earth and Heaven, assume
> Your seats of judgment. Judge ye all in love,
> The love which God the Father hath to you –
> For His Son's sake, and all shall be forgiven.[104]

The last judgment itself is not described. Instead, the scene ends on the Son of God's words:

> The Book of Life is opened. Heaven begins.

And the final scene ('The Heaven of Heavens') opens with Festus being saved:

> *The Recording Angel.* All men are judged save one.
> *Son of God.*   He too is saved.
> Immortal! I have saved thy soul to Heaven.
> Come hither.[105]

The future of the baffled Lucifer is then discussed, and God himself decrees his restoration:

> This day art thou
> Redeemed to archangelic state. Bright child
> Of morning, once again thou shinest fair
> O'er all the starry armaments of light.[106]

Thus in the final triumphal pages of the poem, God is proclaimed not only as 'all in all' but also as being for all:

> *Son of God*. Now all in all are one; and Deified
> All nature as in God.
> *Holy Ghost*.   God, all in all.
> *Son of God*. All God hath made are saved. Heaven is complete.
> *Angel of Earth*. Be glad, O world of worlds! Rejoice, all life,
> And mourn no more. Death, evil, suffering, cease.[107]

Where Bickersteth emphasizes the unity of God and his elect by showing the latter weeping in sympathy with Christ, Bailey includes all mankind, and thus all sinners, in an *eschaton* which could be described as the 'one far-off divine event, / To which the whole creation moves' (*In Memoriam*, Epilogue).

Bailey's *Festus*, first published in 1839, was very much a product of its time. The work that Bailey himself described as a 'dramatic poem' owed much to Byron, whose verse dramas have always enjoyed a higher reputation on the Continent than in Britain. *Festus* also appeared at the end of a decade which had witnessed a revival in (mainly historical) verse drama, with plays by Bulwer, Knowles, Landor, Talfourd, and Sir Henry Taylor. In retrospect, however, it is to Browning's contributions to this revival, in *Strafford* (1837) for example, that literary historians have turned with most interest, in order to chart the poet's development from the early, and unsuccessful experiments with a purely 'reading' drama to the dramatic monologue.[108] One aspect of that development – the move towards experiential 'incarnations' of individual consciousnesses undergoing some kind of spiritual crisis – is of relevance here, with respect to nineteenth-century ideas on divine judgment. For in Browning's *Christmas-Eve and Easter-Day* (1850) we find a vision of judgment which differs radically from those in the extensive forms of the epic and the verse drama.

Whereas Pollok's, Bickersteth's, and Bailey's concepts of judgment are integral to their grandiose cosmological explanations of God's whole providential scheme, before, during, and after 'the course of *time*' (*chronos*), Browning's *Easter-Day*, which takes the form of a one-sided dialogue, turns upon a privileged moment of vision in an individual life at a specific time or 'season' (*kairos*) – the climax of the Christian year. Instead of Milton or Dante, Browning's precursors are St Augustine and Bunyan, perhaps the most influential writers of 'spiritual autobiography'. In both the *Confessions* and *Grace Abounding* the relationship between Christ and the individual sinner is direct, immediate, personal, and unique. In a famous passage from *Grace Abounding* (1666), for example, which recalls the New Testament accounts of the conversion of St Paul, Bunyan records a moment of revelation on the 'Sabbath-day' when God breaks into time suddenly, catastrophically, and unignorably:

the same day, as I was in the midst of a game at Cat, and having struck it one blow from the Hole, just as I was about to strike it the second time, a Voice did suddenly dart from Heaven into my Soul, which said, *Wilt thou leave thy sins and go to Heaven, or have thy sins and go to Hell?* At this I was put to an exceeding Maze. Wherefore, leaving my Cat upon the ground, I looked up to Heaven, and was as if I had, with the Eyes of my understanding, seen the Lord Jesus looking down upon me, as being very hotly displeased with me, and as if he did severely threaten me with some grievous Punishment for these and other my ungodly Practices.[109]

The impact of the 'crisis-autobiography', and particularly the *Confessions*, on English Romantic literature is central to M. H. Abrams's argument in *Natural Supernaturalism* (1971).[110] Victorian autobiographical and pseudo-autobiographical writing shares the same inheritance. Tennyson's lyric 95 in *In Memoriam*, for example – 'By night we linger'd on the lawn' – can be read in relation to a mystical tradition which came down from Augustine.[111] Teufelsdrockh's account of his spiritual crisis in Carlyle's *Sartor Resartus* (1833–4) represents a more radical revision of the spiritual autobiography in the *absence* of the divine 'voice', and the professor's consequent reliance upon the self and the will. As in Tennyson's roughly contemporary 'Supposed Confessions' (1830), this absence is registered in the subjunctive mode:

Had a divine Messenger from the clouds, or miraculous Handwriting on the wall, convincingly proclaimed to me *This thou shalt do*, with what passionate readiness, as I often thought, would I have done it, had it been leaping into the infernal Fire . . .

To me the Universe was all void of Life, of Purpose, of Volition, even of Hostility . . .

Full of such humour . . . was I, one sultry Dog-day, after much perambulation, toiling along the dirty little *Rue Saint-Thomas de l'Enfer* . . . when, all at once, there rose a Thought in me, and I asked myself: 'What *art* thou afraid of? . . . Well, Death; and say the pangs of Tophet too, and all that the Devil and Man may, will or can do against thee! . . . Let it come, then; I will meet it and defy it!' And as I so thought, there rushed like a stream of fire over my whole soul; and I shook base Fear away from me forever.[112]

Carlyle's treatment of 'The Everlasting No' would have been of interest to Browning, not only as an account of the purging of Calvinist paranoia in a 'Baphometic Fire-baptism', but also in its narrative technique, whereby personal experience is mediated through the two filters of the Teufelsdrockh persona and the Editor persona.[113] Like Carlyle and Tennyson, Browning understood the kind of Protestant tradition in which dreams and visions, and prophetic voices and writings were taken to be admonitory signs of the imminent danger of being judged and found wanting on the last day. All three writers adapt apocalyptic language and conventions to their own specific purposes. Browning, however, moved and influenced by the nonconformist piety of both his wife and his mother (who had recently died),[114] is in *Christmas-Eve and Easter-Day* unusually direct in his treatment of the Christian faith and sympathetic towards Evangelical doctrine.[115]

In the first poem, *Christmas-Eve,* the speaker tells how he came to witness the different responses of three religious traditions to the mystery of the incarnation. First, having hovered 'irresolute' in the porch, 'Partitioned off from the vast inside' (line 18), he joins the strange assortment of frail humanity who make up the 'elect' of Mount Zion chapel. Unable, however, to listen patiently to the dissenting 'preaching man's immense stupidity' (144), he escapes to the freedom of the common where, in his 'own church' of nature (272), the sudden appearance of a moon-rainbow in the sky heralds a firsthand encounter with Christ himself: 'All at once I looked up with terror. / He was there' (430–1). Christ then takes him to see the midnight mass at St Peter's in Rome, but he finds himself 'left outside the door', sitting 'on the threshold-stone' (596–7). Again, while the Straussian 'hawk-nosed high-cheek-boned Professor' delivers his Christmas-Eve discourse in Göttingen, he is left 'Alone, beside the entrance-door' (784). The speaker eventually finds himself back in the chapel again, having in reality fallen asleep and dreamt during the sermon (1238–45). An outsider in Rome and Göttingen, and, as he believed, in Mount Zion, he discovers that he has in fact been inside all the time. For all the limitations of dissent, he can now affirm, 'I choose here!' (1341), and the poem ends with his putting

up his pencil and joining the congregation in a hymn, thus marking his
membership through a communal act of worship.

Like Bunyan in the middle of his game of cat and Tennyson seated
alone in the garden at night, the speaker in *Christmas-Eve* is trans-
ported – freed from the limits of space and time in a moment of spiritual
crisis. Having crossed the threshold of organized religion, he is open to
an unmediated 'Vision' which he can claim to be 'true', and in which
he encounters the Christ who is 'Very man and very God' (586). When
he has effected the transition from outsider to insider he can see that
Christ is indeed present where two or three are gathered together, and
that the 'veil' which conceals him from sight is thin even where the
human material which embodies his Church is least physically
attractive:

> I then, in ignorance and weakness,
> Taking God's help, have attained to think
>   My heart does best to receive in meekness
> That mode of worship, as most to his mind,
>   Where earthly aids being cast behind,
> His All in All appears serene
>   With the thinnest human veil between,
> Letting the mystic lamps, the seven,
>   The many motions of his spirit,
> Pass, as they list, to earth from heaven.   (1301–10)

What the speaker describes in *Christmas-Eve* is his passage through
a classic liminal phase: he moves from the threshold of Mount Zion
chapel (cf. Revelation 14.1) to membership of its elect via a vision
which reduces him to a state of ignorance, weakness, and meekness.
The function of the vision in such a passage is familiar to readers of the
great mystics: it is theophanic rather than epiphanic.[116] The unmediated
personal encounter with God, the emphasis laid upon making a decision
for Christ, and the rejection of rationalism in favour of the leap of faith
are also strongly reminiscent of Browning's contemporary, Kierkegaard,
as Philip Drew has shown.[117] William De Vane rightly argues that the
revelation of divine love in the life and death of Christ links *Christmas-
Eve* and *Easter-Day*.[118] Equally important, however, is the shared theme
of the (Kierkegaardian) paradox of incarnation, which in *Easter-Day* is
conveyed through an apocalyptic vision of judgment.

The main speaker in *Easter-Day* makes the poem's central statement
in the opening lines: 'How very hard it is to be / A Christian!' Having

developed this theme in conversation with his more shadowy 'easy Christian' interlocutor, he prepares to relate a 'dread' event – an encounter with God which, he implies, is as 'solemn' and 'strange' as Moses's on Sinai:

> I still
> Stand in the cloud and, while it wraps
> My face, ought not to speak perhaps;
> Seeing that if I carry through
> My purpose, if my words in you
> Find a live actual listener,
> My story, reason must aver
> False after all – the happy chance! (350–7)

Three years ago this Easter-night he crossed 'The common, where the chapel was, / Our friend spoke of, the other day' (374–5). Turning over in his mind the kind of problem he has just been discussing, he asked himself a question that would not be out of place in *Grace Abounding*:

> 'How were my case, now, did I fall
> Dead here, this minute – should I lie
> Faithful or faithless?' (396–8)

Behind this question lies a biblical text that was often cited in nineteenth-century eschatological debates: 'if the tree fall toward the south, or toward the north, in the place where the tree falleth, there it shall be' (Ecclesiastes 11.3). Newman, for example, refers to the text in the *Essay on Development* when discussing what Coleridge and Farrar deprecated as the 'wresting of texts':

In religious questions a single text of Scripture is all-sufficient with most people . . . to prove a doctrine or a duty in cases when a custom is established or a tradition is strong . . . 'Where the tree falleth, there shall it lie,' shows that our probation ends with life.[119]

That our probation ends with life is to be a central theme in *Easter-Day*.

For the moment, however, the speaker relates how he merely toyed with such profound matters as the contingency of mortal life, the wish that 'God's kingdom come', and the possibility that that time or season (*kairos*) might coincide with Easter:

> And it shall dawn, that day,
> Some future season; Easter may
> Prove, not impossibly, the time –

> Yes, that were striking – fates would chime
> So aptly! Easter-morn, to bring
> The Judgement!   (461–6)

In putting flesh on his idle speculations, the speaker playfully adopts the kind of traditional apocalyptic language beloved of Robert Pollok and E. H. Bickersteth: the skylark, 'taken by surprise', shall 'recognize / Sudden the end' (471–3); ' 'At night it cometh like a thief'' (476); 'I fancy why the trumpet blows' (477); and so on. But one of his ideas suggests a further parallel between Browning, the mystics, and Kierkegaard – the 'father of Existentialism':

> From repose
> We shall start up, at last awake
> From life, that insane dream we take
> For waking now, because it seems.   (478–81)

At the very moment, however, in which he dismissed this train of thought (which had finally led him into childhood reminiscences) it was authenticated in an outward and visible form:

> And as I said
> This nonsense, throwing back my head
> With light complacent laugh, I found
> Suddenly all the midnight round
> One fire . . .
> Sudden there went,
> Like horror and astonishment,
> A fierce vindictive scribble of red
> Quick flame across, as if one said
> (The angry scribe of Judgment) 'There –
> Burn it!'   (501–14)

When he felt the 'Judgement-Day' begin, he knew that he could not go back: 'There, stood I, found and fixed, I knew, / Choosing the world. The choice was made' (552–3). In his own defence he pointed out that to have rejected utterly the world in all its beauty would have been 'too hard' (575), but in a final universal conflagration a voice beside him said:

> 'Life is done,
> Time ends, Eternity's begun,
> And thou art judged for evermore.   (594–6)

He looked up, saw only the common and the sky as before, and tried to dismiss the 'waking dream' (609) by recalling that not all the features of the last judgment described in the Revelation had been present: 'And where had place the great white throne? / The rising of the quick and dead?' (615–16). As in *Christmas-Eve*, however, an unmediated vision of God himself silenced all doubts:

> HE stood there. Like the smoke
> Pillared o'er Sodom, when day broke, –
> I saw Him . . .
>
> Motionless, thus, He spoke to me,
> Who fell before His feet, a mass,
> No man now.   (640–55)

God reminded the speaker that in the 'probation' that is mortal life he had chosen the world of his own free will, and that now, 'Judgement done', he could have the world but was 'shut / Out of the heaven of spirit' (696–7). In a radical reversal of the 'threshold' theme in *Christmas-Eve*, God said of the world:

>   'Expend
> Eternity upon its shows,
> Flung thee as freely as one rose
> Out of a summer's opulence,
> Over the Eden-barrier whence
> Thou art excluded. Knock in vain!'   (729–34)

Again the speaker found himself on the common, and consoled himself, first with the thought that nature's delights are inexhaustible, then those of art, and then those of the mind. The 'voice', however, unsettled him by saying that the earth is only 'God's antechamber' (752), while 'royalties' are in store 'one step past the entrance-door' (754–5), and that all 'displays / Of power and beauty intermixed' are merely 'needful furniture / For life's first stage' (816–20). Finally, the speaker acknowledged his error:

>   'Behold, my spirit bleeds,
> Catches no more at broken reeds, –
> But lilies flower those reeds above:
> I let the world go, and take love!'   (931–4)

He cowered before God, pleading to be allowed to go on, 'Still hoping ever and anon / To reach one eve the Better Land!' (1002–3), and, after a final revelation of divine love, 'lived again' in the Easter dawn on the common. As in most mystical experiences, his first thought was to dismiss the vision as a mere dream. Three years later, however, and back in the poem's narrative present, his closing comments leave the question open:

> 'Condemned to earth for ever, shut
> From heaven!'
>   But Easter-Day breaks! But
> Christ rises! Mercy every way
> Is infinite, – and who can say?'   (1037–40)

Whereas Pollok adopts a narrative device whereby 'the course of time' is viewed retrospectively from the privileged (other-worldly) perspective of heaven, Browning's *Easter-Day* begins and ends within the (this-worldly) horizon of the present. From an opening statement of difficulty and limitation, however – 'How very hard it is to be / A Christian' – the speaker has moved back in time through a retrospective narrative, to return to a changed present in which continued uncertainty ('and who can say?') is held in tension with a truth claim ('Christ rises') which, being both specific and universal, of this time and of all eternity, is as all-embracing as the epic scope of Bickersteth's title: *Yesterday, To-Day, and For Ever*. But unlike in Bickersteth's poem, that truth claim has been worked for in the text. Within the narrative past, an apocalypse enacted in the name of divine love precipitated the speaker into a liminal phase from which he emerged in a new state of knowledge.[120] The speaker's former defensive rhetorical strategies, whereby God was kept at bay and his judgment deferred to a distant end-time ('it shall dawn, that day, / Some future season'), reserved as only a possibility ('How were my case, now, did I fall'), or ironized ('This nonsense'), were dissolved in the simple present of a vision in which the 'season' was now: 'thou art judged for evermore'. The teleological is displaced by the immanent, *chronos* disrupted by *kairos*. It is only, of course, in the recalled present (which in this-worldly terms is past, absent) that the full presence of God is described. The collapse, however, of temporal categories at the end of the poem releases the concept of divine judgment from the teleological limit of 'last' into the immanent 'present' of life as a period of probation or a 'preparatory state'.

Both *Christmas-Eve* and *Easter-Day*, then, describe moments of choice in a spiritual crisis. Only in the latter poem, however, are the several meanings of *krisis* – separation, judgment, turning-point – brought into ironic interplay. In *Christmas-Eve* an ambiguous vision reveals some of the disturbing paradoxes of the kingdom.[121] *Easter-Day* is even more challenging, drawing upon a Protestant tradition of authority in which the individual has direct access to the divine, and yet mediating its vision of judgment through the indeterminate form of narrative recollection. Most modern critics of Browning have found these transitional 'problem poems' an embarrassment, and have gratefully moved on to the securer ground of *Men and Women*.[122] One of the first reviewers of *Christmas-Eve and Easter-Day* has thus been proved wrong in his prophecy that, although essentially different from *In Memoriam*, which was published in the same year (1850), they were 'both destined to an earthly immortality'.[123] Read as a linked pair of mid-nineteenth-century crisis poems, however, they are central rather than marginal works.

FICTION AND THE SENSE OF AN ENDING

For those mid-Victorian critics who emphasized the moral function of fiction, the authorial narrator was a God-like judge within the realist novel's horizon of the this-worldly, who not only proposed but also disposed through the deaths of characters and through narrative endings.[124] The concluding chapter of Trollope's *The Warden* (1855) – a one-volume novel – begins in a self-conscious manner that is reminiscent of Jane Austen:

Our tale is now done, and it only remains to us to collect the scattered threads of our little story, and to tie them into a seemly knot. This will not be a work of labour, either to the author or to his readers; we have not to deal with many personages, or with stirring events, and were it not for the custom of the thing, we might leave it to the imagination of all concerned to conceive how affairs at Barchester arranged themselves.   (21)

While promising closure here, the authorial narrator shared with the contemporary reader the embarrassment of ending, although that reader was not to know that a sequel was in prospect. In the previous chapter, the narrator declares of Archdeacon Grantly that 'we have seen only the weak side of the man', and thus prepares the ground for the character to be developed in a more complex way in later novels. Mr Harding and his friends are not declared fictionally dead or brought to judgment at the end of *The Warden*; rather they are left in a kind of limbo, from which they are later to be rescued in *Barchester Towers*.

In *The Last Chronicle of Barset* (1866–7), however, some kind of last judgment is appropriate, and it takes the form of 'dealing' with various characters in their dying. Deliberately to die standing up, as Patrick Brontë did for example, can signify stoic fortitude or stubborn wilfulness. Mrs Proudie's grotesque sudden death, however – she is found standing with one arm clasped round a bed-post, the mouth rigidly closed, the eyes open and apparently staring (66: 'Requiescat in Pace') – represents in a final tableau her ultimate isolation from her husband the Bishop, with whom she has just had a distressing argument. Dying at the margin of the site in which, it is hinted in an earlier novel, she dominated her husband, Mrs Proudie provides a foil against which Mr Harding's peaceful deathbed scene can be written towards the end of the novel. With those he loved alongside him, he 'seemed to sleep' near the end, and finally 'he was praying' (81). Mrs Proudie's funeral is not described. Mr Harding's represents the ideal easy transition from deathbed to grave:

They buried him in the cathedral which he had loved so well . . . and all Barchester was there to see him laid in his grave within the cloisters. There was no procession of coaches, no hearse, nor was there any attempt at funereal pomp. From the dean's side door, across the vaulted passage, and into the transept, – over the little step upon which he had so nearly fallen when last he made his way out of the building, – the coffin was carried on men's shoulders. It was but a short journey from his bedroom to his grave.

Whateley's strictures upon the popular idea of the 'happy death' were based upon the perception that it was unscriptural.[125] For the novelist, however, working in a secular form, it provided excellent material.

Turning to overt references to *post-mortem* judgment in Victorian fiction, we find in Thackeray's novels, which Trollope much admired, that the death of a character can draw the reader into a recognition of a shared and fallen humanity. Old Sedley in *Vanity Fair* (1847–8) dies a broken man, supported by his daughter Amelia who is comforted by her father's 'resignation, and his future hope' (61). To die in debt, 'help-less and humble', praying for forgiveness 'with a contrite heart, at the feet of the Divine Mercy', is a 'better ending' than that of the worldly, the prosperous, and the famous. The sense of a common humanity which will finally come into the divine presence is also emphasized at the end of *The Newcomes*, where three generations of the family pray together before the little boy is – in an ambiguous phrase – 'laid to rest' for the night (41). Old Colonel Newcome's day is approaching 'when he should be drawn to the bosom of the Eternal Pity', and in the following and final chapter of the novel his death at Grey Friars, his old school, is described in schoolboy terms:

At the usual evening hour the chapel bell began to toll, and Thomas New-come's hands outside the bed feebly beat time. And just as the last bell struck, a peculiar sweet smile shone over his face, and he lifted up his head a little, and quickly said, 'Adsum!' and fell back. It was the word we used at school, when names were called; and lo, he, whose heart was as that of a little child, had answered to his name, and stood in the presence of The Master.

Thackeray's emphasis upon God's mercy and pity in his references to the future life is typical of the major Victorian novelists, who were all liberal or agnostic on the question of divine judgment. The more extreme liberal views, however, could raise difficulties for the novelist, who was expected to 'judge' characters. Elizabeth Gaskell, for example, as a Unitarian who did not believe in hell or the last judgment, was criticized for her failure finally to condemn even her more reprehensible characters. (*Mary Barton* and hell are discussed in Chapter 4.) Dickens, like Thackeray, often exploits the tension between Christian values and those worldly values upon which many aspects of Victorian plotting are based, such as ownership, land, power, and physical attractiveness. At Magwitch's trial, for example, the divide between the 'innocent' and the 'guilty', the 'judge' and the 'criminal' is dissolved in a reference to the 'greater Judgement that knoweth all things and cannot err' (*Great Expectations*, 56). Trials in courts of law figure in many novels, including *Paul Clifford*, *Pickwick Papers*, *Bleak House*, *Mary Barton*, *Alton Locke*, and *Felix Holt*. In most cases a critique of the law serves to strengthen the authority of the novelist; and even where characters are handed over to the higher authority of divine mercy, as in Dickens and Thackeray, a large measure of authorial control is in play.

The whole project of serious fiction in the early- and mid-Victorian periods is judgmental, both of individuals and of the society in which they live and die. The rejection of this moral function of fiction in later generations of novelists is reflected in the handling of the biblical language of judgment, and particularly from the Revelation. Whereas in *Hard Times* (1854) Dickens's use of apocalyptic symbolism is as central to his vision as Blake's or John Martin's, Hardy's ironic reference to a 'Last Day luridness' in the confession scene in *Tess of the d'Urbervilles* (1891; 34) is as marginal as the teaching of the church itself to the novel's judgment of Tess as 'A Pure Woman'. Samuel Butler's revisionary account of English religious practice in *The Way of all Flesh* (1903) was written mainly in the 1870s, soon after the publication of *Middlemarch* and the last major revival of millenarian expectation in England. Overton, the narrator, recalls how things were back in 1811, when the bell tolled for old Mrs Pontifex and his nurse terrified him by saying that he too could be struck with paralysis and 'taken straight off to the Day of Judgment':

The Day of Judgment indeed, according to the opinion of those who were most likely to know, would not under any circumstances be delayed more than a few years longer, and then the whole world would be burned, and we ourselves be consigned to an eternity of torture, unless we mended our ways more than we at present seemed at all likely to do . . . .

. . . we were astonished to find that Napoleon Buonaparte was an actually living person. We had thought such a great man could only have lived a very long time ago, and here he was after all almost as it were at our own doors. This lent colour to the view that the Day of Judgment might indeed be nearer than we had thought, but nurse said that was all right now, and she knew.   (3)

Theobald Pontifex, who comforts a dying and frightened old woman by informing her that she will be 'lost' if she doubts that 'we shall all appear before the Judgment Seat of Christ, and that the wicked will be consumed in a lake of everlasting fire' (15), is himself brought to another kind of (Butleresque) judgment when his wife Christina is dying and, being afraid of the day of judgment, seems to question his efficacy as a clergyman (83). In Ernest Pontifex's final rejection of his parents' narrow Evangelical religion, Butler represents his own, and the century's coming of age.

Returning, however, to the mid-century period in which many writers of the former generation – including Tennyson, Browning, Dickens, the Brontës, and Ruskin – were producing their most significant work, and in which the influence of Carlyle's prophetic writings was probably at its height, we find that the language of apocalypse is an aspect of their shared culture and a potent force in their writing. For Romantic novelists, such as Dickens, and Charlotte and Emily Brontë, the language of the Revelation was an aspect of their 'poetry'.

One of the main limitations of realist fiction in the nineteenth century was that, unlike the heavenly spectators in Evangelical epic poems, for example, narrators could not penetrate the veil which separates 'this side' from 'that side': even their so-called 'omniscience' is restricted to time and space. Yet many of the key passages in realist Victorian fiction are precisely those in which the gradual uncovering of events in an orderly and chronological sequence in the narrative is displaced by the kind of catastrophist structures and language normally associated with Romantic forms such as the Gothic novel or the 'sensation' novel. George Eliot's sensational treatment of the Bulstrode/Raffles plot in *Middlemarch*, for example, is reminiscent of Dickens or Charlotte Brontë in its demonstration that at moments of crisis, when a man is judged, the reality of a concealed past is illuminated with an unrelieved, unaccustomed, and lurid brilliance. Furthermore, as in experiential or confessional poetry in which the horizon is ostensibly this-worldly, such moments of stress or fracture in the narrative can also allow the other-worldly to be issued in, usually through visionary or some other spiritual experience. It is, however, in the romances of Charlotte and Emily Brontë that this 'vertical' dimension of narrative is exploited most fully, and the theme of judgment explored.

The third and final volume of *Jane Eyre* (1847), for example, which is to focus upon last things, begins with Jane's internal dialogue after the wedding fiasco: 'What am I to do? . . . Leave Thornfield at once' (27). It is not until the end of this chapter, however, in which Rochester gives his account of his married life with Bertha Mason in the 'bottom-less pit' of hell (Revelation 9.1), and tries to persuade Jane to live with him on the Mediterranean, that a visionary figure directs her to leave Thornfield:

I dreamt I lay in the red-room at Gateshead . . . The light that long ago had struck me into syncope, recalled in this vision, seemed glidingly to mount the wall, and tremblingly to pause in the centre of the obscured ceiling. I lifted up my head to look: the roof resolved to clouds, high and dim; the gleam was such as the moon imparts to vapours she is about to sever. I watched her come – watched with the strangest anticipation; as though some word of doom were to be written on her disk. She broke forth as never moon yet burst from cloud: a hand first penetrated the sable folds and waved them away; then, not a moon, but a white human form shone in the azure, inclining a glorious brow earthward. It gazed and gazed on me. It spoke, to my spirit: immeasurably distant was the tone, yet so near, it whispered in my heart –

'My daughter, flee temptation!'
'Mother, I will.'
So I answered after I had waked from the trance-like dream.

Unlike the moon-rainbow in Browning's *Christmas-Eve*, which heralds
the subsequent appearance of Christ beside the speaker, this moon
resolves itself into a figure who represents the 'feminine principle' in the
novel, and who is akin to the Great Mother, the lunar goddess of pagan
religions.

Having escaped from Thornfield and the threatening male domination
of Rochester, Jane is 'as hard beset' by his polar opposite, St John
Rivers, whose reading of Revelation 21 has a powerful influence upon
her:

> never did his manner become so impressive in its noble simplicity, as when he
> delivered the oracles of God; and to-night that voice took a more solemn tone –
> that manner a more thrilling meaning – as he sat in the midst of his household
> circle (the May moon shining in through the uncurtained window, and render-
> ing almost unnecessary the light of the candle on the table): as he sat there,
> bending over the great old Bible, and described from its page the vision of the
> new heaven and the new earth – told how God would come to dwell with men,
> how he would wipe away all tears from their eyes, and promised that there
> should be no more death, neither sorrow nor crying, nor any more pain, because
> the former things were passed away.   (35)

Rivers, a more intelligent Evangelical than Brocklehurst, implicitly
repeats the warnings of that earlier oppressor as he subtly directs at her
the verse on the 'lake which burneth with fire and brimstone, which is
the second death'. In the prayers that follow, he claims 'the boon of a
brand snatched from the burning', and then lays his hand on Jane's
head:

> I stood motionless under my hierophant's touch. My refusals were forgotten –
> my fears overcome – my wrestlings paralyzed. The Impossible – *i.e.* my mar-
> riage with St. John – was fast becoming the Possible. All was changing utterly,
> with a sudden sweep. Religion called – Angels beckoned – God commanded –
> life rolled together like a scroll – death's gates opened, shewed eternity beyond:
> it seemed, that for safety and bliss there, all here might be sacrificed in a second.
> The dim room was full of visions.

Jane's temporary submission to St John is marked by her entry into
his own religious language and mute acceptance of his eschatology.
As the candle dies out, however, and the room floods with moonlight,

her own prayers are answered by Rochester's cry. Escaping from the house, and also from St John's discourse, she interprets the cry as 'no miracle', but 'the work of nature', and seems to penetrate 'very near a Mighty Spirit' when she hurries upstairs to pray in a 'different way' from St John's.

Jane Eyre re-enters St John's language, but now as the narrator, in the last paragraphs of a 'Conclusion' which has promised closure in its famous opening: 'Reader, I married him.' While she and a chastised Rochester (he thanks the God who 'judges not as man judges') find an earthly paradise in family life, Jane anticipates for St John the inevitable end for the missionary in India, and the equally certain reward:

His is the ambition of the high master-spirit, which aims to fill a place in the first rank of those who are redeemed from the earth – who stand without fault before the throne of God; who share the last mighty victories of the lamb; who are called, and chosen, and faithful.

. . . No fear of death will darken St. John's last hour: his mind will be unclouded; his heart will be undaunted; his hope will be sure; his faith steadfast. His own words are a pledge of this: –

'My Master,' he says, 'has forewarned me. Daily he announces more distinctly, – "Surely I come quickly;" and hourly I more eagerly respond, – "Amen; even so come, Lord Jesus!"'

Jane Eyre ends with St John Rivers's 'last words', which are almost the last words in the Bible (Revelation 22.20). In a work of contraries – between novel and romance, spiritual autobiography and Gothic fiction, Evangelicalism and Byronic excess – two kinds of final judgment are held in tension in this Conclusion: a this-worldly ending for Jane Eyre and Rochester which promises male–female equipoise in an earthly future life, and an other-worldly ending for St John which anticipates his dying into eternal life with Christ.

Wuthering Heights, published in the same year as *Jane Eyre* and drawing on similar materials at several points, is more radical in its treatment of traditional teaching on the last judgment. Lockwood's first nightmare in the coffin bed at the Heights is uncannily similar to Browning's *Christmas-Eve*. This dream draws upon Lockwood's reading of the young Cathy's diary, inscribed in a book of sermons, where she describes her and Heathcliff's Sunday services under the direction of the fanatical Calvinist, Joseph, who provided them with books on 'Th' Helmet uh Salvation' and 'T' Broad Way to Destruction' (3). But Lockwood, too, like Nelly Dean before him, is strongly judgmental in his initial response to the inhabitants of the Heights, including the child ghost who visits him in his second dream, and this characteristic, together with his physical and psychological disorientation and his sexual anxieties, is reflected in the paranoid first nightmare. The last words he reads, however, before falling asleep, are the title of Jabes Branderham's sermon on 'Seventy Times Seven, and the First of the Seventy-First' (Matthew 18.22), which Branderham (a brand plucked from the burning?) preaches in the Chapel of Gimmerden Sough in the dream. As Trollope reminds his readers in *Barchester Towers* (6), those who attend a church service are trapped during the sermon, and have to hear it out. Lockwood is 'condemned' to hear Jabes interpret Christ's teaching on forgiveness as if there had been no new dispensation and he were preaching the old Jewish law, until he reaches the *'First of the Seventy-First'*. At this 'crisis', Lockwood 'denounces' Branderham, who in turn 'accuses' him with the words of Nathan to the adulterous David:

'Thou art the Man!' . . . Brethren, execute upon him the judgment written! Such honour have all His saints!

The rapping of the pilgrim staves in the battle that ensues is resolved into the rapping of a branch on the window, which is to resolve itself again into the ghost's tapping as Lockwood drifts back into sleep.

Unlike Browning's linked poems and *Jane Eyre*, this judgment dream deconstructs itself, revealing its sources – both theological and psychological – as it is narrated. Whereas Jane Eyre and Browning's speakers hold in tension a vision of divine judgment and a sense of earthly limitation, Lockwood's dream is self-reflexive, like the retrospective narrative which it precedes and which is to make up the bulk of the novel. Its language of judgment – 'condemned', 'crisis', 'execute', and so on – and the participation of the 'saints' in the act of judgment, are other-worldly counters in a dream of a this-worldly event. The effect of this and the second dream on the subsequent narrative is similar to that of Cathy's dreams, as she describes it to Nelly Dean: 'they've gone through and through me, like wine through water, and altered the colour of my mind' (9). Like Lockwood's, the dream that she presses upon an unwilling listener, in which she finds that heaven is not her 'home' and that she is expelled like the fallen angels, back to her beloved moors, deconstructs itself as it reverses the oracles of religion. These disruptions of 'normal' behaviour and judgment prepare for the famous and much debated ending of the novel, where Lockwood passes a now delapidated kirk to examine the gravestones on the edge of the moors, and to say over them: 'I . . . wondered . . . how anyone could ever imagine unquiet slumbers for the sleepers in that quiet earth' (34). Like Nelly's earlier attempts to understand Cathy and Heathcliff, Lockwood's analysis falls short of the revisionary nature of their idea of heaven. Caught up in the bonds of orthodox judgmental thinking, he cannot comprehend how they have transcended both death and judgment. Here, surely, is one explanation for the failure of most Victorian critics to understand the radical ambiguity and instability of *Wuthering Heights*, although many acknowledged its strange power. Like Nelly Dean and Lockwood, but most especially Joseph, critics generally assumed that Heathcliff was damned.[126]

Of the ninety-nine English translations of the hymn Dies Irae made between 1621 and 1895, eighty-eight are dated after 1800.[127] *Wuthering Heights*, like the other novels and poems we have been considering, was written in a period in which God's wrath and the possibility of imminent judgment were central to orthodox Christian teaching, and were widely accepted commonplaces of popular belief. They were also the subject of debate. The Victorian novel, a fundamentally secular form, engaged in this debate, most obviously in the portrayal of characters such as Joseph or St John Rivers. The Brontës' special significance, however, lies in the fact that, like Browning, they also drew upon literary traditions in which spiritual *experience* is conveyed through dreams and visions. Reference has been made to Augustine and Bunyan as precursors, but both the *Divine Comedy* and *Paradise Lost* (to which Pollok and Bickersteth were indebted), are also 'visions'. And behind all of these is the Revelation itself:

I was in the Spirit on the Lord's day, and heard behind me a great voice, as of a trumpet,

Saying, I am Alpha and Omega, the first and the last: and, What thou seest, write in a book, and send it unto the seven churches which are in Asia . . .

And I turned to see the voice that spake with me. And being turned, I saw seven golden candlesticks . . .   (Revelation 1.10–12)

Like the speaker in Browning's *Easter-Day*, Jane Eyre lifts up her head, sees, and then hears. In both cases the vision is conveyed within a dream, although, unlike in *Wuthering Heights*, where Lockwood remains an inadequate exegete, both figures enter a new state of knowledge through these apocalypses. Whereas the large structures of the epic poem allowed Pollok and Bickersteth to attempt a cosmological explanation of God's judgment upon man through time, the novel and the crisis poem proved to be better vehicles for more provisional and experiential visions of judgment in the nineteenth century.

1 Henry Bowler, *The Doubt: 'Can These Dry Bones Live?'*, 1855

THE POOR MAN'S FRIEND.

2 *The Poor Man's Friend*, from *Punch*, 1845

3　W. I. Walton, *The Last Moments of HRH The Prince Consort*, lithograph, 1862

4 John Everett Millais, *Autumn Leaves*, 1856

5 John Everett Millais, *The Vale of Rest*, 1858

THE SHADOWED HOME *AND* THE LIGHT BEYOND

THE PILGRIM THEY LAID IN A CHAMBER
WHOSE WINDOW OPENED TOWARD THE SUNRISING
THE NAME OF THE CHAMBER WAS PEACE
WHERE HE SLEPT TILL BREAK OF DAY *Pilgrim's Progress*

BY THE REV.
EDWARD HENRY BICKERSTETH

6 Cover design for Edward Henry Bickersteth, *The Shadowed Home*, 1875

7 John Martin, *The Last Judgment*, 1853

8 John Martin, *The Plains of Heaven*, 1853

9 Dante Gabriel Rossetti, sketch for illustration to 'The Raven', *c.* 1847

10 Dante Gabriel Rossetti, preliminary sketch for *The Blessed Damozel*, 1876

11 Dante Gabriel Rossetti, *The Blessed Damozel*, 1878

12 Dante Gabriel Rossetti, centrepiece from *The Seed of David*, 1864

13 Sandro Botticelli, *Mystic Nativity*, c. 1500

14 W. Read, *Drawing the Retorts at the Great Gas Light Establishment, Brick Lane, from The Monthly Magazine*, frontispiece, 1821

CHAPTER 3

Heaven

Holy, Holy, Holy! all the Saints adore Thee,
  Casting down their golden crowns around the glassy sea;
Cherubim and Seraphim falling down before Thee,
  Which wert, and art, and evermore shalt be.
                              Bishop Heber (1826)[1]

Divine judgment, the subject of the last chapter, is perceived in the nineteenth century as process, either cosmically, as part of a providential plan for mankind which is to be fulfilled in the last days, or experientially, via unmediated moments of *krisis* (both turning-point and separation/judgment). In the former case, judgment is enacted in, through, and at the end of time. Features of the formalized rites of passage associated with the dying process, such as deferral, anticipation, and hopeful expectation, also characterize the process of judgment and the movement towards the final or fixed state. Other kinds of liminal experience too, such as intimations of judgment where a figure is taken out of this-worldly limits into an other-worldly state and precipitated back to the this-worldly, are described as journeys, but in a 'vertical' dimension. Although often problematic as a subject for the writer, either theologically or in terms of the numinous quality of visionary experience, judgment is narratable as process or journey.

Heaven comes into the picture as the reward of the blessed; it is the goal, the fulfilment, the consummation of the Christian's 'lively hope'. The writer of 1 Peter refers to 'an inheritance incorruptible . . . reserved [*tetērēmenēn*: lit. having been kept] in heaven [*ouranois*: lit. heavens] for you, Who are kept [*phrouroumenous*: lit. being guarded] by the power of God through faith unto salvation ready to be revealed in the last time' (1.4–5). For the Jewish mind, the commentators remind us, endings are inextricably associated with beginnings. Thus 'when the Jew wished to designate something as predestined, he spoke of it as already existing in heaven', and the perfect tense in verse 4 'brings out the thought that the custody of the inheritance has been from all time'.[2] E. H. Bickersteth wrote in his commentary on the New Testament: 'This heritage – which is nothing less than the fruition of the favour of God for ever, in his likeness, in his service, in his presence – is safely stored in the heavens for the saints.'[3] Such an inheritance, however, reserved in heaven for some, implies the exclusion of others, and we have seen how in *Yesterday, To-Day, and For Ever*, for example, Bickersteth involves the risen saints in the judgment of the lost.

All this is suggestive of completion and narrative closure. Heaven is a place or a state (which, is a matter of debate) rather than a process; and, being a final place or state, it is often thought of in static rather than dynamic terms. Heaven is sometimes defined as or characterized by the beatific vision of the deity, which is in itself unnarratable. Another model of heaven is as a place of everlasting songs of praise, where saints 'cast down their golden crowns'. Here again, the subject does not lend itself readily to narrative, although it has lyrical possibilities. Both major movements in the religious revival of the early nineteenth century – Evangelicalism and Tractarianism – developed a typological under-standing of heaven as the eternal sabbath; as the future blessedness of which holiness in this life is an earnest; as the eucharistic feast of which the worshipper has a foretaste in this life. And in their hymns – the most enduring and widely familiar form of Victorian lyric verse to this day – heaven is treated as a transcendent spiritual dimension rather than a projection of earthly desires.

Although there are potential contradictions between heaven as beatific vision and heaven as worship,[4] for example, all the models mentioned so far are theocentric, and emphasize both the eternal nature of the church as the body of Christ and the continuity of the kingdom 'from this world to the next'. Other models, however, are anthropocentric, and stress the continuity of personal identity and thus of interpersonal relationships. As Colleen McDannell and Bernhard Lang have shown, from the mid eight-eenth century, when Swedenborg began to record his visions of heaven and hell, the anthropocentric heaven of human love and spiritual progress steadily gained ground on the more static theocentric heaven which had been in the ascendant in Western European theology since the Reformation.[5] Perhaps the most characteristic Victorian ideas of heaven are of a place in which family reunions and 'the recognition of friends' are to be achieved after death, and (more radically Romantic) of a site in which lovers are reunited as couples. Worked upon by imaginations less powerful than Blake's, such heavens are often more like a middle-class suburb in the sky than the city of God; less like the mystical marriage of Christ with his church than the consummation of erotic desire in an idealized form of safe sex. It is not difficult to see why such individualistic and exclusive heavens were scorned as pie-in-the-sky by working-class radicals in the social-problem novels of the period, and provided Feuerbach and Marx with easy targets in their critiques of religious belief and practice in the mid-nineteenth century.[6]

Whereas a modern theologian who believes in a post-mortem existence can acknowledge without embarrassment that all the traditions relating to it 'cannot be fitted together',[7] it was difficult to adopt such a position in the nineteenth century, when many Christian writers clearly felt obliged to attempt an account of the heavenly state that was both coherent and complete. For there was strong popular interest in 'what heaven is like'. Robert Weaver, a Congregational minister, distinguished between two readerships in his sub-title to a book published in the year of Victoria's accession: *Heaven: A Manual for the Heirs of Heaven; Designed for the Satisfaction of the Inquisitive, as well as for Assistance to the Devout. Also, on Angels and their Ministry* (1837). In reality the devout were also all too often inquisitive. Questions which were often asked, even after the publication of Weaver's ostensibly definitive 'manual', included several that were of general interest and concern: Are we to be conscious in heaven? Will we be reunited with friends and family? How will we spend our 'time'? In joining the heavenly choir, are we to give up our earthly assumption that all forms of life are associated with growth and change?

The Victorians' obsessive interest in post-mortem existence has of course been widely ridiculed in our own century. Although the activities of the Society for Psychical Research have been the subject of serious scholarly study in recent years, the broader subject of spiritualism is generally treated as a somewhat quaint aspect of the Victorian cult of death.[8] Ulrich Simon, in *Heaven in the Christian Tradition* (1958), is scornful of the 'uncosmic celestialism' which was a product of the subjectivization and secularization of heaven in the West after Goethe. A socially useful refuge from appalling conditions in this life, heaven came to mean 'anything from unusual happiness to the life after death', and Victorian hymns brought themes of consolation and reward to the fore. As in Pre-Raphaelite art, Simon argues, the greater the effort of 'descriptive realism', the emptier the result: 'The verbiage of "angel faces, hosts of light, and stars upon their way" fails miserably.'[9]

Now as Simon points out, one solution to the problem of accommodating the ancient Christian heaven in a modern scientific world-view is to 'ignore and even to refuse to state it', as Schleiermacher did in abandoning the 'original, cosmic claims' of Christianity.[10] In the light of the 'indefinite' or 'purely figurative' nature of the Redeemer's teaching on the future life, Schleiermacher argued, Christians can gather only that it is essentially 'the persistent union of believers with the Redeemer'.[11] Yet in England some theologians continued to attempt a reconciliation between science and a traditional biblical cosmology, and in both theological and imaginative writings two ideas of the heavenly state – as worship and as community – proved to be particularly resilient to cultural change. For heaven still fulfilled its traditional function of providing a site in which love, both sacred and profane, could be said to find its perfection, or completion, or consummation. At the very least it was possible to mount a defence of writing about heaven in a scientific age by treating it as an expression of the highest spiritual and moral priorities in this life. The interest in the nineteenth century in guardian angels, the recognition of friends in heaven, and the singing of hymns in the heavenly choir reflect a longing for different *kinds* of continuity between this world and the next. Such interest in that which lies beyond the veil raises questions of religious language that are by now familiar. Rather surprisingly, however, we will see that even some of the Evangelical writers who solemnly plotted the topography of heaven were sensitive to the question of the provisionality of the figurative language they used.

Having first reviewed some of the traditional concepts and terms related to this area of Christian eschatology, we will examine Victorian ideas and descriptions of heaven, with special reference to religious language. We will then focus upon devotional and literary works in which these themes are treated in a particularly significant way: first, Victorian hymns which convey a synchronic heaven – the site of perpetual worship; and secondly, the poetry of Dante Gabriel and Christina Rossetti, Coventry Patmore, and Francis Thompson in which heaven is the site of a final reconciliation between sacred and profane love.

HEAVEN, PARADISE, AND THE KINGDOM

Although 'heaven' is occasionally used as a periphrasis for God in the Judaeo-Christian tradition,[12] it is generally taken to be God's realm, created by him, subject to him, and thus distinguished from him.[13] Heaven is above us, both physically, as a synonym for the sky, and metaphysically, as the abode of God who is above all things. In the Old Testament, God's interventions are from 'above', and prophecies in Isaiah of a cosmic collapse and the creation of a new heaven and a new earth draw heaven increasingly into 'soteriological ideas'.[14] Christ's saving mission can be represented in mythic terms as that of a sky god whose incarnation, death, burial, and ascension describe a great circle which begins and ends in heaven.[15] During his ministry on earth he teaches his disciples to pray to 'Our Father, which art in heaven'. The creeds describe the Father as 'maker of heaven and earth', and the Son, Jesus Christ, as he who 'ascended into heaven' and 'sitteth on the right hand of God the Father Almighty'.

Bultmann comments on the fact that in the twentieth century we 'no longer believe in the three-storied universe which the creeds take for granted'.[16] The cosmological framework within which the New Testament writers worked had, of course, been displaced long before the nineteenth century, during which the findings of science and the Higher Criticism raised new questions concerning the creation of the universe and the mythic nature of biblical cosmology.[17] We will see, however, that there was serious discussion in the nineteenth century on the question of the location of heaven: perhaps it is *below* the earth? When this and other issues, such as the nature of the spiritual body in heaven, are discussed, reference is often made to the tension between the literal and the metaphorical, or the physical and the metaphysical, or the this-worldly and the other-worldly in religious language. Only in heaven itself could such tensions be resolved, it is assumed. For Ulrich Simon, however, an imaginative reading of the Bible is the soundest basis for discussion of such questions, as in the Bible 'extremes of literalism are balanced by extremes of metaphorical symbolism'.[18] We ourselves, he argues, 'oscillate between literal fanaticism and liberal vagueness', and we must bear in mind the freedom behind the scriptures (which we have lost) in order 'to understand the immense richness to be found there with respect to Heaven'.

'Richness' in the Bible, as Simon knows, is often synonymous with complexity, and we can see this in one of the key passages in the New Testament concerning heaven. Paul's account of his 'visionary rapture to paradise' brings several of the issues mentioned above into sharp relief, raises the important question of the distinction between heaven and paradise, and is of further interest as another prototype of the kind of visionary experience described in Browning's *Christmas-Eve and Easter-Day*, for example:

> I knew a man in Christ above fourteen years ago, (whether in the body, I cannot tell; or whether out of the body, I cannot tell: God knoweth;) such an one caught up to the third heaven [*hēos tritou ouranou*].
> And I knew such a man, (whether in the body, or out of the body, I cannot tell: God knoweth;)
> How that he was caught up into paradise [*paradeison*], and heard unspeakable words, which it is not lawful for a man to utter. (2 Corinthians 12.2–4)

'Paradise' derives from a Persian word meaning an enclosure, and thence a nobleman's park, which was borrowed by both the Hebrew and Greek languages.[19] Andrew Lincoln comments: 'Most frequently [paradise] is heavenly in character but it can also be earthly . . . or even combine elements of both.'[20] In nineteenth-century literature the tradition of the 'earthly paradise' was exploited by Romantic and Utopian writers, ranging from Coleridge to William Morris, whose dreams were of a new order in the here-and-now.[21] The millennium was generally understood as Eden (or 'paradise') reinstated upon earth.[22] (Such thinking helps to explain the concept of the kingdom, to which we will turn in a moment.) Newman, in his Oxford sermons, also considered the intermediate state (or 'paradise') to be like Eden, that other paradise which, 'though pure and peaceful, visited by angels and by God Himself, was not heaven'.[23] The *garden* of Eden also reinforces the helpful organicist symbolism of the graveyard in the nineteenth century.

The Eden parallel is to be found in Revelation 2.7, one of only three texts in the New Testament in which the word 'paradise' is used: 'To him that overcometh will I give to eat of the tree of life, which is in the midst of the paradise of God.' The second usage is in Christ's promise on the cross to the penitent thief (Luke 23.43), and the third is our present text, where Paul refers both to 'paradise' and the 'third heaven'. Modern commentators offer a variety of glosses on the third heaven, some of which allow the term to be synonymous with paradise.[24] The Anglican Newman and others in the nineteenth century distinguished between paradise, meaning the intermediate state, and heaven, meaning the final state of glory. In other contexts, however, paradise and heaven were equated.[25]

Finally, turning to the ineffable nature of the experience described by Paul, it has been claimed that the event 'may be thought of as an anticipation of the final transference of believers to heaven, or Paradise'.[26] The conclusion that can be drawn from this is highly significant in relation to the visions described in Browning's *Christmas-Eve and Easter-Day* and Tennyson's *In Memoriam*: 'Mystical and apocalyptic-eschatological religion are not as far apart as is sometimes supposed.' The difficulty of finding words to describe such experiences is a common theme in mystical writing, and the repetitive and halting manner of the passage in 2 Corinthians 12 probably reflects this as much as any private embarrassment to which it has been attributed.[27] Verse 4, however, also indicates that Paul is restrained from describing such a sacred event, and commentators have disagreed about the degree to which this is usual in such cases.[28]

Heaven- and paradise-language, then, were problematic in early Christian tradition, and by the nineteenth century an accretion of conventions and interpretation had complicated matters still further. Kingdom-language, on the other hand, could be applied to a wide range of nineteenth-century beliefs concerning the nature of eternal life, and is still widely used in contemporary theology. This is perhaps partly because the kingdom is less cosmological than heaven in its associations. Although the phrase 'the kingdom of heaven' (which is virtually unique to Matthew) might be thought to underline the contiguity between the Father and heaven (his special creation and domain), a modern authority informs us that the essential meaning is 'reign' rather than 'realm', and that by definition this reign does not arise by human effort.[29] The ambiguity of the 'reverential periphrasis' as explained in the *Catholic Dictionary* (1884) suggests parallels with the several different meanings of 'paradise':

the phrase 'Kingdom of the Heavens' does not necessarily imply a kingdom in another world than this. Nevertheless the expression lends itself of its very nature to a certain ambiguity and the context will have to decide the exact formality of its use in any given passage. Sometimes it is the Messianic kingdom of God on earth, sometimes the apotheosis of that kingdom in heaven, sometimes the recognition of God's royal rights by the individual soul. The perspectives will often merge since the kingdom on earth is designed as the antechamber to the kingdom in heaven, e.g. 8:11–12.[30]

Messianic expectation in the Old Testament that the kingship of God was imminent prepared the ground for the more spiritual and inward kingdom-language of Christ, who described the kingdom through parables. Unlike the term 'paradise', however, which can mean Eden, the intermediate state, and the final state of glory, the several meanings of 'kingdom' all proclaim the eternal divine king-ship.

The two most important models of heaven in the nineteenth century – heaven as worship and heaven as community – were in many respects difficult to reconcile. F. D. Maurice's emphasis, however, in *The Kingdom of Christ* (1838; rev. 1842) upon love and fellowship offered a means of drawing these concepts together, through kingdom-language. With reference to the epistles of Peter and the doctrine of John, Maurice writes:

For that men are not to gain a kingdom hereafter, but are put in possession of it now, and that through their chastisements and the oppositions of their evil nature they are to learn its character and enter into its privileges, is surely taught in every verse of the one; and that love has been manifested unto men, that they have been brought into fellowship with it, that by that fellowship they may rise to the fruition of it, and that this fellowship is for us as members of a family, so that he who loveth God must love his brother also, is affirmed again and again in express words of the other.[31]

The 'dynamic dialectic' of Maurice's idea of the church which shaped his Christian Socialism is beyond the scope of this study.[32] There are, however, important parallels between *The Kingdom of Christ* and Maurice's later ideas on the nature of the heavenly reward. In a lecture of 1861 on the Revelation, for example, he anticipates objections to the millennium by focusing upon its value in emphasizing that the earth is redeemable:

'We have been taught to look for a heavenly state; you want us,' they say, 'to fix our hope upon an earthly paradise. We have been looking forward to a reward which is to greet those who have served God faithfully here when they have passed the boundary of death; you point us to a blessed condition which may befall this world generally. . .'

. . . To me it seems that the hope of good for this earth is essentially involved in all the promises of God; that we must suppress the most obvious statements in Scripture, and kill the best wishes in our own hearts, if we refuse to cherish it.

. . . The deliverance of the earth is assuredly [the Apocalypse's] subject – but the deliverance of the earth, from the sensual masters who had degraded it, by its true spiritual Lord. The idea of a Kingdom of Heaven, which has been developing itself through every part of the New Testament, now reaches its completion.[33]

Maurice's argument that the kingdom is continuous between this world and the new heaven and earth that are to be revealed is compatible with Paul's 'paradise now and not yet', which implies that there is no break between an order already established in heaven but as yet only immanent on earth, and that which is to be fulfilled. Similar negotiations between past, present, and future revelations are transacted in Protestant and Roman Catholic liturgies of the eucharist, and in Victorian hymns. Liturgy and hymnody will be discussed later in this chapter. For the moment, however, the content of the popular views cited by Maurice should be examined in some detail: 'We have been taught to look for a heavenly state . . . We have been looking forward to a reward which is to greet those who have served God faithfully here when they have passed the boundary of death.' In the Victorian period there was great interest in and much discussion on the nature of heaven. After what was known as the 'spirit-rapping' craze of mid-century,[34] much popular interest in the subject was channelled into various aspects of parapsychology. 'Glimpses of a Brighter Land' via 'Spiritual Intercommunion' were not, it was believed by some spiritualists, incompatible with Christian teaching on heaven.[35] The 'reluctant doubters' who founded the Society for Psychical Research aimed not only to prove that there is spiritual 'survival', but also to investigate the nature of existence on the 'other side'.[36]

The recurrent implied question, then, was: What is heaven like? A prior question for the theologian, however, was: Is heaven a state or a place? Roman Catholicism regarded heaven as a place without claiming to know anything of its spatial characteristics or its relation to the physical universe. The theological argument as presented in the *Catholic Dictionary* is that as 'the sacred humanity is not omnipresent, heaven is a definite place in which Christ and the Blessed Virgin exist, and in which the angels and blessed souls are gathered together'.[37] Whereas this account set aside the question of the location or locality of heaven, some of the books on heaven recommended to Protestant millenarian readers in the late 1850s and 1860s acknowledged a difficulty here even as they skirted around it. The aptly named John Angell James of Birmingham, for example, argued in 1859 that

we are accustomed to think of heaven more under the idea of a state than a place, because we can render it more apprehensible to ourselves under the former, than under the latter; but some place there is, unvisited perhaps by human imagination, unthought of, where the King of Glory dwells, and gathers round His throne His chosen and redeemed people.[38]

Two years later William Branks, Minister of Torpichen, began the first of his three popular (but anonymous) books on heaven with a chapter entitled 'Heaven a Locality'.[39] (This book, entitled *Heaven our Home*, was said to have been read by Queen Victoria and Albert in the last six months of the Prince Consort's life.[40]) Similarly, in 1866 the view that heaven 'is not a particular locality, designed as the final residence of the pious; but merely that equable and blessed state of mind to which men are brought by the spirit of holiness' was attacked in an anthology of writings on *The Recognition of Friends in Heaven*.[41]

To argue against the idea that heaven is merely a state of *mind* is to address only a narrow, and probably untenable part of the case for heaven as a state.[42] Having claimed, however, that heaven is a specific, if unknown place, the author, who is not identified, goes on to discuss the various 'allusions by which heaven is represented to our faith': Mount Zion, a magnificent temple, the 'green pasture', and so on. He implies, then, that the 'Divine Word' refers or alludes to earthly things, using our limited earthly language, in order to make heavenly things accessible to us through the scriptures. 'By such *metaphors*', he suggests, 'is the place of our future rest described' (my emphasis).[43] E. H. Bickersteth comes to a similar conclusion about biblical symbolism in his prose discourse on the 'Estate and Employments of the Risen Saints', written at the same time as his epic poem. Heaven is defined as a state. It is a state of personal perfection, both of body and spirit; of eternal rest and refreshment; of combined royalty and service; of social perfection; of perfected communion with God in Christ; of perpetuity and yet of progression; and saints 'will there receive the reward of the inheritance'. The Bible, he argues, exhausts 'all the images of the purest and the deepest human joy' in describing the heavenly state. When he tested whether 'all the happiest scenes of earth' are used in the Bible to 'prefigure the good things to come', he 'found that in every case Holy Scripture had appropriated the figure'.[44] These scriptural 'figures' included several that Victorian writers of hymns and consolatory verse made their own: a happy home, rural delights, the joy of harvest, the 'social pleasures of a well-ordered city', and so on. Bickersteth, however, is aware not only of the intrinsic limitations of language in relation to heavenly things, but also of the dangers of literalism in the appropriation of biblical language. He himself believes, for example, that the 'almost uniform testimony of Scripture points to Hades as a region below'. But those who think that it is 'actually situate within the crust of our terrestial globe' should remember that the Bible's 'Divine language may only be an accommodation to our earthly thoughts of height and depth'.[45]

Bickersteth's caveats about figures of speech and the dangers of literalism clear the ground for his own writing project, both in prose and poetry: to interpret what the Bible reveals of the estate and employments of the risen saints. With or without such caveats, however, this and similar projects were open to the kind of attack mounted by the secularist Austin Holyoake, whose pamphlet *Heaven & Hell: Where Situated?* (1873) appeared at the end of the last major revival of popular interest in the subject:

> What is the Christian's Heaven? Where is it situated? In what part of the so-called Sacred Writings shall we find a clear and intelligible description of this abode of bliss – this promised land of never-ending pleasures, which is to be the reward of all true believers? It appears to be situated, by common consent, up above – beyond the clouds – beyond immeasurable space – and yet in the clouds. Whether in the torrid or the frigid zone, we are not informed. What its climate will be no man knoweth . . . How will the Englishman live and be happy, where the African can thrive, or the Russian of the wilds of Siberia will be at home? Are we to be dumb there, or are all to speak one language?[46]

The argument is crude and can easily be demolished. (It ignores, for example, the whole question of religious language and its function of mediating an established system of belief in a transcendent reality.) Yet Holyoake's short pamphlet touches upon several of the major issues considered so far in this study, including the nature of the resurrection of the body and the question of authority in Roman Catholic and Protestant traditions. By adopting a literalist approach to scripture, however, Holyoake draws the debate about the future life into the only arena in which secularism can and wishes to fight, namely within the horizon of this world and our mortal life. He exploits the fact that Christian apologetics draw upon scriptural 'figures' which attempt to describe heaven in this-worldly terms, but ignores the fact that apologists themselves recognize the limits of language.

Like the Roman Catholic definition of heaven as a 'place', quoted earlier, Tractarian writing on the subject of the 'unseen world' was cautious, reflecting a reserve which was intended partly to protect revealed doctrines from 'human judgment'. Both Newman and Keble emphasized the 'mystery' of the 'hidden truth' in the scriptural revelation concerning the 'unseen world'.[47] Tractarians also attached great significance to the holiness of those who are to enter heaven – a secret hidden with God.[48] Whereas the Tractarians emphasized the relationship between holiness and religious discipline, liberal Protestantism took a broader view. Thomas Erskine of Linlathen, for example, whose work influenced F. D. Maurice and initially impressed Newman,[49] argued in *The Unconditional Freeness of the Gospel* (1828) that heaven is 'the joy of God', and that we 'cannot enter into the joy of God without entering into the character of God': indeed, heaven is 'the name for a character conformed to the will of God'.[50] Fifty years later, F. W. Farrar mounted a very similar argument in *Eternal Hope*: 'Is it not a state rather than a place? . . . is it not *to be something* rather than to *go somewhere*? Yes, this, this is Heaven.'[51] 'To go *there*', he added, 'you must *be thus*', and we should not think of heaven as 'some meadow of asphodel beside the crystal waters, or golden city in the far-off blue'.[52]

The note of impatience here, which is also to be found in other writers in the 1870s, perhaps reflects the extent to which such symbolic language had been over-used, and indeed misused, during the third quarter of the nineteenth century.[53] That images of heaven will always fall short of its perfection is a commonplace in the nineteenth century.[54] One corollary of this is the argument put forward by Branks: 'It is not *one* type alone, but the *various figures* of the Scriptures *combined*, that give us the truest view of heaven.'[55] A second addresses the question of the nature of these figures which, in Robert Weaver's view, 'all have a spiritual signification'.[56] A third, expressed by Christina Rossetti in a poem entitled 'Paradise', takes the view that what are now images (here in a dream) will in heaven be wonderful realities.[57]

The dream images described in 'Paradise' are flowers, songs, the 'Fourfold river', the 'Tree of Life', the 'gate called Beautiful', and glimpses of the heavenly city. The reconciliation of rural and urban images that Christina Rossetti achieves in her dream poem by drawing upon the Revelation is more problematic in some other contexts. Indeed, the organic associations of country churchyards spoke to an increasingly urban society not least because they pointed to a heaven that was rural, and that thus represented an ideal which *contrasted* with prevailing conditions in the world.[58] Heavenly 'views' or 'landscapes', however, are often those of the illustrated family Bible, with the inevitable palm trees to shade those who are 'at rest'.[59] Traditional symbolism which represents the dying as passing over a great sea to the 'eternal shore' beyond is widely adopted in Victorian poetry and hymnody.[60] It is difficult, however, to hold both of these images *and* images of the heavenly Jerusalem in the consciousness together. Characteristically, John Martin made the attempt in his painting, *The Plains of Heaven* (illustration 8). Here the faintness in the original of the mirage-like heavenly city in the background is the visual equivalent of Pollok's and Bickersteth's sketchy accounts of the 'many mansions' or the 'highest heaven' at the end of their epic poems.[61] Jerusalem, with its vast domes that could be mistaken for clouds or, as in Jewish tradition, the highest mountain,[62] is thus accommodated by a vision of heaven which is predominantly rural by having its city-like features disguised.

Difficulties in interpreting the heavenly Jerusalem were recognized by Augustine.[63] E. H. Bickersteth saw 'the heavenly Jerusalem' as 'both real and typical – an actual city, of which every part typifies the spiritual temple of living stones'. He also believed that the details of the celestial city in the Revelation 'awaken conceptions of delight which we cannot always define or describe'.[64] In *Yesterday, To-Day, and For Ever* the city which the Messiah has built for his Bride, the Church, is described as 'A city, or a temple, or a home, / Or rather all in one' (XII, 298–9). In drawing together traditional Jewish ideas concerning Jerusalem as the final home of Israel, when paradise will come again, and the eschatology of the Revelation, he grounds the most common Victorian idea of heaven – 'the long home' – in biblical typology.[65]

In its popular conception, heaven as home often had materialist associations, yet the home/house/city nexus seems to have been more helpful than rural associations for those writers who saw heaven as the site in which all earthly types are fulfilled, and who emphasized what Isaac Taylor called the 'correspondence between the present and the future employment of the active principle of human nature'.[66] The question, What is heaven 'like'? could be said in the strictest sense to invite an analogical answer, and William Branks, like Taylor, commented upon the centrality of analogy to his argument that 'a state of grace upon earth is a state of glory begun'.[67] Clough wrote of the hope that 'What here is faithfully begun / Will be completed, not undone.'[68] Kant's emphasis upon 'moral improvement' had led him to think in terms of a state in 'the course of things to come' where 'the creature who has remained true to his nature and who has made himself worthy of happiness through morality will actually participate in this happiness'.[69] For Robert Pollok, happiness in heaven would be impossible without activity in 'meet pursuit',[70] and when Archibald Tate lost his son, then a young clergyman, he drew consolation from the thought that God wanted him 'for some work elsewhere, that [he] might serve in His own immediate Presence in the Heavenly Sanctuary'.[71]

Each of the different states or activities implied in these descriptions reflects an idea of progress, or development, or completion. Such thinking raises a number of difficulties. Tennyson expressed his concern lest the soul of Arthur Hallam should in some way develop in heaven to the point at which reunion was no longer a possibility.[72] It is not easy to imagine continued identity without continued sexuality, or to reconcile the idea of family reunions with New Testament teaching on there being no marrying in heaven.[73] The idea that heaven is 'greatly made up of little children'[74] represents a limited interpretation of the kingdom of heaven described in Matthew 19.14, and was the subject of many popular hymns.[75] To emphasize children in heaven (as John Martin literally does in *The Plains of Heaven*) is to stress innocence and thus to defer the question of adult sexuality. Children, it was generally agreed, would not somehow grow to 'adulthood', and those who wrote on the 'recognition of friends in heaven' consoled bereaved parents by stating that their children would be 'among the first to welcome' them on their arrival.[76]

A hope of reunion in heaven was frequently expressed in nineteenth century literature and theology, and treatises discussing this particular kind of continuity between earthly and heavenly existence were taken seriously by many educated readers.[77] Isaac Taylor's *The Physical Theory of Another Life* (1836), which deeply impressed the young Marian Evans,[78] includes a chapter entitled 'The Survivance of Individual Character, and of the Moral Consciousness', in which he develops his argument on the mutual dependence of the physical and moral nature. After the 'passage from the present, to another mode of existence', there will naturally be a settling-in period, and here the book begins to read like one of Murray's guides: 'A short season probably, will be enough to impart to us an easy familiarity with our new home, a ready use of our corporeal instruments, and a facility in joining in with the economy around us.'[79] William Branks saw his own argument that heaven would be social above all, a 'home' with a '*great and loving family in it*', as a counterbalance to the negative and unsocial views of heaven given by most divines.[80] Similar ideas were preached in a novel by the American writer Elizabeth Stuart Phelps entitled *The Gates Ajar* (1868),[81] which proved to be so popular in Britain that an irate, but unnamed Dean of the Church of England felt compelled to denounce it as manuscriptural, sensational, and spiritualist in its teaching.[82] Other approaches to the topic were more reserved. Keble, for example, wrote in *The Christian Year* of the 'store' of 'friends out of sight',[83] while F. D. Maurice, who, as we have seen, thought of the kingdom as a family, recorded that he could not read the account of the raising of Lazarus 'without feeling that, among those things in heaven and earth that are so to be restored, the sympathies and affections of the family are some of the chief'.[84]

We saw earlier that for E. H. Bickersteth, Christ's use of 'heaven's language', or 'the Divine style', or a 'celestial dialect' in the story of the raising of Lazarus was a mark of his divinity.[85] On the widely accepted view that entry into heaven is also entry into knowledge of God and his will, many Victorian commentators argued that the saved would immediately and without difficulty acquire 'heaven's language', which was before Babel and will be for evermore. Interestingly, however, Pollok in *The Course of Time* emphasized the continuity between *personal* earthly and heavenly existence by having the Bard of Earth explain that although all languages can be understood in heaven, as all are 'perfect here in knowledge', traces of earthly languages remain in a form of dialect:

> for each in heaven a relish holds
> Of former speech, that points to whence he came.
> But whether I of person speak, or place . . .
>
> . . . the meaning still,
> With easy apprehension, thou shalt take.[86]

This aspect of what Isaac Taylor called the 'economy' of another life emphasizes heaven as community, the site of idealized interpersonal relations in which love of neighbour is apotheosized. Is it to be assumed, however, that the perfected strains of the celestial choir of angels and risen saints mask any traces of earthly dialects, as heavenly worship (or love of God apotheosized) is in 'one voice'? In this as in other respects, the two main Victorian models of heaven as community and heaven as worship are no more compatible than the rural and urban imagery used to describe heaven. Kingdom-language, however, can be applied meaningfully to both traditions, while also suggesting earthly-heavenly continuities such as that of fellowship. It is in relation to continued fellowship that the communion of saints also accommodates both models, taking love of neighbour up into the corporate expression of love of God in worship.

As a doctrine, the communion of saints is particularly cherished by those clergy and religious for whom the daily round of work and worship is a divine office understood in relation not only to the church visible but also to the church invisible. Some sense of this is conveyed in a letter of condolence from B. F. Westcott, then Bishop of Durham, to William Michael Rossetti, concerning the death of Christina Rossetti in December 1894. No overt reference is made to the communion of saints, but the doctrine clearly shapes Westcott's thinking:

Not a week passes, I think, when I do not find some real pleasure from fragments of your sister's works. And my experience is, I am sure, that of very many. Those who so teach us and reveal themselves to us cannot be lost. However hard it is to realise as yet that the fact that they pass out of sight makes them unchangeable, at least I know – this house with its Chapel tells me so every day – that some of the friends who are dearest to me and help me most have entered on a fuller life. May you feel the consolation of this eternal companionship which *knows no break* in the presence of God [my emphasis].[87]

Sixty years earlier, Newman preached a sermon on the communion of saints in which he affirmed that the 'heavenly Jerusalem is the true Spouse of Christ and virgin Mother of Saints', and that 'this *invisible* body is the *true* Church, because it changes not, though it is ever increasing'.[88] In another sermon entitled 'The Invisible World' he wrote of the 'world of spirits', though unseen, being 'present': 'It is not above the sky, it is not beyond the grave; it is now and here; the kingdom of God is among us.'[89] Thus a 'world of Saints and Angels, a glorious world, the palace of God, the mountain of the Lord of Hosts, the heavenly Jerusalem, the throne of God and Christ, all these wonders, everlasting, all-precious, mysterious, and incomprehensible, lie hid in what we see'.[90] Among the great divines of the nineteenth century, Newman had the strongest sense of the ministry of angels, those 'inhabitants of the world invisible' about whom, on his argument, we know more than about the faithful departed, as they are active, rather than resting from their labours. Although they are so wonderful that we could not bear to look at them, if that were possible, they are 'our "fellow-servants" and our fellow-workers, and they carefully watch over and defend even the humblest of us, if we be Christ's'.[91]

It is important to emphasize that although Newman wrote of the kingdom of heaven being among us and of angels as our fellow-workers, the 'invisible world' is by definition hidden and utterly *different* from this world, in which we can discern only signs of its presence. Heaven for Newman 'is not like this world', but much more like a church, 'because both in the one and the other, there is one single sovereign subject – religion – brought before us'.[92] Heaven 'would be hell to an irreligious man', because in heaven every man must 'do *God's* pleasure' rather than 'choose and take his *own* pleasure'.[93] Other writers of different religious persuasions put forward similar arguments in the nineteenth century, but no teaching was more influential than Newman's on 'Holiness Necessary for Future Blessedness'.[94] Perhaps the most interesting counter-argument was F. D. Maurice's in his lecture on 'The Vision of Heaven' in the Revelation:

Oftentimes it has been said in Christian pulpits, that heaven is but the continuance of the worship upon earth. Those who have found that worship on earth very dreary and unsatisfactory, have said that they should prefer any Greek Elysium or Gothic Walhalla to such a heaven. I think if we take St. John as our guide – if we accept his revelation as the true revelation – we may see a meaning in the assertion of the divine, and a meaning in the protest of the layman. All is worship there, because all are pursuing the highest good in contemplation and action; because all are referring their thoughts and acts to one centre, instead of scattering and dispersing them by turning to a thousand different centres; because each thinker and each doer is forgetting himself in the object which he has before him, in the work which is committed to him.[95]

'Work is Worship', that favourite tag of Thomas Carlyle, Maurice's sceptical fellow-worker in the labouring house of the world, here finds its apogee in a Christian Socialist heaven where worship and work know no division.[96]

Maurice's subsequent description of Hooker's announcement on his deathbed that he was going to 'a world of order' as a 'thrilling statement' reflects a deep sense of what Matthew Arnold in 'The Scholar Gipsy' called the 'sick hurry' and 'divided aims' of modern life.[97] Although in danger of suggesting a tidy, somewhat claustrophobic heavenly state, talk of 'order' is characteristic of a period in which heaven as a state of 'harmony' and completion was commonplace.[98] Only in Victorian hymnody, however, to which we now turn, were such ideas conveyed in a liturgical context which proclaimed heaven as worship.

HYMNODY: HEAVEN IN THE PRESENT TENSE

A formal act of public worship constitutes a corporate rite of passage in and through time. Following a general confession of sins committed in time past, for example, forgiveness or reconciliation may be declared in time present, before a congregation is sent back into the world of time future with a blessing and the saying of the grace. Lessons from the Old Testament, the epistles, and the gospels may be linked typologically, and the fulfilment of history-like events in later history-like events related to the lives of a congregation in time present and time future via a sermon or homily. Although diachronic, however, in its internal dynamics and its engagement with a revelation that is historical, an act of worship is synchronic in relation both to the divine reality and to the universal church, each of which is in a different sense 'present'. This is reflected in the dominance of the present tense in liturgy, as in the words 'I believe in God', 'Give us this day our daily bread', and 'We are not worthy so much as to gather up the crumbs under Thy Table.' Victorian hymns exploit both the diachronic and the synchronic potentialities of liturgical language in order to speak of heaven within the present of an act of worship.[99] Heaven may be now, or not yet, or now and not yet.[100] The continuities and discontinuities between this fleeting world and heaven are conveyed in the language of hymnody through special uses of tense and syntactic construction.

Within the dominant present tense of hymnody, three kinds of present can be distinguished: first, what we can call the 'eternal' present of heaven as an affirmed transcendental reality; secondly, the 'locutionary' present in which the hymn is sung; and thirdly, the 'existential' present of a mortal lifespan, as opposed to a future *post-mortem* existence. All three are to be found in this short version of one of J. M. Neale's *Hymns for Children* (1842):

Around the Throne of God a band
Of glorious Angels ever stand;
Bright things they see, sweet harps they hold,
And on their heads are crowns of gold.

Some wait around Him, ready still
To sing His praise and do His will;
And some, when He commands them, go
To guard His servants here below.

Lord, give thy Angels every day
Command to guide us on our way,
And bid them every evening keep
Their watch around us while we sleep.

So shall no wicked thing draw near,
To do us harm or cause us fear;
And we shall dwell, when life is past,
With Angels round Thy throne at last.[101]

The transition in verses 2 and 3 from the evoked eternal present of heaven (cf. Revelation 5) to the locutionary and existential present is characteristic of Victorian hymnody. Here it is effected through reference to the dual role of angels: in verses 1 and 2, some 'ever' (or, in a later version, 'always')[102] stand in heaven ready 'still' (in the sense of 'always') to obey God's will; in verses 2 and 3, some are sent 'here below' to guard us day and night, and, by analogy, in life and death. In the first two verses, traditional items in heaven are simply and directly described in the authoritative tone of hymnic affirmation. Then the petitionary form of 'Lord, give' in the third verse briefly establishes the hymn's locutionary present, which modulates into the continuous existential present of time future in the construction 'give . . . every day . . . bid . . . every evening', as in H. F. Lyte's 'Abide with me'.[103] Finally, the fourth verse affirms a blessed future in both this world and the next, where, as the hymn ends where it began, we will dwell 'at last' with angels who always stand around the throne of God.

The use of the first person singular can enhance the sense of immediacy in the locutionary present of Victorian hymnody, although the characteristic unction of pious ejaculations on the subject of heaven can be excessive:

O Paradise! O Paradise!
I want to sin no more,
I want to be as pure on earth
As on thy spotless shore;
Where loyal hearts and true
Stand ever in the light,
All rapture through and through,
In God's most holy sight.[104]

Like Newman, F. W. Faber, who wrote this hymn fifteen years after his conversion to Roman Catholicism in 1846, placed great emphasis upon holiness being necessary for future blessedness. Heaven is attainable only after a lifelong struggle against sin, which is dramatized in the repeated words 'I want' in the locutionary present.

James Montgomery, like Faber, believed that the existential present of a human lifespan should be dedicated to expectant preparation, as expressed in his hymn 'Songs of praise the Angels sang' (1819):

> Saints below, with heart and voice,
> Still in songs of praise rejoice;
> Learning here, by faith and love,
> Songs of praise to sing above.'[105]

On a universal scale, however, the whole of creation, past, present, and to come, looks forward to the end of the present order which Montgomery's contemporary, Robert Pollok, called the 'course of time'. For it is not until the last day that the blessed will enter into the full glory of heaven:

> Heav'n and earth must pass away,
> Songs of praise shall crown that day;
> God will make new heavens and earth,
> Songs of praise shall hail their birth.

Thus the worshipper's expectation in the existential present is taken up into a universal eschatological vision of God's providential plan for mankind.

These terms to describe different aspects of the present in Victorian religious language can now be applied to the strategies whereby the spiritual qualities of the heavenly state are conveyed in hymns. As we have seen, kingdom-language was less problematic than heaven- or paradise-language in the nineteenth century. A hymn by F. T. Palgrave, editor of the *Golden Treasury,* entitled 'Kingdom of God within', begins with these words:

> O Thou not made with hands,
>   Not throned above the skies,
> Nor walled with shining walls,
>   Nor framed with stones of price,
> More bright than gold or gem,
> God's own Jerusalem!
>
> Where'er the gentle heart
>   Finds courage from above;

> Where'er the heart forsook
> Warms with the breath of love;
> Where faith bids fear depart,
> City of God, thou art.[106]

The Pauline source, 'an house not made with hands' (2 Corinthians 5.1), refers, in Andrew Lincoln's view, to the 'heavenly resurrection body'.[107] For Palgrave, however, the negative form of the famous phrase simply provides a suitable scriptural basis for a hymn which marginalizes transcendental interpretations of the kingdom of heaven in order to earth the kingdom in the 'gentle heart', and to emphasize the locutionary and existential present of his final verse:

> Not throned above the skies,
> Nor golden-walled afar,
> But where Christ's two or three
> In his name gathered are,
> Be in the midst of them,
> God's own Jerusalem!

Palgrave's hymn was published in 1867, when the publication of books describing heaven, often in literalist terms, was at its height. In internalizing the Book of Revelation, however, it denies the other worldly side of the familiar liturgical parallel between worship in church and worship in heaven, in sentences such as 'Therefore *with* Angels and Archangels, and *with* all the company of heaven, we laud and magnify Thy glorious Name.' This kind of synchronic parallelism was exploited by hymnists of several different traditions in the nineteenth century. The revised (1827) version of Bishop Reginald Heber's Advent hymn, 'Hosanna to the living Lord', for example, celebrates the continuity between heaven, the 'house of prayer', and the human heart, via the workings of the Holy Spirit in 'God's temple':

> Hosanna to the living Lord!
> Hosanna to the Incarnate Word,
> To Christ, Creator, Saviour, King,
> Let earth, let heaven Hosanna sing,
> Hosanna in the highest!
>
> O Saviour, with protecting care
> Abide in this Thy house of prayer,
> Where we Thy parting promise claim,

> Assembled in Thy sacred Name.
>   Hosanna in the highest!
>
> But, chiefest, in our cleansed breast,
> Eternal, bid Thy Spirit rest;
> And make our secret soul to be
> A temple pure and worthy Thee.
>   Hosanna in the highest![108]

The repetition of 'Let' in the fourth line brings earth and heaven into syn-chronic harmony: 'Let earth, let heaven Hosanna sing'. The subsequent movement from verse to verse, however, is inwards, and it is possible that the second verse in the original (1811) version was later omitted in order to clarify this. What the missing verse brings out though is the continuity between the church militant and the church triumphant, and the syn-chrony between the eternal present of heaven and the locutionary present of the hymn as sung in church. Again this is achieved through repetition, although here the effect in the first two lines is antiphonal:

> Hosanna, Lord! thine angels cry;
> Hosanna, Lord! thy saints reply;
> Above, beneath us, and around,
> The dead and living swell the sound;
>   Hosanna! Lord! Hosanna in the highest![109]

Similar techniques are adopted in the opening verses of L. B. C. L. Muirhead's hymn, published in his friend Robert Bridges's *Yattendon Hymnal* of 1899:

> The Church of God a kingdom is,
>   Where Christ in power doth reign;
> Where spirits yearn till, seen in bliss,
>   Their Lord shall come again.
>
> Glad companies of saints possess
>   This Church below, above:
> And God's perpetual calm doth bless
>   Their paradise of love.[110]

From the eschatological perspective of the first verse, the hymn moves into a confident affirmation of the transcendent in the second, and the directness of description which is continued in subsequent verses could be read (if not sung) as a description of the altar piece on which it is

said to be based.[111] The delicate equipoise in the second verse between
the church militant here on earth and the church triumphant in heaven
is achieved by a contiguity ('This Church below, above') which suggests
a coincidence of opposites and accommodates all three kinds of present
currently under discussion.

Such strategies were well adapted to the aims of hymnists who wished
to emphasize the sacramental in their treatment of the heavenly state,
as we can see in three hymns from different traditions, but all written
in 1854–5. Horatius Bonar, a member of the Free Church of Scotland,
treats the eucharist as a direct encounter with the divine in his communion hymn:

> Here, O my Lord, I see Thee face to face;
>   Here would I touch and handle things unseen;
> Here grasp with firmer hand th'eternal grace
>   And all my weariness upon Thee lean.
>
> Here would I feed upon the Bread of God;
>   Here drink with Thee the royal Wine of heaven;
> Here would I lay aside each earthly load;
>   Here taste afresh the calm of sin forgiven.[112]

Following the confident affirmation of the first line, which is in the
existential present and the first person singular, present and future are
conflated in the 'would' which acknowledges that the bread and wine
are no more than first fruits. To drink *with* Christ the 'royal Wine of
heaven' suggests partaking of the heavenly feast. Hedged about with
cautious Protestant modifiers that emphasize the opposition of 'my' sin
and 'thy' grace, Bonar's hymn ends, as it began, in the present tense:
'Here is my robe, my refuge, and my peace, – / Thy Blood, Thy right-
eousness, O Lord my God'.

As the earthly sabbath is a type of the 'eternal sabbath' of the millennium or of heaven itself as a state of repose, so the eucharist is a foretaste
of a heaven that is future. Faber's communion hymn, 'Jesu, gentlest
Saviour', which is often sung to Stainer's 'Eucharisticus' (1875), begins
in the locutionary present:

> Jesu, gentlest Saviour,
>   Thou art in us now,
> Fill us with Thy Goodness,
>   Till our hearts o'erflow.[113]

'Till' already hints at future development in the spiritual life, and this is emphasized in subsequent verses where the gift of the eucharist is seen as a taste of the heavenly bliss for which we must wait in the existential present:

> Oh, how can we thank Thee
>   For a Gift like this,
> Gift that truly maketh
>   Heav'n's eternal bliss!
>
> Ah! when wilt Thou always
>   Make our hearts Thy home?
> We must wait for Heaven;
>   Then the day will come.

Finally, in William Bullock's 'We love the place, O God', revised by Sir Henry Baker for *Hymns Ancient and Modern* (1861), each aspect of church worship reflects God's presence among his flock: the two major sacraments of the Church of England, in 'the sacred Font', where the 'Holy Dove' pours out 'His blessings from above' (verse 3), and 'Thine Altar', where 'We find Thy Presence near' (4); and the 'Word of life', that tells of peace and ceaseless joys (5).[114] In the fifth and penultimate verse, however, an exclamation dramatizes the fact that these earthly forms fall short of heavenly worship:

> We love to sing below
>   For mercies freely given;
> But, oh, we long to know
>   The triumph-song of Heav'n.

And the final verse is a simple prayer for grace:

> Lord Jesus, give us grace
>   On earth to love Thee more,
> In Heav'n to see Thy Face,
>   And with Thy Saints adore.

These sacramental hymns, then, proclaim a heaven that is now and not yet, seen or tasted in the eucharist but to be enjoyed fully only after the last day. Newman's view that heaven would be like a church became a commonplace in Victorian hymnody, where the 'courts' of earth and heaven are often compared, as in Lyte's famous hymn:

> Pleasant are Thy courts above
> In the land of light and love;
> Pleasant are Thy courts below
> In this land of sin and woe:
> Oh, my spirit longs and faints
> For the converse of Thy Saints,
> For the brightness of Thy face,
> For Thy fulness, God of grace.[115]

As in Bullock's hymn, the emphasis falls upon 'longing' for heaven as the fulfilment of that to which earthly worship points. An alternative strategy is to set a hymn in the eternal present itself, as in Frances Cox's translation from the German of H. T. Schenk. The question posed in the first verse is based upon Revelation 7, where the past tense of the narrative account of the vision ('And one of the elders answered') gives way to the present in the reply ('What are these which are arrayed in white robes?'):

> Who are these like stars appearing,
>   These before God's Throne who stand?
> Each a golden crown is wearing,
>   Who are all this glorious band?
>   Alleluia, hark! they sing,
>   Praising loud their heavenly King.[116]

The answers explain the present in relation to the past: 'These are they who have contended / For their Saviour's honour long'; 'These are they whose hearts were riven, / Sore with woe and anguish tried.' The final verse celebrates the special kind of continuity between a priest's earthly vocation and heavenly reward by making two durative verb forms rhyme:

> These, the almighty *contemplating,*
>   Did as priests before Him stand,
> Soul and body always *waiting*
>   Day and night at His command:
>   Now in God's most holy place
>   Blest they stand before His Face.

The immediacy of the eternal present brings 'these' into the locutionary present, in the same way that constructions such as 'See . . .' and 'Hark . . .' can make angels 'present' in Victorian hymns.

Perhaps the most impressive triumphalist vision of the period, however, is Matthew Bridges's great hymn of praise to the risen Christ, written three years after his conversion to Roman Catholicism in 1848:

> Crown Him with many crowns,
> The Lamb upon His Throne;
> Hark! how the heavenly anthem drowns
> All music but its own:
> Awake, my soul, and sing
> Of Him Who died for thee,
> And hail Him as thy matchless King
> Through all eternity.[117]

Here synchrony between the eternal present and the locutionary present is established through the ambiguity of 'heavenly' in the third line: the anthem that is sung in heaven, *and* this earthly hymn which is like that in heaven. Thus the worshipper enacts the crowning (cf. Revelation 19.12.; Hebrews 2.9) as he or she has been enjoined, and in the third verse emulates the angels' heavenly reserve:

> Crown Him the Lord of love:
> Behold His Hands and Side,
> Those Wounds yet visible above
> In beauty glorified:
> No Angel in the sky
> Can fully bear that sight,
> But downward bends his burning eye
> At mysteries so bright.

'Crown Him with many crowns' is suitable for Ascensiontide, the season in which the nature of heaven as the realm 'above' and the separation of the risen Christ from his disciples are major themes. The Victorians inherited Charles Wesley's great hymn, 'Hail the day that sees Him rise', for example, where Christ's entry into glory and his preparation of our 'place' is described in the eternal present as 'the first-fruits of our race'.[118] The translation in the nineteenth century of ancient ascension hymns from the Latin or Greek made it possible to sing of the old three-storied universe, as, for example, in the third verse of J. M. Neale's 'O Lord most High, Eternal King':

> To Thee the whole creation now
> Shall, in its threefold order, bow,

Of things on earth, and things on high,
And things that underneath us lie.[119]

Bishop Christopher Wordsworth's highly scriptural ascension hymn, 'See the Conqueror mounts in triumph' (1862), is characteristically conservative in its typological and cosmological treatment of the subject:

While He lifts His Hands in blessing, He is parted from His friends;
While their eager eyes behold Him, He upon the clouds ascends;
He Who walk'd with God, and pleased him, preaching truth and doom to come,
He, our Enoch, is translated to His everlasting home.[120]

In contrast, Emma Toke's 'Thou art gone up on high' (1852), represents a simple and highly personal plea:

Thou art gone up on high,
    To mansions in the skies;
And round Thy Throne unceasingly
    The songs of praise arise;
But we are lingering here,
    With sin and care oppress'd;
Lord, send Thy promised Comforter,
    And lead us to Thy rest. [121]

It is fitting, however, to end this section with a brief examination of the hymn which was liked by Tennyson better than most,[122] and which supplied the epigraph for this chapter: Bishop Heber's 'Holy, Holy, Holy', appointed for Trinity Sunday. Like Frances Cox in her translation of Schenk's hymn, Heber adapts passages from the Revelation to his own purposes. The use of tenses in the Authorized Version reflects a difficulty which confronted the translators. Their additions to the original Greek are marked with square brackets in the following quotation:

And immediately I *was* in the spirit: and, behold, a throne was set in heaven, and [one] sat on the throne . . .

And before the throne [there was] a sea of glass like unto crystal: and in the midst of the throne, and round about the throne [were] four beasts full of eyes before and behind

. . . and [they were] full of eyes within: and they *rest* not day and night, saying, Holy, holy, holy, Lord God Almighty, which was, and is, and is to come.

And when those beasts *give* glory and honour and thanks to him that *sat* on the throne, who *liveth* for ever and ever,

The four and twenty elders *fall* down before him that *sat* on the throne, and worship him that liveth for ever and ever, and cast their crowns before the throne, saying,

Thou art worthy, O Lord, to receive glory and honour and power: for thou hast created all things and for thy pleasure they *are* and *were* created.

(Revelation 4.2, 6, 8–11; my emphases)

Some idea of the problem can be conveyed by comparing the Authorized Version with a literal translation of verse 9:

Kai hotan dōsousin ta zōa doxan kai timēn kai eucharistian tō kathēmenō epi tō thronō to zōnti eis tous aionas tōn aiōnōn . . .

And whenever shall give the living creatures glory and honour and thanks to the [one] sitting on the throne[,] to the [one] living unto the ages of the ages . . .[123]

And when those beasts give glory and honour and thanks to him that sat on the throne, who liveth for ever and ever . . .

Thus both 'give' *and* 'sat' (AV) are durative, conveying the sense of what was earlier identified as the eternal present of heaven.

Having put the words of the four living creatures in the mouth of the worshipper in the locutionary present of his first line, Heber suggests a promise of continued and regular earthly worship through the durative 'shall' in his second:

> Holy, Holy, Holy! Lord God Almighty!
> Early in the morning our song shall rise to Thee:
> Holy, Holy, Holy! Merciful and Mighty!
> God in Three Persons, Blessed Trinity![124]

Continuity between the locutionary and eternal present is established in the second verse:

> Holy, Holy, Holy! all the Saints adore Thee,
> Casting down their golden crowns around the glassy sea;
> Cherubim and Seraphim falling down before Thee,
> Which wert, and art, and evermore shalt be.

In the Revelation it is the *elders* who cast down their crowns, and the elders are differentiated from the transfigured saints and the angels.[125]

Heber's adaptation, however, strengthens the parallel between the earthly congregation and the heavenly 'host' of the redeemed. Several of the hymns quoted earlier invoke the various senses of 'crown' and 'crowning' in the Revelation: 'Songs of praise shall crown that day' (Montgomery); 'on their [the angels'] heads are crowns of gold' (Neale); 'Each [of the redeemed] a golden crown is wearing' (Cox); 'Crown Him with many crowns' (Bridges). The line 'Casting down their golden crowns around the glassy sea' is, however, one of the most vivid and memorable lines in nineteenth-century hymnody, and one that epitomizes the sense of synchronic worship in heaven that has been illustrated in this section. The rhyming of the durative 'casting' and 'falling' reinforces given temporal universality in the echoing triple structure of the line, 'Which wert, and art, and evermore shall be.'

Verse 3 returns to the locutionary present, and in the final verse a universal song of praise to the Trinity broadens to a *benedicite* offered on behalf of the three-fold creation of 'earth, and sky, and sea':

> Holy, Holy, Holy! though the darkness hide Thee,
>   Though the eyes of sinful man Thy glory may not see,
> Only Thou are Holy, there is none beside Thee
>   Perfect in power, in love, and purity.
>
> Holy, Holy, Holy! Lord God Almighty!
>   All Thy works shall praise Thy Name, in earth, and sky,
>   and sea;
> Holy, Holy, Holy! Merciful and Mighty!
>   God in Three Persons, Blessed Trinity!

HEAVEN IN POETRY OF SACRED AND PROFANE LOVE

The opposition earth/heaven, which in secular contexts suggests mutual separateness and inaccessibility (earth *or* heaven), takes on the sense in some Victorian hymns of mutual interaction and continuity (earth *and* heaven). In Muirhead's lines, 'Glad companies of saints possess / This Church below, above', for example, the comma signifies addition, both by substituting for 'and' (below and above) and by bringing opposing signs (below/above) almost into contiguity. In a liturgical context, Victorian hymns which 'spoke' of the kingdom could affirm the communion of saints as being at once below and above by establishing a continuity between the locutionary present and the eternal present.

Similar effects could be achieved in non-liturgical writing, such as E. H. Bickersteth's epic poem, for example, by introducing an angel visitant – a messenger of God who can speak in the narrative's present tense of that other angelic vocation, the endless worship of God in the eternal present of heaven. In other narrative forms such as the dramatic monologue, access to the eternal present is often via descriptions of dreams and visions, inserted into a standard past tense narrative. Traditional religious dream or vision narratives (the *Commedia*, *Piers Plowman*, the *Pilgrim's Progress*), like the New Testament sources upon which they draw (Paul's account of the third heaven, the Book of Revelation), are framed in the past tense, but can move into the present tense via dialogues between earthly and heavenly voices. This convention is followed by Browning in *Christmas-Eve and Easter-Day*.

The poetry to be considered in this section explores the major traditional *topos* of sacred and profane love, using not only some of the techniques that are characteristic of Victorian hymnody, but also some of those associated with dream narratives. Dante Gabriel Rossetti adapts Edgar Allan Poe's narrative technique in 'The Raven' to his own purposes in 'The Blessed Damozel', that ambiguous vision of lovers separated by death, yet able, even if fleetingly, to communicate across the bar of heaven. In contrast, three other poets write of earthly love in specifically theological terms: Christina Rossetti, in her fervent poems of renunciation and Christian hope; Coventry Patmore, in his bereavement odes which attempt to harmonize remarriage and the heavenly reward; and Francis Thompson, in his odes on unmediated religious experience, interpreted in relation to platonic human love. Although these four writers' treatments of sacred and profane love are different, each of them uses subtle modulations in tense and mode to convey intimations of a heaven which is both now and not yet.

Poe's 'The Raven' (1845) produced a sensation in England, and clearly impressed the young Gabriel Rossetti. Whether or not he planned 'The Blessed Damozel' (1847) as a companion piece, parallels between the two poems are too strong to be ignored.[126] At the end of the first stanza of 'The Raven', which opens in the traditional past tense of a Gothic narrative ('Once upon a midnight dreary'), the present tense comes through in the conventional form of a reported statement: ' " ' 'Tis some visiter," I muttered, "tapping at my chamber door – / Only this and nothing more".'[127] At the end of the second stanza, however, the modulation from past to present has the quite different effect of placing the 'lost Lenore' in the eternal present of heaven:

> Eagerly I wished the morrow; – vainly I had sought to borrow
> From my books surcease of sorrow – sorrow for the lost Lenore –
> For the rare and radiant maiden whom the angels name Lenore –
> Nameless *here* for evermore. (9–12)

The last word of the stanza prepares for the Raven's only word, 'Nevermore', the varied contextualizing of which in later stanzas registers a deepening disturbance in the mind of the narrator – Poe's real subject.[128] The possibility that the bird will leave the narrator 'nevermore' (60), suggesting an apparently endless earthly future, contrasts with the poem's central fact – the lover's presence nevermore, registered in the future tense: the 'cushion's velvet lining' she 'shall press, ah, nevermore!' (76–8). The narrator's later use of the present tense in his interrogation of the creature he takes to be some kind of supernatural visitant (' "Is there – *is* there balm in Gilead? – tell me – tell me, I implore!" ', 89), is ominously fragile in this penultimate line of the stanza, as the last word immediately evokes the expected rhyme of 'Nevermore' from the Raven (90). The subsequent construction in future and (eternal) present tenses, where the narrator asks the Raven to tell 'this soul' if it shall 'clasp a sainted maiden whom the angels name Lenore', by now seems shaped to draw out the only possible answer, 'Nevermore' (93–6). His last use of the past tense, in describing his 'upstarting' and shrieking at the bird (' "Take thy beak from out my heart, and take thy form from off my door!" / Quoth the Raven, "Nevermore" ', 101–2), leads into the continuous present of a fixed state in the final stanza, where is sketched a ghastly and, to the narrator, hellish mockery of an 'evermore':

> And the Raven, never flitting, still is sitting, *still* is sitting
> On the pallid bust of Pallas just above my chamber door;
> And his eyes have all the seeming of a demon's that is dreaming,
> And the lamp-light o'er him streaming throws his shadow on the floor;
> And my soul from out that shadow that lies floating on the floor
> Shall be lifted – nevermore! (103–8)

Rossetti's pencil and ink sketches of 'The Raven' (*c.* 1847) experiment with different ways of conveying a sequence of events in a single scene – a problem that was to be central to Victorian narrative painting. The most Dantesque treatment of the subject is that in which Lenore leans yearningly towards the narrator as she passes underneath the Raven in a procession of angels (illustration 9).[129] Whereas in the poem, which moves through time, the narrator's separation from Lenore is conveyed partly through play with two different and, here, irreconcilable kinds of present tense – the existential present of the bereaved narrator and the eternal present of Lenore in heaven – the sketch conveys the idea of separation by bringing the Raven and the two figures together in the same scene (as they are in the narrator's imagination), but with the central figures separated spatially at the point of her departure. Heaven itself, as other and elsewhere, is only *in posse*. During Rossetti's subsequent career as a poet-painter he explored the ironic relationship between *eros* and *thanatos* through the use of both narrative/temporal and pictorial/spatial mediums. The resulting contiguity of human beings and angels, the mortal and the immortal, makes his treatment of heaven profoundly ambiguous.

'The Blessed Damozel' is a highly problematic poem for critical analysts, not only because of the numerous changes that Rossetti introduced in the different versions which appeared during his lifetime, but also because no one version is stable in its perspectives on life and death, earth and heaven. According to D. M. R. Bentley, for example, the early Pre-Raphaelite version, published in *The Germ* in 1850, justifies Swinburne's conception of the implied Pre-Raphaelite poet as a Christian.[130] For Bentley, the reader-spectator 'comes to participate in an awareness of the Catholic Middle Ages' in this early version.[131] Yet even this critic acknowledges that a 'mercurial amalgam' can be sensed behind the 1850 version, written by a poet who 'knew about religious doubt as well as medieval faith, about personal misgiving as well as idealistic vision, about despair as well as hope'.[132]

This and later versions, including those of the 1870s, when Rossetti was working on the famous painting of the same name, reflect a radical insecurity in his thinking on the subject of heaven.[133] The poem's structure suggests that Rossetti attended not only to Poe's treatment of a disturbed mind at work but also to his handling of tense. Again the poem is framed in the past tense of traditional narrative forms ('The blessed Damozel leaned out / From the gold bar of Heaven', 1856), although here the place is apparently otherworldly – the matter being in some doubt initially because of the fleshly qualities of the damozel, with her hair 'yellow like ripe corn' and bosom that 'must have made / The bar she lean'd on warm'.[134]

Between these two uses of the word 'leaned' in the main narrative is its second use in the poem, where the interpolated voice of the lover states – parenthetically, in the present tense, and in a specific earthly site – that whereas to those the damozel left what seemed her 'day' in heaven had counted as ten years,

> (To *one* it is ten years of years.
> . . . Yet now, and in this place,
> Surely she lean'd o'er me – her hair
> Fell all about my face . . .
> Nothing: the autumn fall of leaves.
> The whole year sets apace.)

For the moment a very recent and transient sense of the damozel's presence is denied, the experience being explained away in terms of nature's annual and thus unremarkable signs of decay and death – important symbols for Keats, Tennyson, and the Pre-Raphaelites – autumn leaves.

Back in the main narrative the damozel's heavenly site is described in more detail, first in the past tense ('It was the rampart of God's house / That she was standing on'), and then in the (eternal) present:

> It lies in Heaven, across the flood
> Of ether, as a bridge.
> Beneath, the tides of day and night
> With flame and darkness ridge
> The void, as low as where this earth
> Spins like a fretful midge.

Here the sense of the separation of heaven from earth suggested by 'rampart' (an improvement on the too modern and domestic 'terrace' in *The Germ*, 1850) is greatly intensified by the modulation from past tense to present, whereby the contrast between the monumental stability of the bar of heaven and the restless mobility of the earth seems to be eternally ordained. Yet while the damozel leans over the fixed bar, looking longingly towards the earth from which her lover's soul will journey, all around her is life and movement in heaven. The final (1881) version of the relevant stanza reads:

> Around her, lovers, newly met
> 'Mid deathless love's acclaims,
> Spoke evermore among themselves
> Their heart-remembered names;

> And the souls mounting up to God
> Went by her like thin flames.

This version of the stanza opens up the poem's central dichotomy between a Romantic idea of heaven as the site of erotic reunion between lovers and a more 'spiritual' idea implied in the 'thin flames'. Rossetti's preliminary sketch (1876) for the background of his painting *The Blessed Damozel* (illustration 10) shows a number of couples meeting, two women in the left foreground in a sisterly kiss-of-peace embrace, the remaining man/woman couples in a variety of amatory embraces. The version of the fourth line of the stanza as quoted at the foot of the sketch, in which the lovers speak 'Their rapturous new names' (1872, 1873), emphasizes the idea of heaven as erotic bliss. For the lovers are enraptured by each other (heaven as reunion and community), not by the experience of the divine presence (heaven as worship). The more pietistic 1850 version in *The Germ* was different in emphasis:

> Heard hardly, some of her new friends,
>   Playing at holy games,
> Spake, gentle-mouthed, among themselves,
>   Their virginal chaste names;
> And the souls, mounting up to God,
>   Went by her like thin flames.

The contrast cannot be explained simply in terms of Rossetti's conscious secularizing of his early work, as 'virginal chaste names' was kept in until 1870. In all versions, however, without her lover the blessed damozel still leans out, not unlike Cathy in her dream in *Wuthering Heights* (9), published in the year that the poem was written, although Cathy's longing was to return to earth. The damozel's sense of longing is expressed in her opening words:

> 'I wish that he were come to me,
>   For he will come,' she said.
> 'Have I not pray'd in Heaven? – on earth,
>   Lord, Lord, has he not pray'd?
> Are not two prayers a perfect strength?
>   And shall I feel afraid?
>
> 'When round his head the aureole clings,
>   And he is clothed in white,
> I'll take his hand and go with him

> To the deep wells of light,
> And we will step down as to a stream,
> And bathe there in God's sight.'   (1856)

Although she is already 'one of God's choristers', her heaven is not a place of worship in Newman's sense. Her prayers are not expressions of praise or thanksgiving, as Beatrice's are in Dante, but petitions for reunion with her lover. Her anthropocentric and Romantic vision of how heaven will be then is that of a virgin ('She had three lilies in her hand') who is still unfulfilled. The eroticism which in a Christian poem might be of the kind expressed in the Song of Songs, and directed towards Christ the Bridegroom, is here channelled into the thought of 'lying' with the lover in heaven. The continuity for which the damozel longs is that between an earthly and a heavenly *paradise*, rather than that of the kingdom as expressed in, say, the doctrine of the communion of saints.

The crucial transition in the final (1881) version of the poem is reminiscent of Tennyson's *In Memoriam*, lyric 41. When the lover actually hears the damozel's words, his interpolated response to her talk of 'we two' being in heaven together in the future is anxious, as he doubts whether their former earthly union could ever be regained:

> (Alas! We two, we two, thou say'st!
>   Yea, one wast thou with me
> That once of old. But shall God lift
>   To endless unity
> The soul whose likeness with thy soul
>   Was but its love for thee?)[135]

In the main narrative the damozel then continues her description of an imagined future bliss for 'we two' in the presence of Christ and of Mary (who, like some tolerant 'Mother' will 'approve' her 'pride' in her lover), after which there are two concluding stanzas in the poem:

> 'There will I ask of Christ the Lord
>   Thus much for him and me: –
> Only to live as once on earth
>   With Love, – only to be,
> As then awhile, for ever now
>   Together, I and he.'

> She gazed and listened and then said,
>   Less sad of speech than mild, –

'All this is when he comes.' She ceased[.]
   The light thrilled towards her, fill'd
With angels in strong level flight.
   Her eyes prayed, and she smil'd.

(I saw her smile.) But soon their path
   Was vague in distant spheres:
And then she cast her arms along
   The golden barriers,
And laid her face between her hands,
And wept. (I heard her tears.)   (1881)

Whereas the apocalyptic prayer of the church militant is for Christ's presence ('Even so, come, Lord Jesus', Revelation 22.20), the damozel's last words in heaven, where Christ is already present, apply to the lover, and have erotic overtones. Her longing to be 'As then awhile, for ever now / Together I and he' is for a future that is not to be realized. For the earthly lover's final parenthetical statements, registering his seeing as well as hearing her, are in the past tense, quietly suggesting that there is no future for them. The damozel is left in a tragic gap between past and future, on the very margin of eternal bliss. Desire remains unfulfilled, heaven, in all versions of the poem, ambiguous.

Rossetti's career as a painter is characterized by an obsessive interest in the idealized female form which signifies the transforming, or perhaps transfiguring power of eroticism which issues in death. The different versions of the seventh stanza of 'The Blessed Damozel' (37–42) reflect a lifelong struggle with this ideal/real paradox, now openly confronted, now suppressed. In the famous oil painting, executed in the 1870s, paradoxes abound (illustration 11). Heaven is presented as a place of life and sexuality, with a deadly-alive damozel who is unsmiling. But then so too are the angels beneath her (only potential mediators between heaven and earth, sited in the space between the bar of heaven and the parallel framing bar beneath them), the lovers behind her, and the figures in Rossetti's other paintings. In March 1878 he deliberately 'brightened' the picture with 'flowers in hedges, aureoles round heads etc.'.[136] The tomb-like arrangement of the predella, however, is suggestive of death, the male figure (like Adam associated with the earth) in a recumbent position, his weapon sheathed (he will not 'come'), the landscape dark and bloomless.

That the idea of a transcendental heaven was problematic for Rossetti is also reflected in his treatment of the nativity in the triptych commissioned for Llandaff Cathedral, and entitled *The Seed of David* (1858–64; illustration 12). Technical problems in executing decorative art of this kind delayed him for years, but the finished design of the central canvas reflects a sympathy with the subject of God made flesh, with angels walking on the earth. Rossetti himself described the arrangement of the angels who figure in three of the canvas's four vertical divisions (marked by three characteristically bold horizontal lines) in these terms:

An Angel . . . leads by the hand a King and a Shepherd, who are bowing themselves before the manger on which the Virgin Mary kneels, holding the infant Saviour. . . other Angels look in through the opening round the stable, or play on musical instruments in the loft above.[137]

It is instructive to contrast the cramping of his angels, and the narrow limits within which Rossetti set what he himself described as 'not a literal reading of the event of the Nativity, but rather a condensed symbol of it',[138] with, say, Botticelli's apocalyptic *Mystic Nativity* (*c.* 1500; illustration 13). Here both the enlarged figure of the madonna, and the strong vertical hierarchy which elevates the angels in heavenly glory above the earthly scene, privilege the transcendent. Through the spatial equivalent of the eternal present, Botticelli's mystic nativity folds earthly time and space into a vision of that new heaven and new earth when 'we shall see clearly'.[139] Rossetti's vertical hierarchy, on the other hand, follows earlier models in stopping at the level of the loft, itself more a prototypical musicians' gallery or organ-loft than a glimpse of heaven. (One recalls Browning's Bishop at Saint Praxed's.) Rossetti's nativity scene signifies incarnation but not resurrection, earth as the site of 'heavenly' love but not of a new heaven and a new earth. Rather it was his sister Christina who looked for the coming of the kingdom, and whose cry was 'Come, Lord Jesus.'

Christina Rossetti commented that 'The Blessed Damozel' fell short of expressing the 'highest view'.[140] The contrast between her theological perspective on heaven and her brother's more fleshly view is reflected in their different experiments with tense. Like the Victorian hymnists, Christina Rossetti uses the locutionary present, the existential present, and the eternal present in her poetry which treats of heaven. One of her most important forms of syntactic play in this context (as in the poetry of Coventry Patmore and Francis Thompson) is her future constructions. Here she exploits the fact that terms such as 'will' or 'shall', 'when' and 'then' can be omitted in English after their first use in a sentence or clause, thus allowing subsequent verbs which are primarily to be read as future also to suggest or establish some kind of present reality, in this case the eternal present. The nearest that one finds to the effect in 'The Blessed Damozel' is in the second and last lines of this stanza:

> 'When round his head the aureole clings,
>   And he is clothed in white,
> I'll take his hand and go with him
>   To the deep wells of light;
> We will step down as to a stream,
>   And bathe there in God's sight.'   (73–8)

The first and fifth lines contain strong future constructions ('When . . . clings', 'We will'), whereas in the second and sixth lines, which are syntactically and typographically separated from the initial 'when' or 'will', the sense of future is weakened, although not sufficiently to suggest a secondary reading of these lines as if they stood alone; that is, as if written in the present tense. In the work of Christina Rossetti, however, this syntactic feature is used to make the anticipated heavenly consummation that is not yet, also now.

Whereas Gabriel Rossetti's blessed damozel undergoes no form of judgment, but, soon after death, leans on the bar which divides heaven from the void and the restless world, Christina Rossetti writes of the bar to which the soul will be brought at the last judgment, beyond which heaven is possible. This is the subject of her poem 'After this the Judgment' (MS title 'In Advent'), written during Advent in 1856 and published ten years later. The poem (the first of three of Christina Rossetti's to be examined here in some detail) explores the nature of its own art as heavenly song (the speaker longing to 'take up her part' in harmony with the heavenly choir), and is grounded syntactically in present tense constructions similar to those of hymnody and scripture. It begins with a series of familiar analogies of the spiritual quest for heaven, the doors of which are described (as in Newman, cf. Revelation 21.25) standing open for all who would enter:

> As eager homebound traveller to the goal,
>   Or steadfast seeker on an unsearched main,
> Or martyr panting for an aureole,

My fellow-pilgrims pass me, and attain
That hidden mansion of perpetual peace
　　Where keen desire and hope dwell free from pain;
That gate stands open of perennial ease;
　　I view the glory till I partly long,
Yet lack the fire of love which quickens these.　　(1–9)

The existential present of the first four lines ('pass', 'attain') modulates into the eternal present of heaven ('dwell', 'stands') before returning to the existential ('long', 'lack', 'quickens') via the ambiguous 'view', which only hints at the eternal present. Unlike in 'The Blessed Damozel', it is in the existential present of this mortal life that desire and hope are felt, whereas in heaven they 'dwell free from pain'.

It is through the mediation of a heavenly messenger that the existential and the eternal are to be unified:

O passing Angel, speed me with a song,
A melody of heaven to reach my heart
　　And rouse me to the race and make me strong;
Till in such music I take up my part
　　Swelling those Hallelujahs full of rest,
One, tenfold, hundredfold, with heavenly art,
　　Fulfilling north and south and east and west,
Thousand, ten thousandfold, innumerable,
　　All blent in one yet each one manifest;
Each one distinguished and beloved as well
　　As if no second voice in earth or heaven
Were lifted up the Love of God to tell.　　(10–21)

Taken up into the theocentric heaven that is everlasting worship, the speaker's 'voice' will ultimately remain unique and yet be 'blent in one', as it never can be within the limits of earthly language. Indeed, the merging of the future construction after 'Till' (13) into the eternal present represents no more than a foretaste of a heaven that is not yet.

Divine love, which subsumes the highest expressions of profane love ('Be Husband, Brother, closest Friend to me; / Love me as very mother loves her Son', 28–9), also includes judgment, without which heaven is impossible (36ff.). Within the projected future of that judgment ('Shall meet me at the inexorable bar', 44) the omission of later 'shalls' also suggests that it is a present spiritual reality:

How shall I then stand up before Thy face . . .

> . . . when no rock
> Remains to fall on me, no tree to hide,
> But I stand all creation's gazing-stock,
> Exposed and comfortless on every side,
> Placed trembling in the final balances
> Whose poise this hour, this moment, must be tried? –

(40, 49–54)

The judgment 'after this' of the title, expressed in terms of future time
(*chronos*), is also experienced now, in the season of penance that is
Advent (*kairos*).

The final section of the poem draws upon the farewell discourses
in the fourth gospel in which the present tense is that of the 'hour'
which 'was come that he should depart out of this world unto the
Father' (John 13.1) and of the season in which the disciples are to
be tested:

This is my commandment, That ye love one another, as I have loved you.

Greater love hath no man than this, that a man lay down his life for his
friends.

Ye are my friends, if ye do whatsoever I command you.

(John 15.12–14)

A poem of petitions ('speed me with a song', 'Draw Thou mine eyes')
now concludes with a prayerful meditation on the passion which is
reminiscent of Hopkins in its spiritual intensity:

> Ah Love of God, if greater love than this
>   Hath no man, that a man die for his friend,
> And if such love of love Thine Own Love is,
>   Plead with Thyself, with me, before the end;
> Redeem me from the irrevocable past;
>   Pitch Thou Thy Presence round me to defend;
> Yea seek with pierced feet, yea hold me fast
>   With piercèd hands whose wounds were made by love;
> Not what I am, remember what Thou wast
>   When darkness hid from Thee Thy heavens above,
> And sin Thy Father's Face, while Thou didst drink
>   The bitter cup of death, didst taste thereof
> For every man; while Thou wast nigh to sink
>   Beneath the intense intolerable rod,

> Grown sick of love; not what I am, but think
>   Thy Life then ransomed mine, my God, my God.   (55–70)

This prayer draws both past and future into the urgent immediacy of its present tense: pleading for the redemption of past sins at the future judgment, it recalls both the historical reality and the eternal efficacy of Christ's death and passion. The voice which addresses God in the present of a projected future judgment is also located in the poem's locutionary present. Thus specific petitions such as 'Pitch Thou Thy Presence round me to defend' are for today, but also for yesterday, and for ever.

This theme of judgment is also central to a poem which has been described as making up a pair with 'The Blessed Damozel', namely 'The Convent Threshold', written in July 1858 and published four years later.[141] The poem opens with a reference to yet another bar:

> There's blood between us, love, my love,
> There's father's blood, there's brother's blood;
> And blood's a bar I cannot pass:
> I choose the stairs that mount above,
> Stair after golden skyward stair,
> To city and to sea of glass.   (1–6)

While her lover looks 'earthward' and sees a pagan earthly paradise (30–7), the speaker, acknowledging that her 'lily feet are soiled with mud' (7), looks up to the heaven of the martyrs:

> I see the far-off city grand,
> Beyond the hills a watered land,
> Beyond the gulf a gleaming strand
> Of mansions where the righteous sup . . .   (18–21)

This contrast between the sacred and the profane becomes more pressing, however, when the poem takes on a strongly Adventist note: 'The time is short and yet you stay' (46).

It is in a later passage that 'The Convent Threshold' most clearly locates itself in relation to 'The Blessed Damozel':

> How should I rest in Paradise,
> Or sit on steps of heaven alone?
> If Saints and Angels spoke of love
> Should I not answer from my throne:

> Have pity upon me, ye my friends,
> For I have heard the sound thereof:
> Should I not turn with yearning eyes,
> Turn earthwards with a pitiful pang?
> Oh save me from a pang in heaven.   (69–77)

The dramatic impact of the locutionary present in this last line is prepared for in line 73 ('Have pity upon me'), where the present is that of a projected future paradise and heaven, the provisionality of which is indicated by the use of the subjunctive mode. Other projections follow, this time in the past tense of a remembered series of dreams, the second of which brings *eros* and *thanatos* into contiguity through Gothic play with the idea of the grave as a bed (110–25). Having prayed for her lover in words she cannot write (130), the speaker has emerged from this dark night of the senses with pinched face and grey hair, and with frozen blood on the sill (134–5).

This shuffling of tenses, which is characteristic of dream narratives, prepares for the remarkable final section, where the eternal present of heaven is brought into the locutionary present of the poem, more in the manner of hymnody:

> If now you saw me you would say:
> Where is the face I used to love?
> And I would answer: Gone before;
> It tarries veiled in paradise.
> When once the morning star shall rise,
> When earth with shadow flees away
> And we stand safe within the door,
> Then you shall lift the veil thereof.
> Look up, rise up: for far above
> Our palms are grown, our place is set;
> There we shall meet as once we met
> And love with old familiar love.   (137–48)

In the first lines quoted it is a present, earthly meeting rather than a future, heavenly reunion that is imagined in the subjunctive mode. Within that present the lover's looking back into the past ('the face I used to love') contrasts with the speaker's 'Gone before'. This elegant use of the familiar consolatory euphemism opens up both the present and future constructions which alternate in the subsequent lines (141–4), in a manner which is reminiscent of the Revelation, the subject of Christina Rossetti's devotional commentary, *The Face of the Deep*

(1892).[142] It also prepares for the conflation in line 140 ('It tarries veiled in paradise') of the existential present of the liminal conventual life referred to in the poem's title and the eternal present of the intermediate state of paradise in which, after death, she will wait for the last judgment and eventual reunion in heaven. For the speaker, the reconciliation of sacred and profane love is possible only when the God of love is all in all, at the end of time. Only through renunciation in this life, the speaker believes, can she and her lover avoid the danger of sin, and thus anticipate in certain hope the 'safe' reward that is reserved for them even now in heaven. Only through her grappling with past and future realities, as in the poem's penultimate line, can the anticipated eternal present of the final line speak of the love that is ultimately to be expressed only in heaven.

Four months after writing this poem, Christina Rossetti produced one of her most fully developed dramatized accounts of heaven in verse. The title 'From House to Home' sends us back to that favourite Victorian idea of heaven which provided material for consolatory manuals by writers such as William Branks and E. H. Bickersteth, and which Jane Eyre misinterpreted at Helen Burns's deathbed. As in 'After This the Judgment', the poem rejects an 'earthly paradise supremely fair' (7), although here the 'pleasure-place', which is within her soul, is described in wonderful detail, rivalling that of Tennyson in 'The Palace of Art', to which it clearly refers. Continuing in the narrative past tense, the speaker describes her 'angel' companion and how he left her when she denied his 'Tonight' with 'Tomorrow' (65–8). Again her renunciation of sexual love changes her overnight (78), but 'something' whispers, 'You shall meet again, / Meet in a distant land' (91–2).

It is through the speaker's vision of a woman 'in a certain place', however, again described in the past tense, that this distant land is mediated in the poem. As she suffers, voices call out on her behalf, the last of which answers, 'Rend the veil, declare the end, / Strengthen her ere she goes' (159). In the description of the apocalypse which follows, all the stages of the last days to which Pollok and Bickersteth devote whole books in their epic poems are drawn together in one mighty consummation – of the world, of the mystic marriage of Christ with his church, and, it is implied, of all profane love. The past tense in which the vision is recalled complements the allusiveness of a passage which draws upon the Revelation and, in a beautifully weighted pun on 'rose', the *Paradiso*:

Multitudes – multitudes – stood up in bliss,
Made equal to the angels, glorious, fair;
  With harps, palms, wedding-garments, kiss of peace,
And crowned and haloed hair.

They sang a song, a new song in the height,
  Harping with harps to Him Who is Strong and True:
They drank new wine, their eyes saw with new light,
  Lo, all things were made new.

Tier beyond tier they rose and rose and rose
  So high that it was dreadful, flames with flames:
No man could number them, no tongue disclose
  Their secret sacred names.

As tho' one pulse stirred all, one rush of blood
  Fed all, one breath swept thro' them myriad-voiced,
They struck their harps, cast down their crowns, they stood
  And worshipped and rejoiced. (165–80)

In 'After This the Judgment', unity in difference, when voices are 'All blent in one yet each one manifest', remains future. Here, through the use of the narrative past tense and through simile ('As tho' one pulse stirred all'), it is already achieved.

From 'all' the speaker moves to 'each':

Each face looked one way like a moon new-lit,
  Each face looked one way towards its Sun of Love;
Drank love and bathed in love and mirrored it
  And knew no end thereof.   (185–8)

F. D. Maurice, that other admirer of Dante and commentator on the Revelation, defends the idea of heaven as worship by arguing that 'all is worship' there, 'because all are referring their thoughts and acts to one centre'.[143] Where Maurice strives to reconcile work and worship in heaven, the vision in 'From House to Home' points to a reconciliation between sacred and profane love:

Glory touched glory on each blessèd head,
  Hands locked dear hands never to sunder more:
These were the new-begotten from the dead
  Whom the great birthday bore.

Heart answered heart, soul answered soul at rest,
　　Double against each other, filled, sufficed:
All loving, loved of all; but loving best
　　And best beloved of Christ.

I saw that one who lost her love in pain,
　　Who trod on thorns, who drank the loathsome cup;
The lost in night, in day was found again;
　　The fallen was lifted up.   (185–96)

Some of the favourite clichés of the writers of sacred poems for mourners, and of novelists such as Mrs Henry Wood in England and Elizabeth Stuart Phelps in America – 'hands locked dear hands', 'the great birthday', 'heart answered heart' – here regain vigour and authority in their true eschatological context, where profane love is fulfilled in the consummation that is a theocentric heaven of everlasting worship, and the language of *eros* ('Double against each other, filled sufficed') is taken up into the mystical language of heaven's *agape* – precisely the opposite of Dante Gabriel Rossetti's 'transvaluation' of the Christian idea of divine love.[144] Like the woman who has 'fallen' on thorns, the fallen language of this world is here 'lifted up'.

In the poem's closing section the speaker makes this vision the basis for her argument to her lover, in the here-and-now of the existential present: 'Therefore in patience I possess my soul' (205). The biblical metaphor of the vine with which the poem ends is here sacramental in emphasis:

Altho' today He prunes my twigs with pain,
　　Yet doth His blood nourish and warm my root:
Tomorrow I shall put forth buds again
　　And clothe myself with fruit.

Altho' today I walk in tedious ways,
　　Today His staff is turned into a rod,
Yet will I wait for Him the appointed days
　　And stay upon my God.

The eucharist at once anticipates and partakes in the feast of the heavenly reward. As in 'After This the Judgment', that reward is for those who have been 'pruned' and who have felt the 'rod' which signifies the love of God as judge. Yet will the speaker wait for Him the appointed days, and stay(s) upon her God.

Through subtle changes of tense and mode, then, Christina Rossetti's eschatological poetry folds present renunciation into future judgment, future heaven into present vision. Where her brother looked for the transfiguration of the body through the erotic in the here-and-now, she anticipated the transformation of the spiritual body described by St Paul, and the deferred consummation of all earthly longings in the mystical marriage of Christ with his church in the *eschaton*. Coventry Patmore, an associate of the Pre-Raphaelites from the beginning of the movement, attempted in his most important poetry a reconciliation of ideas which are broadly similar to these two positions. 1 Corinthians 15.46, a verse which is often overlooked, was a favourite text: 'that was not first which is spiritual, but that which is natural; and afterward that which is spiritual'.[145] Like two friends of his early years in the British Museum library – Dante Gabriel Rossetti and Alfred Tennyson – he thought of the incarnation as the greatest 'secret' of all: 'an event which is renewed in the body of every one who is in the way to the fulfilment of his original destiny'.[146] He is perhaps closest to Gabriel Rossetti when he argues that the 'spiritual body, into which the bodies of those who love and obey God perfectly are from time to time transfigured, is a prism'.[147] Yet although this Victorian laureate of married love, who believed in the chastity of marriage, was strongly influenced by Swedenborg, he was aware with Aquinas that, in J. C. Reid's words, 'the sacramental quality of marriage does not lie in intercourse'.[148] A major shift in his thinking in later life brought him closer to the position of the Rossetti whose name was taken by his daughter when she became a nun:

In Patmore's progress beyond and through the sanctified analogy of married love to a wider acceptance of love in which, mystically, the body is made holy through rejection of the pleasures of the body, and in which, while married love is still accepted as a great and holy love, a foreshadowing of the union with God, dedicated celibacy is a love of at least equal and perhaps higher virtue, Sister Mary Christina's example was paramount.[149]

Whereas much of Christina Rossetti's poetry resists autobiographical readings,[150] Patmore's bereavement odes almost invite them. The death of his first wife Emily in 1862 proved to be the fulcrum around which both his life and work turned, occurring after the completion of *The Angel in the House*, which she had inspired, and releasing in him much of his best writing, in a way which anticipates Thomas Hardy's development as a poet fifty years later.[151] Yet two years after Emily's death, Patmore converted to Roman Catholicism, as she had prophesied he would, and remarried, as she had wanted him to. His change of project from the spiritualizing of human love in *The Angel in the House* to the humanizing of divine love in *The Unknown Eros*[152] represented not only a reversed perspective on the same subject, as the incarnation might be treated in a theological treatise, but also an attempt to justify (primarily to himself) his remarrying so soon after the wife he had idealized, and who was now in heaven, had 'departed' with 'sudden, unintelligible phrase'.[153]

One of the most successful of Patmore's early bereavement odes, which was to be placed immediately before 'Departure' in *The Unknown Eros* (1877), was 'The Azalea', a poem based upon an actual experience.[154] A number of familiar elements of Victorian domestic elegiac writing are present: a misinterpretation as the central narrative event; a dream; a letter written by the dead person. So too is the domestic interior, in this case the married couple's bedroom:

> There, where the sun shines first
> Against our room
> She train'd the gold Azalea, whose perfume
> She, Spring-like, from her breathing grace dispersed.
> Last night the delicate crests of saffron bloom,
> For this their dainty likeness watch'd and nurst,
> Were just at point to burst. (1–7)

The sense of daily recurrence in the first four lines, brought quietly into question by the shift from the present tense to the past, is interrupted in the specificity of 'last night' and the expectancy of 'just at point to burst'. The line that follows echoes Wordsworth's 'Lucy' poem:

> At dawn I dream'd, O God, that she was dead,
> And groan'd aloud upon my wretched bed,
> And waked, ah, God, and did not waken her,
> But lay, with eyes still closed,
> Perfectly bless'd in the delicious sphere
> By which I knew so well that she was near,
> My heart to speechless thankfulness composed. (8–14)

Ironically the scent which the speaker associates with his wife is described in line 12 in terms which would better describe his wife's

fixed state in heaven than his fool's paradise in a liminal phase between
sleep and consciousness:

> Till 'gan to stir
> A dizzy somewhat in my troubled head –
> It *was* the azalea's breath, and she *was* dead!
> The warm night had the lingering buds disclosed,
> And I had fall'n asleep with to my breast
> A chance-found letter press'd
> In which she said,
> 'So, till to-morrow eve, my Own, adieu!
> Parting's well-paid with soon again to meet,
> Soon in your arms to feel so small and sweet,
> Sweet to myself that am so sweet to you!'   (15–25)

Following the descent from a dream state to waking reality with which
the past narrative had to end, the epistolary form in lines 22–5,
grounded in the present, introduces a future dimension which, in this
context, can be read off as hope of (erotic) reunion in heaven, thus
reversing the flow of the irony in line 12.

Whereas the subtext in 'The Azalea' is suggestive of the Romantics'
heaven of reunion, the second of the three Patmore odes to be considered
here overtly draws upon New Testament eschatology in relating this
bereavement and the possibility of remarriage to Christ's passion and
resurrection, a central *topos* of Roman Catholic devotions.[155] In 'Tired
Memory', one of the odes originally printed for private circulation in
1868, three of the poem's four turns from the past tense of the narrative
to the present tense of direct speech foreground this intertextual relationship. The speaker's prayers to keep his 'vows of faith' having proved
empty, he has also failed to find an outlet for 'duteous love':

> But, kneeling in a Church, one Easter-Day,
> It came to me to say:
> 'Though there is no intelligible rest
> In Earth or Heaven,
> For me, but on her breast,
> I yield her up, again to have her given,
> Or not, as, Lord, Thou wilt, and that for aye.'

Just as the women and the eleven had to 'yield him up' on the first
Good Friday, and again after the resurrection, so the speaker must let his
first wife go. He must also leave in God's hands the mystery embodied in

the problem text with which Patmore most frequently wrestled: 'they which shall be accounted worthy to obtain that world, and the resurrection from the dead, neither marry, nor are given in marriage' (Luke 20.35).

Having for the first time dreamt of 'possessing' his 'most Dear' in 'gay, celestial beauty nothing coy', and experienced 'fresh despair' on waking, the speaker records his further attempt to pray in his own Gethsemane:

> In agony, I cried:
> 'My Lord, if Thy strange will be this,
> That I should crucify my heart,
> Because my love has also been my pride,
> I do submit, if I saw how, to bliss
> Wherein She has no part.'
> And I was heard,
> And taken at my own remorseless word.

In a radical reversal of the norm, the 'bliss' that primarily signifies the other-worldly (marriage in heaven) is here to be 'submitted to' in this world, through remarriage. (Where Christina Rossetti's way of the cross involved renouncing the love of two men on religious grounds, Patmore's led to two further marriages.)

The final passage of direct speech is the first wife's reply to her husband's question:

> O, my most Dear,
> Was't treason, as I fear?
> 'Twere that, and worse, to plead thy veiled mind,
> Kissing thy babes, and murmuring in mine ear,
> 'Thou canst not be
> Faithful to God, and faithless unto me!'
> Ah, prophet kind!
> I heard, all dumb and blind
> With tears of protest; and I cannot see
> But faith was broken.

The simplicity of the wife's words, suggestive in their eternal present of life with and in God, has great authority for the speaker in his troubled and confused state, following his intimations of Gethsemane and Golgotha. The speaker's Lucan parallels now reach their logical culmination in a road-to-Emmaus event, when, 'Dead of devotion and tired memory', he recognizes 'a strange grace' of his dead wife in a 'fair stranger', whom he describes as her 'Sister sweet':

> So that I lived again,
> And, strange to aver,
> With no relapse into the void inane
> For thee;
> But (treason was't) for thee and also her.

Already in parenthesis, the sense of betrayal in the poem's final line will, it is suggested, fade in the resurrection life of his 'living again'.

Like the followers of Jesus after his death and burial, the speaker, caught between despair and hope, is given a sign. With extraordinary boldness, Patmore relates the speaker's spiritual renewal to the resurrection life of the early church, when men and women held all things in common, in anticipation of the coming of the kingdom. Thus, on a biographical reading, the possibility that conversion to Roman Catholicism would eternally separate Patmore from his first wife is gently denied in the speaker's description of the 'fair stranger' as his dead wife's 'sister'. The theology which informs this description is more overtly spelt out in Patmore's devotional odes such as 'Deliciae Sapientiae de Amore', also printed in the anonymous volume of 1868, and later placed in Book II of *The Unknown Eros* (IX). Here the speaker is not in a domestic setting where he can perceive only intimations of heaven. Sited instead 'by the Porch / Of the glad Palace of Virginity', he invites all to 'behold / The dainty and unsating Marriage-Feast'. Again reversing the norm, heavenly music in praise of 'the Husband of the Heavens' is played upon 'the harps they bore from Earth, five-strung', thus sanctifying the profane. The Blessed Virgin Mary is then seen in glory:

> And how the shining sacrificial Choirs,
> Offering for aye their dearest hearts' desires,
> Which to their hearts come back beatified,
> Hymn, the bright aisles along,
> The nuptial song,
> Song ever new to us and them, that saith,
> 'Hail Virgin in Virginity a Spouse!'
> Heard first below
> Within the little house
> At Nazareth;
> Heard yet in many a cell where brides of Christ
> Lie hid, emparadised,

And where, although
By the hour 'tis night,
There's light,
The Day still lingering in the lap of snow.

'The Azalea' explores the ironies of loss and bereavement via the perfume which the dead wife's 'breathing grace dispersed'. 'Tired Memory'
records a moment of uncanny recognition through a 'strange grace' of
the wife in a 'fair stranger'. Here hymnody in the eternal present of the
heavenly 'nuptial song' echoes for ever both the yesterday of the first
Ave (Luke 1.28) and the today of the sisters who repeat it ('Hail Mary,
full of grace') in their hidden lives as brides of Christ, their condition
on earth akin to the intermediate state of paradise, their convent cells
reminiscent of the humble little house at Nazareth.

Patmore's belief in the chastity of marriage is reflected in the lines
that follow:

Gaze and be not afraid
Ye wedded few that honour, in sweet thought
And glittering will,
So freshly from the garden gather still
The lily sacrificed

. . .

'Tis there your Hymen waits!

In heaven the limits of earthly language fall away, and 'each to other'
sighs, 'Twas this we meant!' Similarly, wholeness in the form of virginity
could in Patmore's view be regained through penitence and turning to
God in love.[156] Thus of the holy virgins, none 'Save One' looks 'fairer'
than Mary Magdalene, and all who love God are, in the poem's final
lines,

Heirs of the Palace glad,
And inly clad
With the bridal robes of ardour virginal.

'Deliciae Sapientiae de Amore' is not about progress or development
in heaven but rather the heavenly state as the consummation of the
earthly life. Indeed, 'consummation', or the relationship between its
different kinds of completion — of marriage, of earthly life, of the temporal world — is often the implicit subject of his and the Rossettis'
writing. In Patmore's Marian 'Deliciae', the other-worldly consumma-

tion is mediated through a vision described by a speaker located in a privileged site 'above'. In other poems the perspective is this-worldly, and heaven is mediated through a variety of means: in Dante Gabriel Rossetti by making heaven 'fleshly'; in Christina Rossetti via the sacraments, or the seasons of the Christian year which formalize the 'seasons' of God's relationship with man, or visions seen in the here-and-now; in Coventry Patmore through the 'grace' of a perfume, or of a physical likeness which indicates sisterhood. Like these precursors, Francis Thompson adapts the syntactic resources of tense and mode to his own special purposes in writing different kinds of mediating vision of heaven. For Thompson, however, it is primarily the *kingdom* of heaven which the incarnation has inaugurated, and which perfectly expresses the love of God for man, or the grace which operates from God's side to man's, from the other-worldly to the this-worldly.

It was on the basis of *The Unknown Eros* that Francis Thompson became a respectful admirer of Coventry Patmore.[157] Alice Meynell (the Roman Catholic poet who pointed out that Patmore's 'Angel' was not his wife Emily, but rather Love) and her husband Wilfrid brought the two men together in Patmore's last years, when he shared his 'secret self' with Thompson.[158] As Patmore aged, in the early 1890s, a group of young Capuchin Franciscans came to see Thompson, their contemporary, as the natural heir to their former 'prophet'.[159] If this reflects the poets' shared opinions concerning the interrelationship between the spiritual and material worlds, other aspects of their writing reveal differences between them. Compared to Patmore's domestic bereavement odes, which, like much of the Rossettis' poetry, are somewhat claustrophobic in atmosphere, Thompson's poetry is positively bracing. Patmore could not have described marriage as '*mere* knocking at the gates of union', as the bachelor Thompson did:

Therefore sings Dante, and sing all noble poets after him, that Love in this world is a pilgrim and a wanderer, journeying to the New Jerusalem: not here is the consummation of his yearnings, in that mere knocking at the gates of union which we christen marriage, but beyond the pillars of death and the corridors of the grave, in the union of spirit to spirit within the containing Spirit of God.[160]

Nor does Patmore's poetry convey a strong sense of the kingdom of heaven that is within and among us, a sign of God's king-ship in the world, as Thompson's does.

Indeed, Francis Thompson's genius – like Gerard Manley Hopkins's – was to internalize what other poets earlier in the nineteenth century had attempted to describe as some kind of external reality. The classic example is 'The Hound of Heaven' (1890):

> I fled Him, down the nights and down the days;
> I fled Him, down the arches of the years;
> I fled Him, down the labyrinthine ways
>   Of my own mind; and in the mist of tears
> I hid from Him, and under running laughter.
>   Up vistaed hopes I sped;
>   And shot, precipitated,
> Adown Titanic glooms of chasmed fears,
>   From those strong Feet that followed, followed after.   (1–9)[161]

Thompson's late Victorian Catholic baroque internalizes the kind of sublime landscape that the nineteenth-century Protestant epic had located as external, remotely 'above' or 'below', other-worldly. As in Augustine and the medieval mystics, Thompson's subject is the I/ Thou relationship between man and God, whose love pursues its 'prey'.[162] Heaven itself is only 'dimly guessed' (143), the 'battlements of Eternity' rarely emerging from the mists (145). So intimate is the love expressed to the speaker in the present tense of the poem's closing lines that the favourite Victorian idea of heaven reads quite naturally as a homely sign of what is 'stored' for him (cf. 1 Peter 1.4). In contrast to the haunting 'shadow' of Poe's Raven, it is God's hand that will shade him:

> 'All which thy child's mistake
> Fancies as lost, I have stored for thee at home:
>   Rise, clasp My hand, and come!'
>   Halts by me that footfall:
>   Is my gloom, after all,
> Shade of His hand, outstretched caressingly?
>   'Ah, fondest, blindest, weakest,
>   I am He Whom thou seekest!
> Thou dravest love from thee, who dravest Me.'   (174–82)

Line 181 recalls Mary Magdalene's recognition of her risen Lord ('Woman, whom seekest thou?', John 20.15) and Peter's self-identification after his vision, when he hears the voice of the Lord ('I am he whom ye seek', Acts 10.21). It is in the now of God's presence that what has been a pursuit becomes a completion or consummation, here marked by the past tense of the poem's final line.[163]

Thompson himself thought that 'The Hound of Heaven' was the greatest of his odes because it 'embodies a world-wide experience in an individual form of that experience: the universal becoming incarnated in the personal'.[164] Although more culturally specific, two of the odes which explore the mystery of the passion of the incarnate Son also 'incarnate' the subject in the personal, treating it with a vigorous excess reminiscent of seventeenth-century religious verse. 'Ode to the Setting Sun' (1890) reflects Thompson's reading of Crashaw for an essay he completed shortly before writing the poem[165] The 'Prelude' establishes in the present tense a specific moment in time – 'The wailful sweetness of the violin / Floats down the hushed waters of the wind' (1–2) – and earths the poem in a specific place, based on the 'Field of the Cross' at the Praemonstratensian Priory at Storrington (at this time his home), where the cross is actually 'planted' (17). Taking up Patmore's theme in 'Winter' (*The Unknown Eros*, I.III), whose 'dim cloud' has 'less the characters of dark and cold / Than warmth and light asleep', the ode announces that 'It is the falling star that trails the light, / It is the breaking wave that hath the might' (8–9). From its initial claim that 'The fairest things in life are Death and Birth, / And of these two the fairer thing is Death' (3–4), the ode works towards its last words – 'and Death is Birth' (238) – via meditations on the setting sun/Son, the hill, like the cross, standing 'black as life against eternity' (203). The universal is made personal in the poem's 'After-Strain', where the poems' spatial and temporal setting is again made vividly present – 'One step, and lo! the Cross stands gaunt and long / 'Twixt me and yet bright skies, a presaged dole' (3–4). Yet the first-person plural of line 6 is both specific (of this community) and universal (of all humankind): 'Even so, O Cross! thine is the victory. / Thy roots are fast within our fairest fields' (5–6).

Thompson began work on the 'Ode to the Setting Sun' in the Field of the Cross at Storrington, and finished it 'ascending and descending Jacob's Ladder' – the local name for a steep path built into the side of the downs.[166] This other favourite symbol of mediation between earth and heaven figures prominently in one of his later poems, written in the early years of the twentieth century, which should be quoted in full:

> O world invisible, we view thee,
> O world intangible, we touch thee,
> O world unknowable, we know thee,
> Inapprehensible, we clutch thee!

Does the fish soar to find the ocean,
The eagle plunge to find the air –
That we ask of the stars in motion
If they have rumour of thee there?

Not where the wheeling systems darken,
And our benumbed conceiving soars! –
The drift of pinions, would we hearken,
Beats at our own clay-shuttered doors.

The angels keep their ancient places; –
Turn but a stone, and start a wing!
'Tis ye, 'tis your estranged faces,
That miss the many-splendoured thing.

But (when so sad thou canst not sadder)
Cry; – and upon thy so sore loss
Shall shine the traffic of Jacob's ladder
Pitched betwixt Heaven and Charing Cross.

Yea, in the night, my Soul, my daughter,
Cry, – clinging Heaven by the hems;
And lo, Christ walking on the water
Not of Gennesareth, but Thames!
                    ('The Kingdom of God: "In no Strange Land"')

The subtitle is a quotation from Coventry Patmore's poem 'The Three Witnesses'. As Brigid Boardman points out, however, Thompson does not 'commit the error which he had feared in Patmore's too-ready identification between the natural and the supernatural, carried dangerously further by his Capuchin friends'.[167] Like Newman in the 1830s, Thompson writes of the kingdom of God 'now and here', and 'among us', but also as other, and ultimately mysterious.[168] The poem's immediacy, reminiscent now of Vaughan, now of Blake, is achieved through the use of an existential present which presses towards the eternal present of the penultimate stanza, where the constant mediatory 'traffic' of the angels (in the old sense of commerce) between earth and heaven promises to break through into the modern world of London with its 'traffic' (in the new, nineteenth-century sense of vehicular movement). This imagined future mediation prepares for the revelation in the final stanza, where the durative present of 'clinging' and 'walking' is reminiscent of the eternal present of the Apocalypse and of Victorian hymnody. As in the sacrament of the eucharist, the mystery of the incarnation is constantly renewed in each generation.

In Francis Thompson's 'Ode for the Diamond Jubilee of Queen Victoria, 1897', the 'long Victorian line that passed with printless tread' is headed by the 'holy poets, two on two' (17–18). Along with Tennyson, Robert and Elizabeth Barrett Browning, and Matthew Arnold are three other poets. Dante Gabriel Rossetti comes on 'disranked', his heart stirring within his breast 'like lightning in a cloud, a Spirit without rest' (48–50). Elizabeth Barrett's 'fervid breathing' breaks on Christina Rossetti's 'gentle-taken breath' (46–7). Coventry Patmore, Thompson's friend and co-religionist, is honoured above all, walking alone as the 'throngs' give room to him (57–8), until he turns away to find his 'station in the dim, / Where the sole-thoughted Dante waited him' (70–1).

It would be misguided to look for clues to Thompson's idea of a future life in this highly formalized processional ode, which goes on to celebrate a wide range of Victoria's pantheon of departed national heroes. His choice and treatment of the 'holy poets' discussed in this section is, however, of some interest. That he should have associated only Patmore with Dante, for example, and not the Rossettis, is suggestive of partiality. What Thompson himself shared with these poets was a sense of the centrality of the incarnation to the theology of heaven, paradise and the kingdom in the nineteenth century. Whereas Victorian hymns tended to work within a comparatively narrow syntactic range, being grounded in the locutionary present which a liturgical context dictated, the odes and dramatic monologues of these poets modulate from past to future tense, from existential to eternal present, from indicative to subjunctive mode, as they explore the relationship between sacred and profane love within the horizon of eternal life.

CHAPTER 4

Hell

And is there in GOD's world so drear a place,
Where the loud bitter cry is rais'd in vain?
Where tears of penance come too late for grace,
As on th'uprooted flower the genial rain?
John Keble, *The Christian Year*[1]

Edward Henry Bickersteth, that most prolific of Evangelical writers on the four last things, held firmly to what F. W. Farrar described as the 'common view' of salvation, and would have responded as the High Churchman Keble did to his own rhetorical question in the epigraph above: ''Tis even so.' Written in the middle of a period in which belief in everlasting punishment declined, Bickersteth's epic poem *Yesterday, To-Day, and For Ever* (1866) again provides a helpful point of reference, reflecting in its treatment of the subject the kind of views which fuelled fierce theological controversy during much of Victoria's reign.[2]

Having made his 'Descent to Hades' (Book I), the Seer is shown the 'Paradise of the Blessed Dead' (II) by Oriel, who then leads him to 'The Prison of the Lost' (III). This 'realm of night' (98), the 'awarded prison / Of darkness, till the judgment trumpet sounds' (171–2), is grave-like in its subterranean position, its darkness, and its transitional nature. A 'world o'ershadow'd with the pall of death, / The sepulchre of life' (103–4), it will be emptied on the last day. Crucially – and here was a stumbling-block for many in the nineteenth century – there is no possibility of avoiding the ultimate doom that is Gehenna after the last judgment. Thus 'there is no path / From hell to heaven, from heaven to hell direct' (158–9).

Later in Book III, Oriel relates the story of one of the lost souls, Theodore, who in the fourth century renounced his Christian faith, married a pagan, and was almost immediately killed in battle. Citing

Matthew 16.18 and Dante's *Inferno*, many nineteenth-century writers invested the gates of hell with particular symbolic significance, and here Bickersteth makes Oriel describe his leading Theodore up to the great 'iron gates' (499) which 'recoil'd / Back, slowly back, with ponderous noise' (513–14). These gates and the walls of hell are, as Bickersteth's precursor Robert Pollok emphasized in *The Course of Time* (1827), 'Above all flight of hope'.[3] Thus when Theodore asks for Christ's mercy, Oriel tells him that his plea cannot possibly be answered: the only way in which he can serve his maker is in 'passive submission' (592). Now he and the other lost souls 'wait their sentence' at the judgment which is 'beyond' (594).

When he first entered the prison of the lost, Theodore caught a glimpse, 'permitted him by God', of paradise in the distance (624), and Oriel had to remind him of 'the deep inexorable gulf' (650) described in the parable of Dives and Lazarus (Luke 16). Fifteen centuries later, Theodore, who has always had paradise in view (809), has undergone a 'solemn change'. But here Oriel makes an important general observation:

> Lost souls of every type were there: and yet
> The hell of one was not another's hell.
> Nor needed separate prisons to adjust
> The righteous meed of punishment to each.
> As they had sinn'd, they suffer'd . . .   (906–10)

and the 'native idealities of men' remain 'immutable for ever' (987).

The first three books of *Yesterday, To-Day, and For Ever* are anticipatory, like the intermediate states in Hades that they describe (v.669–81). Before, however, the description of the last judgment and the dismissal of the damned to Gehenna in the poem's final books, Bickersteth's treatment of the 'Redemption' (VII) reflects the close identity between hell and the atonement that one would expect to find in the work of a nineteenth-century Evangelical. He criticized Milton elsewhere for describing the war in heaven as taking place before the creation of man, instead of after Christ's ascension.[4] For Bickersteth, the focus of the battle between God and Satan, good and evil, love and death, in human history was Christ's redemptive act upon the cross (VII.777–94). Even before the deposition, Christ 'traversed the dark avenue that leads / Straight to the adamantine doors of hell' (844). When those detained in the prison of the lost, seeing him without strength, tried to detain him in order to secure their own release, he was drawn by his Father across the gulf that separates the two halves of Hades. The awful final destination of the damned was then disclosed, when fissures opened up to reveal 'A lower depth of fire unquenchable, / Gehenna's lake, soon hidden' (888–9).

In 'The Last Judgment' (XI), the prison of the lost is emptied and destroyed, falling 'sheer into the bottomless pit':

> But huge
> As was that ruin, loom'd more huge, more vast
> That shoreless fathomless abyss of fire,
> Which swallow'd up in its remorseless waves
> Whatever lay beyond the mighty gulf
> Coasting the triple wall of Paradise.   (XI.534–9)

Like Pollok, Bickersteth gives much more space to the damned than to the risen saints in his account of the last judgment, emphasizing 'the terrors of the wrath to come' (511) rather than the hope of heaven. The description of Gehenna follows Matthew 25: even Satan's 'apostate spirits' could only answer,

> 'Thou art righteous, Lord:'
> And, as the awful sentence fell on each
> Of chains and everlasting banishment
> To his own portion in the lake of fire,
> As by the Spirit of holiness compell'd
> We and the blessed angels said, Amen.   (700–5)

Satan is then crushed under the 'burning heel' of his conqueror, the 'crystal empyrean' opens beneath him, and he and his rebel armies fall into a 'yawning gulf':

> Standing upon its rugged edge we gazed
> Intently' and long down after them; and there
> They sank and sank, the forms more indistinct,
> The cries more faint, the echoes feebler, till
> The firmamental pavement closed again:
> And silence was in heaven.   (740–5)

(Again there are parallels with the grave, the angels looking down as if into the deepest of graves.) The 'millions of the dead', the lost, are then also judged, beginning with Cain and including Theodore, and are finally dismissed to everlasting fire 'Beneath Gehenna's burning sulphurous waves' (879). Sounds of wailing subside as 'His Eye, who is consuming fire' (923) quells the damned into silence, broken only when Satan leads them in praise of God. They are not forgotten in heaven, however, as the 'smoke of their great torment' rises, and is in the presence of the Lamb of God, / For ever and for ever' (918–19). (Unending cremation and final burial from which there will be no rising again are thus uncannily combined.)

On Bickersteth's scheme, then, those who are 'lost' go straight to their, separate prison in Hades after death, where, beyond hope themselves, they can nevertheless see paradise, which is also in Hades. After the last judgment they will suffer everlastingly in the fires of Gehenna, the smoke from which will always be smelt in heaven. In thus sharply differentiating between Hades and Gehenna, Bickersteth avoids some of the problems of translation associated with the use of the word 'hell' in the Authorized Version. It was via this and other problematic key words, however, and particularly those associated with the idea of everlasting punishment, that such traditional schemes were challenged in the second half of the nineteenth century, from the early 1850s (Maurice) to the late 1870s (Farrar) and beyond. While popular religious forms such as Evangelical tracts, Roman Catholic mission sermons, and Salvationist hymns continued to stoke the fires of hell, the Broad Churchmen who questioned the doctrine of everlasting punishment in theological essays were often anticipated in the more informal medium of the novel – in the fiction of the Brontë sisters, for example, and of their contemporary, J. A. Froude.

Complicated as it is by sectarian divisions and variations, the plot of the theology of hell in the nineteenth century has certain clearly discernible lines of development, and these are examined in the third section of this chapter. By 1890 the idea of endless physical punishment had been discredited in the more liberal Protestant traditions, and even moderated in English Roman Catholic circles. (When Gladstone comments in the 1890s, however, that the traditional hell has been relegated to the 'far-off corners of the Christian mind', one assumes that he is referring to the Protestant mind; in our own time David Lodge has placed the disappearance of the traditional hell of Roman Catholics 'at some point in the nineteen-sixties'.)[5] By 1890 an Archbishop of Canterbury had declared that the damnatory clauses in the Athanasian Creed were not taken literally by anybody in the Church of England, and cremation had been legalized, suggesting that those who associated the committal of the body to the flames with hell-fire were becoming a minority. Belief in hell as a spiritual reality, however, was still widespread. Was not the separation from God, who is love, the only possible final state of those who in this life set their faces against divine grace? Thus although belief in everlasting punishment declined, a fear of some kind of hell remained for many, and this is the subject of the second section of the chapter. In the fourth section I will show how language traditionally associated with hell continued to provide Victorian writers – including Kingsley, Gaskell, and Gissing, Meredith, Swinburne, and James Thomson – with a vocabulary with which to describe painful spiritual experiences in this world, and particularly in the treatment of two kinds of 'hell on earth'.

THE FEAR OF HELL

In modern secular societies in the West, fear of death is focused more upon the dying process than what might follow. If there is some kind of life after death, it is often assumed, that life will be wonderful, heavenly. If not, then the future is simply oblivion and, as we will know nothing about it, we will not suffer. In the century of the Nazi death camps, it is often said, hell is experienced by the living. But if there really were to be a *post-mortem* state of hell, it would be for those who have no belief in or desire for God. It may not necessarily take the form of eternal punishment or pain, but perhaps we all experience something of hell in divine judgment? For most people in the late twentieth century, however, 'hell' has come to be used as a 'metaphor based on another metaphor', referring to 'painful states of consciousness, to despair or to alienation'.[6]

Although some humanist and secularist intellectuals held advanced views on these matters in the second half of the nineteenth century, the fear of hell was alive elsewhere. Thomas Hardy, for example, describes Tess Durbeyfield as being 'well grounded in the Holy Scriptures', like all village girls, but he also suggests that other influences contributed to the fears of such girls:

She thought of the child [her baby Sorrow] consigned to the nethermost corner of hell, as its double doom for lack of baptism and lack of legitimacy; saw the arch-fiend tossing it with his three-pronged fork, like the one they used for heating the oven on baking days; to which picture she added many other quaint and curious details of torment sometimes taught the young in this Christian country.   (*Tess of the D'Urbervilles*, 1891; 14)

But not only village girls were vulnerable to the fear of hell. Mark Pattison recalls in his memoirs how an Oxford professor was converted to Christianity unexpectedly, 'not by the seduction of piety, but by the terrors of hell'.[7]

Behind these instances, and indeed behind the fact that the 'decline of hell' was extremely slow (it can be traced from the seventeenth century), lies the use of hell as a moral deterrent.[8] A traditional justification for such practice is that in holding over us the threat of hell, God must have had a moral purpose for us in this life:

If we are always thinking of Hell, we shall not easily fall into it. For this cause God has threatened punishment, for He would not have done so, if there was not great advantage in thinking of it.[9]

The specific nature of that punishment could also be explained on these grounds. Father Furniss, for example, whose penny booklet, *The Sight of Hell* (1861), was designed to save children through pure terror, puts the following words into the mouth of Christ addressing the damned in hell:

It was a mercy that the punishment of Hell was made everlasting. If so many broke my law, knowing that the punishment would be everlasting, how would it have been, if the punishment had not been everlasting? There are millions in Heaven who would not have been there but for the everlasting pains of Hell. They were wise . . .[10]

When hell is seen in this light, the need to save people, and especially young people, from everlasting torment becomes urgent, and Father Furniss devoted much of his ministry to missions to children and the production of booklets which sold in their millions.[11] Furniss drew upon the tradition of St Alphonsus Liguori, the founder (1732) of the Redemptorist order of which he was a member, and the author of devotional writings which were widely read on the Continent in the early nineteenth century, and in Britain after their translation into English by R. A. Coffin.[12] Other models were also available, such as the source of the famous hell-fire sermon in Joyce's *Portrait of the Artist as a Young Man* (1914–15): Pinamonti's *Hell Opened to Christians to Caution them Entering It*, reprinted in 1807 with terrifying woodcuts, and available for most of the nineteenth century.

Furniss chooses as an epigraph for *The Sight of Hell*, however, this quotation from Father Faber's *The Creator and the Creature* (1858):

The false delicacy of modern times in keeping back the searing images of Hell, while in the case of children, it has often marred a whole education, is a formidable danger to the sanctity as well as to the faith of men.

No such false delicacy afflicts Father Furniss, as he addresses the 'little child' with the words,

if you go to Hell, there will be a devil at your side to strike you. He will go on striking you every minute for ever and ever, without ever stopping.[13]

He then invites his young reader to accompany him on a visit to a series of 'dungeons of hell'.[14] In the first is a girl of about eighteen, wearing a terrible dress of fire which burns and scorches her, but can never destroy her. (Similarly Robert Pollok in *The Course of Time* described 'most miserable beings', 'Burning continually, yet unconsumed'.)[15] Furniss has an eye for the unnerving detail. The girl in the dress of fire

counts with her fingers the moments as they pass away slowly, for each moment seems to her like a hundred years. As she counts the moments she remembers that she will have to count them for ever and ever.

Her crime was to have gone to 'dancing-houses and all kinds of bad places' to show off her dress, instead of going to mass. Similarly, a young prostitute, who died aged sixteen as a result of the 'bad life she led', is doomed to stand for ever on a red hot floor, while a young man who on earth frequented 'dancing-houses, public-houses, and theatres' stands immobile in hell, the blood in his veins and the brain in his skull boiling like a kettle. God is 'terrible to sinners in Hell', he says, 'but He is just!' And so the subterranean tour continues.

To read *The Sight of Hell* is to see how Furniss held the attention of his young audiences during missions. Whereas a sophisticated contemplative tradition such as St Ignatius Loyola's is designed to stimulate the adult reader's imagination by asking a limited number of questions in a 'Meditation on Hell',[16] Furniss fills his young readers' minds with detailed descriptions of hell and evokes a strong sense of place, answering every possible question they might have and thus leaving little space for doubt or uncertainty. As well, however, as playing upon the child's emotions by dwelling upon physical pains and repulsive physical properties of hell such as choking smoke and continual noise, Furniss also tackles the more abstract concept of 'everlasting' punishment by using the traditional rhetorical technique of turning the limits of language and cognition to his own advantage, offering a series of analogies which fail to convey the idea:

> Think of a great solid iron ball, larger than the Heavens and the Earth. A bird comes once in a hundred millions of years and just touches the great iron ball with a feather of its wing. Think that you have to burn in a fire till the bird has worn the great iron ball away with its feather. Is this Eternity? No.
>
> . . . How long, then, will the punishment of sinners go on? For ever, and ever, and ever!'[17]

Having thus established a sense of the vastness of eternity, and therefore of everlasting punishment, he later illustrates the 'badness of mortal sin' by explaining that if it is put into one scale and the pains of hell into the other 'you will see that the balance stands equal': '*A mortal sin of one moment deserves the everlasting pains of Hell.*'[18]

Disturbing as it is, the avidity with which Father Furniss contemplates the torments of hell and the awesome idea of everlasting punishment is representative of a strand of Christian tradition which goes back to the second century, and cannot be lightly dismissed.[19] In the modern era, frightening children with hell had long been common practice among English Protestants too, as Isaac Watts's *Divine Songs for Children* (1715) reveals. Like some Roman Catholics, some Victorian High Churchmen used hell as a means of pointing their congregations to heaven. As Pusey wrote, the 'dread of hell peoples heaven: perhaps millions have been scared back from sin by the dread of it'.[20] Wisely, though, Pusey added that the appropriateness of hell-fire preaching depended upon the nature of the congregation. This perhaps helps to explain the success of William Booth, founder of the Salvation Army, who saw the need of such preaching among the people he was called to save.[21]

Why, though, should the fear of hell be so powerful a weapon, at least when used in the appropriate circumstances? As with heaven, there is a problem of language associated with hell. In Pollok's *The Course of Time*, for example, the bard falters as he approaches the subject of the damned: 'What harp of boundless, deep, exhaustless woe, / Shall utter forth the groanings of the damned . . . ?'[22] Yet, like Dante and Milton, Victorian epic writers have more to say about the physical properties of hell than of heaven, and about the condition of those who inhabit hell. For whereas contradictory models of heaven could be said to destabilize the idea of a place of perfect harmony, the contradictoriness of traditional descriptions of hell – a place of fire and water, crowdedness and solitude, noise and silence – is itself an aspect of its horror. Heaven is also more obviously 'other' than hell. Although one can talk of heaven on earth, or of glimpses of heaven in human experience, and although models of heaven as community or worship are necessarily based upon earthly experience, heaven is fundamentally that which is beyond and above earthly experience, as it is the dwelling place of God. Hell, on the other hand, is not only understood, perforce, in anthropocentric terms, but is also the site of God's absence, where the soul is trapped in the damnation that is its own unredeemed nature and those of other lost souls. Just as it is easier to see hell on earth than heaven on earth, so it is easier to see earth in hell than in heaven.

Although specialist writers such as E. H. Bickersteth conceived of an intermediate paradise in Hades, which is beneath the earth, most of the imaginative and descriptive effort of Victorian writers of pious consolatory literature, including Bickersteth's, was focused upon the difficult and mysterious subject of the resurrection of the dead to new life in heaven, which is above. The use of traditional analogies such as the transformation of the worm into the butterfly, and of the dead seed into the ear of corn, proved to be problematic in the nineteenth century, requiring elaborate symbolic reinforcement in Bowler's painting *The Doubt: 'Can These Dry Bones Live?'*, for example (illustration 1). In contrast, parallels between hell and the grave, our common destination, are easy and natural, and would seem to have biblical authority. Where in the Authorized Version the Psalmist is rendered 'if I make my bed in *hell*, behold, thou art there' (Psalm 139.8), modern translators have *Sheol* (RV and NEB) or *the grave* (ASB Liturgical Psalter). Death and the descent to Sheol, or Hades, are often synonymous in the Bible, and the Authorized Version's use of the word 'hell' brings the symbolism of hell and the grave into contiguity: 'Yet thou [Lucifer] shalt be brought down to hell [Sheol NEB], to the sides of the pit [depths of the abyss]' (Isaiah 14.15). Both hell and the grave are 'below' and loathsome, and the two senses of 'hell' – the pareschatological Hades and the eschatological Gehenna – parallel the dual nature of the grave, which is at once transitional (as the site of the resurrection of the body to judgment) and permanent (as the fixed state of physical corruption).

Both death and damnation are traditionally thought of as a downward movement, a descent into the depths. F. D. Maurice, for example, writes of the 'abyss of death', and of 'sinking' into eternal death.[23] Bickersteth refers to the '*crypt* / Which overarch'd the fiery gulf below', and describes how 'the *vault* . . . / Fell sheer into the bottomless *pit*' (XI.530–4; my emphases). Characteristically, however, it is Swinburne who, in the final stanza of 'Dolores', published in the same year as Bickersteth's epic, draws attention to the ambiguity that he exploits:

> We shall know what the darkness discovers
> If the grave-pit be shallow or deep. . .[24]

We have seen that references to worms in Victorian poetry strengthened an association between the fear of death and burial, and the fear of judgment. Bickersteth, in his paper on *The Second Death* (1869), focuses upon the 'undying worm' of scripture (Isaiah 66, Matthew 18), which he interprets as the individual sinner's 'accusing conscience' that torments him in the unquenchable fire of Gehenna.[25] Father Furniss's parallels between the grave and hell are more explicitly repulsive. Worse than the smell of a living body suffering from cancers or ulcers, he reminds his young readers, is the 'smell of death coming from a dead body lying in the grave'. But

St. Bonaventure says that if one single body was taken out of Hell and laid on the earth, in that same moment every living creature on the earth would sicken and die. Such is the smell of death from one body in Hell. What then will be the smell of death from countless millions and millions of bodies laid in Hell like sheep?[26]

Father Furniss's exploitation of parallels between hell and the grave in order to reinforce fears associated with damnation with those associated with death is characteristic of writers who considered that it was their duty to warn their readers of the perils of living in a state of mortal sin. The tide of opinion in the Victorian period turned against this kind of teaching, however. The sources of public criticism are in the main fairly predictable. In Charles Kingsley's Broad Church novel *Yeast* (1848), for example, the authorial narrator offers this aside:

The New Testament deals very little in appeals *ad terrorem*; and it would be well if some, who fancy that they follow it, would do the same, and by abstaining from making 'hell fire' the chief incentive to virtue, cease from tempting many a poor fellow to enlist on the devil's side the only manly feeling he has left – personal courage.   (16)

In the 1870s, the secularist Austin Holyoake argued that the doctrine of hell 'brutalises all who believe in it', and that it 'does *not* make men good';[27] F. W. Farrar concluded that the 'virtue which has no better basis than fear of Hell is no virtue at all';[28] and Samuel Butler began work on his brilliant satire of Evangelical clergy and their use of threats of hell in *The Way of All Flesh* (published posthumously in 1903).

Those who took the high ground, however, on the broad issue of punishments and rewards were themselves vulnerable to criticism. Matthew Arnold rejected the idea of Christianity as nothing but a promise of paradise to the saint and a threat of hell-fire to the worldly man.[29] Similarly, in *Culture and Anarchy* (1869), he commented sadly that Mr Smith, whose suicide had been reported, and who was said to have 'laboured under the apprehension that he would come to poverty, and that he was eternally lost', was 'a kind of type . . . of all the strongest, most respectable, and most representative part of our nation'.[30] H. N. Oxenham's response to Arnold's position in the preface to the first edition of *Catholic Eschatology* (1876) is telling:

It is currently asserted that the doctrine of eternal punishment, and indeed of future retribution altogether, is peculiarly repugnant to the spirit of the age; and I quite believe it. There is something uncongenial to an atmosphere of high intellectual culture and elaborate artificial refinement in an ethical system, like the Christian, based on the acknowledgment of what the Apostle calls the exceeding sinfulness of sin. The conviction of sin, whether original or actual, is abhorrent alike to the pride and sensuality – or sensuousness, if that term be preferred – of the dominant '*Zeitgeist*'.[31]

It was upon the 'sinfulness of sin' that the question of whether it was right to inculcate the fear of hell in believers turned. For although many high-minded people deprecated the methods of popular preachers such as Father Furniss or William Booth, some shared Gladstone's concern, expressed in the 1890s, lest the relegation of hell to 'the far-off corners of the Christian mind' might adversely affect morals, as a sense of the 'terrors of the Lord' could thus be lost.[32] The High Church theologian, J. B. Mozley, for example, wrote in response to Maurice's *Theological Essays*, in 1854:

the belief in eternal punishment is the true and rational concomitant of the sense of moral obligation. Destroy the punishment and you destroy the sin; limit it, and you make sin a light thing.[33]

F. W. Farrar acknowledged that one of his major objections to universalism was its potential impact upon moral behaviour.[34]

Farrar knew, however, from his pastoral experience, that extreme measures such as hell-fire preaching or deathbed calls to repentance were not necessarily effective in the fight against sin, as they took no account of the fact that genuine change in people is usually gradual, and that most die in the manner in which they live. Indeed, one of the most effective defences against the terrors of hell would seem to have been the kind of stubborn resistance that George Eliot portrays in 'Amos Barton' from *Scenes of Clerical Life* (1857).[35] The Revd Barton, a 'university-taught clergyman', has neither a 'flexible imagination' nor an 'adroit tongue', and, when preaching in the workhouse, fails to convey his message to the unlettered poor who sit before him. After the service he notices that old Mrs Brick's snuff box is empty. Whereas a more tactful and broad-minded man might have quietly supplied her with a refill, and thus warmed her heart towards him and his office, Barton simply says in a brusque manner, 'So your snuff is all gone, eh?':

Mrs Brick's eyes twinkled with the visionary hope that the parson might be intending to replenish her box, at least mediately, through the present of a small copper.

'Ah, well! you'll soon be going where there is no more snuff. You'll be in need of mercy then. You must remember that you may have to seek for mercy and not find it, just as you're seeking for snuff.'

At the first sentence of this admonition, the twinkle subsided from Mrs Brick's eyes. The lid of her box went 'click!' and her heart was shut up at the same moment.   (2)

When he then turns his attention to a boy of seven who has misbehaved during the service, he is equally ineffectual, again resorting unthinkingly to the stock threats traditionally employed by clergymen as a means of gaining control over rebellious spirits:

'Do you like being beaten?'
'No-a.'
'Then what a silly boy you are to be naughty. If you were not naughty, you wouldn't be beaten. But if you are naughty, God will be angry, as well as Mr Spratt; and God can burn you for ever. That will be worse than being beaten.'

Master Fodge's countenance was neither affirmative nor negative of this proposition.

As so often in George Eliot's fiction, references to invisible things have little or no impact upon her ordinary simple folk, who are of the earth, earthy.

It is recorded in a defence of Father Furniss against some of the strong criticism which his work received that the children who attended his missions showed many signs of affection towards him.[36] Several possible explanations for this present themselves, including the debt which the children might have felt they owed to the priest who showed so much concern for their salvation. Some no doubt remained impervious to what was said, or, like Jane Eyre, resolved to keep in good health, and not die. Others, while possibly accepting that they would go to hell if they did not attend mass regularly, probably found Furniss's vivid narrative so extreme and foreign to their own experience that they could not fix hell in their minds, and therefore dismissed it as something remote and, in present terms, unreal. It would seem that it is later in life, and specifically during transitional phases such as adolescence, or child-bearing, or the dying process, when a sense of past sins is awakened, that the fear of hell is most acute. Mrs Brick and Master Fodge are less vulnerable to the threat of hell than are Joyce's Stephen Dedalus, or Hardy's Tess Durbeyfield, or the dying cottager's wife in whom the Revd Theobald Pontifex induces a 'paroxysm of fear', in Butler's *The Way of All Flesh* (15). It was through their satirical treatment of this kind of ministry that writers such as Eliot, Hardy, and Butler focused their critiques of a religion which seemed to play cruelly upon the hopes and fears of vulnerable people, and all in the name of a loving God.

THE THEOLOGY OF HELL

Turning from pastoral to more specifically theological questions associated with hell in the nineteenth century, we should first remind ourselves of the two kinds of punishment traditionally believed to be reserved for the damned: the *poena sensus* (the punishment or pain of sense) and the *poena damni* (the punishment or pain of loss). Much of the opposition to hell-fire preaching was grounded in a repulsion from teaching on physical torments, and opinions on the validity and effectiveness of such teaching varied widely. Before the middle of the century the liberal preacher F. W. Robertson of Brighton could state in a sermon that 'we have learned to smile' at the idea of a 'bodily hell', and that 'in bodily awful intolerable torture we believe no longer'.[37] Such ideas were still being disseminated at the end of the century, however, when Gladstone comments that the 'fashion' of describing details of the pains of hell, 'sometimes even approaching to the loathsome', has 'continued, within narrowing limits, down to the present day'.[38] Gladstone cites one Mr Trapp, an English clergyman, as an example of 'a strong element of pure vulgarity' in such writing:

> Doomed to live death, and never to expire,
> In floods and whirlwinds of tempestuous fire,
> The damned shall groan . . .

The idea of *poena damni*, however, was much more widely acceptable in the Victorian period. The loss of heaven, and thus the absence of God, seemed for most who believed in a *post-mortem* judgment to be the inevitable consequence of a willed rejection of Christ in this life. (Universalists and Unitarians, of course, held different views, and the question remained of limbo, and what happened to those who had never heard the name of Christ.) If heaven is to be with God, hell is to be without him, and with the loss of God goes the loss of his spiritual gifts: in hell, 'tears of penance come too late for grace' (Keble epigraph). 'What is Perdition but a loss?', asked Maurice, and Tennyson would quote with approval his friend's view that the 'real Hell was the absence of God from the human soul'.[39] It was easier for liberals to accept what could be thought of as internalized spiritual pain which resulted from man's sinful nature, than some kind of physical pain more obviously inflicted from without by an avenging and punitive God. And here was material with which the novelist or poet for whom the inner life and a sense of the absence of God were primary themes could work.

Again, the great literary precursor was Dante, whose vision of the perpetuation of our sinful nature in death is the subject of A. C. Charity's study:

> by making his shades 'alive' with their human character undiminished, and with real names . . . attached to them, Dante has taken a bold step already. But he has presented them as dead too, inescapably: they no longer have what is essential to Dasein, real human being: they are without a future . . . Their death is the direct subject, and only through death is life seen. But it is seen; life and death are shown as typologically related.[40]

Commenting in the mid-nineteenth century on Dante's hell, Maurice makes a slightly different point. 'Men are in eternal misery', he writes, 'because they are still covetous, proud, loveless', and he adds that 'the thought of His ceasing to punish them, of His letting them alone, of His leaving them to themselves, is the real, the unutterable horror'.[41]

Indeed, in purely temporal terms, *poena damni* can be more daunting than *poena sensus*, which is sometimes conceived of as diminishing. In a fascinating letter addressed to Hallam Tennyson, Aubrey de Vere reports a visit he made to the eighty-nine-year-old Newman, saying that he wished Hallam's father could have been present to hear the Cardinal's words on a religious subject which was of interest to him:

Eternal Punishment, respecting which he remarked that though the 'Pain of Loss' (that of the Vision and Fruition of God) never ceased, yet *Catholic* Theology allowed of a belief entertained by many Theologians, that the '*Poena Sensus*' does not share that Eternity, but gradually diminishes and may wholly cease, as is implied by the expression 'beaten by few *stripes*'. This is wholly opposed to the Calvinist Theology, especially when combined with the teaching that the 'Fire' like the 'Worm' is a *figure*, that Eternity includes no sense of *Succession*, and that the gates of Heaven are always open; so that the reason that the reprobate and impenitent does not enter is because he has no love for God and *does not desire* His presence.[42]

This last point is crucial, and is often made in relation to the *poena damni* in both the Victorian Age and our own. Hans Küng, for example, rejects a mythological understanding of hell, which still implies a place in the upper or lower world, and instead favours a purely theological interpretation as 'an exclusion from the fellowship of the living God', while John Bowker argues that everlasting punishment is impossible in our universe, where time is a statistical effect of entropy, but hell as the absence of God is possible.[43]

The cruder attempts in the nineteenth century to locate hell as a place in the lower world – to Father Furniss, for example, it seemed likely that it is in the middle of the earth[44] – provided easy targets for Austin Holyoake, who asked how hell could be both within the earth and bottomless.[45] In contrast the *Catholic Encyclopedia* was more cautious, stating that 'the Church has decided nothing on this subject; hence we may say hell is a definite place; but where it is, we do not know'.[46] Like heaven, hell could be seen as a state rather than a place, a view which was favoured by spiritualists among others,[47] and this position was again more compatible with the traditional *poena damni* than with the *poena sensus*.

Whereas Roman Catholics referred to 'Holy Church' for their authority on such matters and spiritualists to their sources on the other side, Evangelical Protestants like E. H. Bickersteth naturally turned to the Bible on the subject of the condition of the lost, and it was on this

ground that the great theological battles on the subject were fought in
the nineteenth century. In his paper on *The Second Death* (1869), for
example, Bickersteth uncritically cites Old Testament texts on what he
calls 'these eternal verities'.[48] He then quotes Josephus on the beliefs of
the Jews before the fall of Jerusalem, explaining the 'orthodox' position
of the Pharisees on the existence of an 'everlasting prison', and the
Sadducees' denial of any future state or punishments and rewards in
Hades.[49] Moving on to the New Testament, he begins with John the
Baptist as one of the strongest sources of evidence, quoting texts on 'the
wrath to come' and 'unquenchable fire' (Matthew 3.7,12), and 'the
wrath of God' (John 3.36).[50] In the Sermon on the Mount, Bickersteth
argues, 'the Truth' preaches 'the Pharisaic creed of the everlasting prison
and of a burning Gehenna'.[51] And at the end of his ministry Jesus said,
'Depart from Me, ye cursed, into everlasting fire, prepared for the devil
and his angels' (Matthew 25):

But can this word *everlasting* possibly have a limited meaning in their case?
With what can you compare it? – the duration of the bliss of the saved – 'These
shall go away into everlasting punishment: but the righteous into everlasting
life.' It is, as you know, the same word in both clauses [*aiōnion*] . . . and these
were the last accents of the Saviour's voice, ere He retired to prepare to suffer
and to die.[52]

(A few years later the mistranslation of the word *aionion* was to be a
major plank in Farrar's argument against everlasting punishment.)
Having then quoted from the doubtful verses at the end of Mark (16.16)
as a post-resurrection statement on damnation, Bickersteth finally goes
through the rest of the New Testament, culminating in Revelation 21
and 'the lake which burneth with fire and brimstone: which is the second
death'.[53]

Among the many theological problems with which liberal churchmen
struggled, that of '*everlasting* punishment' was primary: hell and heaven
are fixed states (there are no escalators between them), and the vast
majority of mankind are doomed to go to hell. Such a view was incompatible with their idea of a loving God, and could be challenged on
ethical grounds. Whereas hell had traditionally been explained as an
expression of God's justice, it came to be seen more as an injustice, and
thus not of God, especially as an expanding empire brought home to
people the existence in the world of vast numbers of adherents to other
faiths.[54] Long before Farrar was writing on the subject in the 1870s,

however, J. A. Froude used Markham Sutherland's letters in his novel
The Nemesis of Faith (1849) as a means of expressing his repugnance
from the 'doctrine so horrible':

the largest portion of mankind . . . are to be tortured for ever and ever in
unspeakable agonies. My God! and for what?[55]

People are 'thrown into life' unformed, Markham argues, and if man
is forgiving, how much more must God be. Heaven would be hell
if one knew that even one soul was suffering in hell. Christ went
down to hell, but it was 'to break the chains, not to bind them'.[56]
Like most doctrinal issues, these go back to the question of early
Christian sources, and Markham refers to the early creeds and devotes
a letter to the authority of the Bible. Again, however, it is with a
reminder of the 'sinfulness of sin' that a new note is introduced, and
in a highly dramatic manner. Like Rochester in *Jane Eyre* (27),
published the same year, Markham in his despair comments that hell
could not be worse than this life: 'not that dark sulphurous home
of torture . . . hell itself, could be less endurable than the present'.[57]
When he prepares to commit suicide, however, in order 'to lighten
others' sorrows' and to end his own, he is suddenly interrupted by
a voice that at first he does not recognize:

'Die without *hope* – the worst sinner's worst death – to bear your sin, and
your sin's punishment, through eternity!' (my emphasis)[58]

Frederick Mornington is the Newman figure in a novel in which, unusually, the original is himself described:

sin with Newman was real; not a misfortune to be pitied and allowed for; to
be talked of gravely in the pulpit, and forgotten when out of it; . . . but in
very truth a dreadful monster, a real child of a real devil . . .[59]

The question of hell, then, turns upon our idea of hope, and upon
whether, as for Newman, a suicide for example loses all hope of eternal
life, or, as for Farrar, 'eternal hope' would embrace even the worst of
sinners in the possibility of purgation in an intermediate state.

Markham Sutherland's cast of mind contrasts strongly with that of
Charles Reding in Newman's own novel *Loss and Gain* (1847):

He [Charles] had had some difficulty in receiving the doctrine of eternal punishment; it had seemed to him the hardest doctrine of Revelation. Then he said
to himself, 'But what is faith in its very notion but an acceptance of the word

of God when reason seems to oppose it? How is it faith at all if there is nothing
to try it?' This thought fully satisfied him.   (15)

Charles cannot, however, get satisfactory answers from Mr Upton, a
High Churchman, on the articles and the creeds. Did the anathemas of
the Athanasian Creed, for example, apply to all its clauses? It was on
the Athanasian Creed that a major debate within the Church of England
concerning hell and everlasting punishment was to focus in the 1870s.
The significance of the debate is reflected in the fact that in the monumental *Life* of Archbishop Tait, which includes separate chapters on
major ecclesiastical issues of the day such as the controversies surrounding *Essays and Reviews* and Bishop Colenso, another whole chapter (22) is entitled 'The Athanasian Creed (1870–1873)', and records
that among Tait's books were, 'besides scores of pamphlets, eight separate volumes devoted to this single subject, all of them published between
the years 1868 and 1872'.[60] Why was this creed so contentious?

The rubric of the Book of Common Prayer stated that on certain
major feast days, including Christmas Day, the Epiphany, Easter Day,
Whit Sunday, and Trinity Sunday, the Athanasian Creed was to be sung
or said at Morning Prayer instead of the Apostles' Creed. The creed
includes 'damnatory clauses' concerning, first, the 'Catholick Faith' –
'Which Faith except every one do keep whole and undefiled: without
doubt he shall perish everlastingly' – and, secondly, the last judgment:
'And they that have done good shall go into life everlasting: and they
that have done evil into everlasting fire.' In the early nineteenth century
many easygoing parish churches had let this command slip, but the
Oxford Movement changed this, and congregations were both surprised
by the unfamiliar words and annoyed when clergymen defended the
action by pointing to the rubric.[61] As Anthony Trollope observed in
1866, the question was viewed differently by different generations, the
'old rector' having been ready enough with his belief (and 'he believed
that he believed what he said that he believed'), whereas 'the new parson
has by no means so glib an answer ready to such a question' because
he is 'ever thinking of it'.[62]

The whole question became the subject of a major controversy in the
early 1870s, following the timely appointment of a Royal Commission
to inquire into the rubrics and rituals of the Church of England in 1867.
It preoccupied many clergy for a number of years of largely tedious
debate, and Tait, as Primate, was put in the difficult position of being

lobbied by brother bishops with strongly held but widely differing views. At the heart of the question lay the corollary that those who had never heard the gospel preached were condemned to everlasting punishment. Opinion divided over whether the creed should be excluded from the prayer book altogether, or some explanatory note should be inserted to the effect that 'nothing in this creed is to be understood as condemning those who by involuntary ignorance or invincible prejudice are hindered from accepting the faith therein declared', as Pusey and his fellow professors in Oxford proposed. The intensity of feeling over this issue is reflected in Pusey and Liddon's avowed intention to retire from the ministry even if there were to be a rearrangement of the days on which the creed was compulsorily to be said.[63]

Significantly, Archbishop Tait's own speech in Convocation on the matter addressed the difficult question of religious language, and specifically of literalism. His comments were to be quoted against him for the rest of his life:

The Bishop of Peterborough [W. C. Magee] . . . says every clause is to be taken in the absolute literal sense, and that of all the words of the creed none are so explicit as the damnatory clauses. Very well. We are to take them, then, in the plainest and most literal sense. But we do not. There is not a soul in the room who does. Nobody in the Church of England takes them in their plain and literal sense.[64]

In the end a Convocation of 1873 agreed on a statement that 'the Church in this confession [doth] declare the necessity for all who would be in a state of salvation of holding fast the Catholic faith, and the great peril of rejecting the same'.[65]

It is illuminating to contrast Tait's approach in his speech with that of E. H. Bickersteth in his paper on *The Second Death* (1869), where he argues that the 'Word of God has spoken' on everlasting punishment:

and we have all affirmed that the doctrine of the Athanasian Creed, 'They that have done good shall go into life everlasting, and they that have done evil into everlasting fire,' *'ought thoroughly to be received and believed: for it may be proved by most certain warrants of Holy Scripture'* [Article 8].[66]

Bickersteth no doubt had the creed in mind when he argued in the same paper that the theme of everlasting punishment was 'deeply exercising many minds at this time'.[67] Characteristically, the path that he himself beat through this particular thicket of ecclesiastical argument was narrow and undeviating.

By the 1870s the Athanasian Creed had become something of a litmus test of people's religious views. In 1875 we find Newman, for example, rejoicing in Charles Kingsley's defence of the creed, and 'in his views generally nearing the Catholic view of things'.[68] Several leading Victorian writers, however, held liberal positions on the subject. Anthony Trollope provides an interesting gloss on the Bickersteth position in his perception that the 'fulminating clause of the Athanasian Creed' was an example of the discrepancy between actual beliefs and declarations of faith, pointing out that although few of the clergy believed it, each clergyman declared aloud that he did 'a dozen times every year of his life'.[69] Tennyson followed the lead of his father, who refused to read the creed in church, and Charlotte Brontë described it as 'profane'.[70]

The 'common view' on 'life everlasting' and 'everlasting fire' had traditionally been based upon the Athanasian Creed and a number of scattered proof texts, including Isaiah 33.14, Daniel 12.2, and Matthew 25.46. The parable of Dives and Lazarus (Luke 16) was also a key text, often cited quite uncritically as 'evidence', including in popular religious literature. In an Evangelical miscellany entitled *The Traveller's Guide, from Death to Life* (n.d.), for example, which was reprinted at least fifty-one times, the following is presented as 'A Solemn Fact':

There is a way for any sinner to *keep* out of hell. There is no way to *get* out of hell. Jesus says, 'I am the Way.' But the rich man in hell was told that there was 'a great gulf fixed.'[71]

As late as the 1890s, Gladstone, a keen student of eschatological controversies of the period, simply cited the passage in Luke against an argument for the possibility of spiritual development after death.[72] Yet sixty years earlier Whateley had argued that although such a parable '*may* chance to agree in every point with matter of fact . . . there is no necessity that it should'.[73] A larger question concerning the parable is that of translation. The Authorized Version translates the Greek *hadēs* (Luke 16.23) as 'hell', whereas the emphasis changes if it is understood that both Dives and Lazarus go to Hades. In the preface to the first edition of his Westminster Abbey sermons, *Eternal Hope* (1878), F. W. Farrar shows how the word 'hell' is used to translate three different words in the New Testament: first, the one instance of the Greek version of *tartarus* (2 Peter 2.4), which refers to an intermediate state previous to judgment; secondly, *hadēs*, which is the exact equivalent of the Hebrew *sheol*, and means 'the unseen world', as a place both for the

bad and the good, and which again refers to an intermediate state of
the soul previous to judgment; and thirdly, *gehenna*, a word for the
common sewer of a city where the bodies of the worst criminals were
dumped, and which came to mean punishment, but *never* endless punishment, beyond the grave.[74]

The major crux in relation to translation, however, was the word
aiōniōs. Bickersteth comments on the matter in *The Second Death*:

> some have in all ages tried to evade or escape the force of these Scriptures by
> affirming that the word (*aiōnios*) translated eternal or everlasting, does not
> mean unending, but coextensive with that age or dispensation (*aiōn*) to which
> it refers. To this our simple answer must be, not what may be the possible
> etymological meaning of the word, or what its use by uninspired authors, but
> what is its actual meaning as employed in the New Testament.[75]

Having begged the question of authority by referring to 'uninspired
authors' and 'actual meaning', he goes on to cite a number of New
Testament 'Scriptures' which seem to him 'absolutely decisive against
any theories either of universalism or of annihilation: they declare in
no ambiguous terms that the punishment is without end, and the penal
suffering to continue for ever and ever'.[76]

Precisely the opposite interpretation informs Farrar's main argument
in *Eternal Hope*, published nine years later:

> The word *aiōnios*, sometimes translated 'everlasting,' is simply the word which,
> in its first sense, means *agelong* or *aeonian*; and which is in the Bible itself
> applied to things which have utterly and long since passed away; and is in its
> second sense something 'spiritual' – something above and beyond time, – as
> when the knowledge of God is said to be eternal life. So that when, with your
> futile billions, you foist into this word *aiōnios*, the fiction of endless time, you
> do but give the lie to the mighty oath of that great angel, who set one foot
> upon the sea, and one upon the land, and with hand uplifted to heaven sware
> by Him who liveth for ever and ever that 'Time should be no more.'[77]

Interestingly, he illustrates his argument in a footnote with a quotation
from Newman's verse drama *The Dream of Gerontius* (1865), which
includes the lines 'For spirits and men by different standards mete / The
less and greater in the flow of time'. As in Newman's comment in old
age, cited earlier, on Roman Catholic teaching 'that Eternity includes
no sense of *Succession*', the theological debate turns upon the limits
of our this-worldly ideas of time and eternity. Farrar's former tutor
F. D. Maurice had suggested in *Theological Essays* (1853) that 'Eternity

in relation to God has nothing to do with time or duration', a view which was to impress Tennyson.[78] Farrar himself was to comment on the first page of *Mercy and Judgment* (1881) that he did not deny 'the eternity of punishment', but that he understood 'the word eternity in a sense far higher than can be degraded into the vulgar meaning of endlessness'.[79] More traditional interpretations continued to be expounded until the end of the nineteenth century. Professor Salmond, for example, stated in 1895 that the phrase 'eternal fire' conjures up 'a sufficiently appalling picture of the retributive future, and . . . in using it Christ Himself gives no hint of a termination of the penalty meant by it'.[80] Once the ground had been loosened, however, around these key biblical terms, the decline of hell as a place of everlasting physical pain was accelerated, and by 1879 G. Somers Bellamy could claim that 'thank God, very few of us remain today' who believe in 'endless punishment'.[81]

'FROM FEARFUL HOPE INTO FEARLESS DESPAIR': SOME VERSIONS OF HELL ON EARTH

While the theologians wrangled over key words and doctrines, the leading novelists and poets, most of whom held liberal or radically revisionary views on the subject, continued to find in the language traditionally associated with hell a repertoire of resonances and associations through which to describe spiritual experience in the here-and-now, and particularly in the treatment of two versions of hell on earth. One is associated with the Industrial Revolution and the growth of the great cities, and is to be found mainly in the social-problem novels of the middle of the century and, later, in the fiction of George Gissing. The other is diametrically opposed to the conventionalized 'heaven' of profane love: the 'hell' of love which is dead, or betrayed, and particularly associated with sex where there is no love – a secularized version of the theologians' *poena damni*, perhaps most poignantly explored in George Meredith's sonnet sequence, *Modern Love* (1862), and most ambiguously in Swinburne's 'Laus Veneris' (*Poems and Ballads*, 1866). Whereas for liberal theologians the decline of hell as everlasting punishment is associated with a new emphasis upon the 'lively hope' of a future life with Christ, the more radical secular writers of the 1860s and 1870s deny that hope and argue the need for stoic endurance in a world of pain. This kind of movement 'from fearful hope into fearless despair' (Swinburne)[82] is epitomized in James Thomson's *City of Dreadful Night* (1874).

First, however, let us turn to one of the two versions of hell on earth which provide a context for reading Thomson, namely that associated with industrialization and urbanization in the early nineteenth century. If the Blake who wrote of England's dark satanic mills is the strongest literary precursor of Victorian writings on the subject, it is John Martin's apocalyptic paintings which provide some of the most illuminating contemporary parallels in the graphic arts. Martin's treatment of 'wonderful subjects', mainly from the Bible, in the late 1820s and 1830s coincided with one of the peaks of millenarian activity in the nineteenth century. It was also in this period that the demand for political and social reform in the context of frighteningly rapid urban development during the Industrial Revolution came to a head. In one of Martin's late 'judgment' paintings, *The Last Judgment* (1853; illustration 7), a railway train – that potent symbol of the new age of steam – crashes down a ravine into the abyss of hell. The fears and suspicions concerning the advent of the railway train, which seemed to express in its fire and steam, its weight and apparently resistless energy, a force greater than nature and therefore suggestive of satanic power, are thus embodied in this classic example of the apocalyptic sublime, in which the doomed train conveys a multitude of sinners into the pit.

In his apocalyptic paintings and his illustrations to *Paradise Lost*, Martin was strongly influenced by the shapes and colours of the industrial landscape of the North-East of England where he was brought up, as were other artists included in Francis D. Klingender's classic study on *Art and the Industrial Revolution* (1947). The relationship, however, between such landscapes and hell also works the other way, as Klingender suggests: 'If Martin gave Hell the image of industry . . . contemporary illustrators often gave industry the image of Hell.'[83] Klingender cites as an example of this W. Read's aquatint entitled 'Drawing the Retorts at the Great Gas Light Establishment, Brick Lane' (in London), which provided the frontispiece of the 1821 volume of *The Monthly Magazine* (illustration 14). Remove some of the details such as the products and machinery depicted here, and it would be easy to mistake the picture for a vision of hell. Even the slatted air vent, through which a moonlit sky can be seen, is suggestive of the traditional belief that it is possible for those who suffer in the stifling fires of hell to see heaven in all its glory.

According to his son Leopold, Martin's 'judgment' paintings were inspired partly by a journey through the Black Country at dead of night:

The glow of the furnaces, the red blaze of light, together with the liquid fire, seemed to his mind truly sublime and awful. He could not imagine anything more terrible even in the regions of everlasting punishment. All he had done or attempted in ideal painting fell far short, very far short, of the fearful sublimity.[84]

This statement contains a clue to one of the principal reasons for the decline in the power of images of hell as *poena sensus* in the nineteenth century, for during the Industrial Revolution reality began to exceed the bounds of the imagination, even in the most dramatic visual or poetic versions of hell. This theme was taken up by social commentators on the appalling squalor of the urban slums in the 1830s and 1840s, and by the end of the nineteenth century had become conventionalized. William Booth's ironic response to Stanley's account of his African journeys – *In Darkest England and the Way Out* (1890) – is typical in this respect:

Talk about Dante's Hell, and all the horrors and cruelties of the torture-chamber of the lost! The man who walks with open eyes and with bleeding heart through the shambles of our civilisation needs no such fantastic images of the poet to teach him horror.[85]

Again, the horror of reality at home exceeds the horror of hell, or indeed of darkest Africa, which the Victorian reader can imagine only with the help of the poet or the travel writer.

As in the case of industrial scenes, images of the city were often as suggestive of hell as images of hell were suggestive of the city. In Gustave Doré's illustrations for Jerrold's *London* (1872), for example, published six years after his *Paradise Lost* and *The Vision of Hell* (Dante), the huddled figures in plates depicting the docks and the surrounding brothels, pubs, and opium dens adopt the postures of the damned.[86] Of the many features of urban deprivation and alienation to which social commentators drew their readers' attention, several were reminiscent of hell. Friedrich Engels, for example, focused upon that sense of isolation in a crowd which had always been a traditional feature of hell, as in Dante, in his description of London,[87] and described the Old Town of Manchester as a 'Hell upon Earth'.[88]

Engels was one of several visitors to Britain who were like modern Dantes, penetrating the Inferno of a new industrial age, but without a Virgil at their side. De Tocqueville, for example, when writing on Manchester in 1835, described the polluted streams that wound their way between and beneath the town's appalling slum dwellings as 'the Styx of this new Hades'.[89] Whereas classical allusion in the original Dante reflected the writer's Catholic world view and was central to both his learning and his technique, by the middle of the nineteenth century in England it can have the effect of weakening the specifically Christian connotations of references to hell. Alexander Welsh argues that Dickens's London is like the classical hell, and draws a parallel with S. E. Finer's quotation from *The Times* of 1847:

To investigate the source of a malaria or stench Mr. Chadwick would swim through the stagnant pools of Avernus and enter the pestiferous jaws of Orcus itself: *per loca foeda situ* he would track the secrets of the nether world, to rescue his Eurydice from the reign of Black Dis.[90]

Interestingly, Charles Kingsley's working-class hero, Alton Locke, says '*Facilis descensus Averni!*', when describing as narrator how the tailoring trade was forced to put work out at contract prices, and thus caused unemployment (10). It is the prophetic note of Carlyle's writing, however, that can be heard most clearly in a passage in the previous chapter, where Locke describes the atmosphere of London, bringing together disparate elements of the city as hell on earth:

that was uncongenial enough; crime and poverty, all-devouring competition, and hopeless struggles against Mammon and Moloch, amid the roar of wheels, the ceaseless stream of pale, hard faces, intent on gain, or brooding over woe; amid endless prison walls of brick, beneath a lurid, crushing sky of smoke and mist. It was a dark, noisy, thunderous element that London life; a troubled sea that cannot rest, casting up mire and dirt; resonant of the clanking of chains, the grinding of remorseless machinery, the wail of lost spirits from the pit. And it did its work upon me; it gave a gloomy colouring, a glare as of some Dantean 'Inferno', to all my utterances.   (9)

These are the same materials with which Dickens worked in his social novels of mid-century: the prison walls; the urban desert of resistant brick; the smoke and mist hanging over the city; the grinding machinery of the works; the glare of the furnaces.

Kingsley's application of the language of hell to the city is most fully developed in the chapter entitled 'The Lowest Deep' (35), in which Jemmy Downes's wife and children are found dead, their bodies already gnawed by rats, in a slum dwelling at 'the very mouth of hell', where a dirty gas-lamp just serves to make 'darkness visible'. Downes himself drowns in the 'hell-broth' of a stream that runs under the floor of this room. And who are to blame? The rich, who turn a blind eye to this squalor, and who 'leave the men who make their clothes to starve in such hells on earth' as Locke's workroom (5)? For a Christian commentator, however, there was always a danger that this kind of loose application of the language of hell to social conditions could not be supported theologically. Consider, for example, this passage from William Booth's *In Darkest England*, where he attacks those who 'ruin' girls by forcing them into prostitution:

Her word becomes unbelievable, her life an ignominy, and she is swept downward, ever downward, into the bottomless perdition of prostitution. But there, even in the lowest depths, excommunicated by Humanity and outcast from God, she is far nearer the pitying heart of the One true Saviour than all the men who forced her down, aye, and than all the Pharisees and Scribes who stand silently by while these fiendish wrongs are perpetrated before their very eyes.[91]

Milton's 'bottomless perdition' must be metaphoric here, but what follows is at best ambiguous and at worst blasphemous, hinting at a separation between God and the one true saviour. Booth posed the question: 'Why all this apparatus of temples and meeting-houses to save men from perdition in a world which is to come, while never a helping hand is stretched out to save them from the inferno of their present life?' The relationship between the suffering of sinners on earth, however, and their hope of heaven, remains unclear. For the prostitute who lives in the lowest depths of depravity; the wife of a drunkard who lives at the mouth of hell; the stoker who works near the heat of a furnace; the tailor who labours in a sweat-shop; or the weaver in the mill, deafened by the noise of the machines and with fluff on the lung, to whom it seemed that hell had come on earth, escape was possible only in the respite of limited leisure hours, and in the hope of heaven. A cultural product partly of middle-class guilt and partly of a Christian reformist agenda, the social-problem novelists' hell on earth often fails to resolve or even address the theological issues which its sources in Christian tradition would seem to raise.

An exception to this is Elizabeth Gaskell's *Mary Barton* (1848), in which images of hell on earth are consistent with a Unitarian theology that denies everlasting punishment.[92] The worst fear of the prostitute in this novel, Esther, whose life in this world seems to be lived in 'outer darkness' (22), is that she will be separated from her dead daughter, born out of wedlock, in the world to come. She says to Jem Wilson:

'I've done that since, which separates us as far asunder as heaven and hell can be.' Her voice rose again to the sharp pitch of agony. 'My darling! my darling! even after death I may not see thee, my own sweet one! She was so good – like a little angel. What is that text, I don't remember, – that text mother used to teach me when I sat on her knee long ago, it begins "Blessed are the pure" '–   (14)

The whole thrust of the novel is towards forgiveness, and ideas of the future life are grounded in 'texts of comfort': 'Where the wicked cease from troubling, and the weary are at rest'; 'The tears shall be wiped away from all eyes', and so on (19). When Esther is buried with John Barton, a confessed murderer who has been forgiven by his victim's father, the epitaph is from Psalm 103: 'For He will not always chide, neither will He keep His anger for ever' (38).

The novel's non-judgmental ending, then, suggests that Esther's anxious reference to the parable of Dives and Lazarus was misplaced. In the case of John Barton, however, his perversion of the parable in his set-piece speech in the opening chapter is shown to be blasphemous:

'. . . we pile up their fortunes with the sweat of our brows; and yet we are to live as separate as if we were in two worlds; ay, as separate as Dives and Lazarus, with a great gulf betwixt us: but I know who was best off then,' and he wound up his speech with a low chuckle that had no mirth in it.[93]

Whateley was sceptical about the possible coincidence between this parable and fact, and later in the century F. W. Farrar focused on the problem of translating *hadēs*. Elizabeth Gaskell's handling of the parable is consistent with her Unitarianism. In a sermon on the Gadarene, for example, Theophilus Lindsey (one of the founders of English Unitarianism) attempted to explain how the 'great gulf' of the parable of Dives and Lazarus is part of Jewish tradition, and that the concept of everlasting torment has no place in the New Testament. Discussing the Gadarene's 'devils', he wrote:

St. Luke has it, 'that he would not command them to go out into the deep,' *i.e.* the abyss, the supposed place of wicked spirits betwixt death and the resurrection, in the vulgar estimation . . . Hence Dives, in the parable, is made to talk of a great gulf betwixt him and Abraham, consistently with these Jewish notions; but the scriptures teach no such thing, speak of no such state.[94]

While Esther's anxiety concerning the future state is shown to be misplaced and Barton's misapplication of the parable of Dives and Lazarus is corrected by the novel's theology of forgiveness, Elizabeth Gaskell can still fall back upon a parallel between industry and hell which is very close to that of W. Read and other artists of the Industrial Revolution. Seen through the eyes of three policemen who have never been in a foundry before, Jem Wilson's workplace makes a deep impression:

> Dark, black were the walls, the ground, the faces around them, as they crossed the yard. But, in the furnace-house a deep and lurid red glared over all; the furnace roared with mighty flame. The men, like demons, in their fire-and-soot colouring, stood swart around, awaiting the moment when the tons of solid iron should have melted down into fiery liquid . . .   (19)

That the reference to demons is purely aesthetic perhaps reflects Elizabeth Gaskell's lack of belief in hell, but such references were to become more common with the erosion of belief in everlasting punishment in the second half of the century.

The freedom with which George Gissing treats ideas of hell on earth in his social fiction of the 1880s is explained partly by his agnosticism. It also reflects the fact that by then the major doctrinal battles over everlasting punishment had been fought and won by the more progressive forces in the Established Church of England, and thus the subject had become less problematic in the public mind. Freed from the complications associated with their former doctrinal significance, images of hell take on a new life in his early novels, and from the opening paragraph of *Workers in the Dawn* (1880) to the last paragraph of *The Nether World* (1889) hell is a recurrent controlling metaphor. His close examination of physical conditions in the slums of late-nineteenth-century London, and his more impressive analysis of psychological impoverishment in the depressing environment of mean streets, broadly correspond to the *poena sensus* and *poena damni* of the theologians. Like most of them he sees the *poena damni* as the greater suffering, being a state in which the individual human being is cut off from love and hope.

Dante, the presiding genius of nineteenth-century social commentary, is present here too, where the author-narrator in *Workers in the Dawn* writes like a Henry Mayhew in the role of Virgil in the *Inferno*: 'Walk with me, reader, into Whitecross Street' (1). Flames and a 'reddish light' contrast with 'deep blackness' overhead; through a 'yawning archway' are 'unspeakable abominations'. Whereas in Kingsley, however, the reader tries to relate such language to the writer's Christian Socialist programme, there is no question of discovering in Gissing some kind of providential scheme for mankind, or even any hope of reform. Indeed, there is in *The Nether World* a new sense of hopelessness concerning the masses of the urban poor in London, the 'city of the damned':

> Over the pest-stricken regions of East London, sweltering in sunshine which served only to reveal the intimacies of abominations; across miles of a city of the damned, such as thought never conceived before this age of ours; above streets swarming with a nameless populace, cruelly exposed by the unwonted light of heaven; . . . the train made its way at length beyond the utmost limits of dread, and entered upon a land of level meadows.   (19)

What John Martin said of the sublime power of industry fifty years earlier, Gissing now writes of the enormously expanded East End of London, where reality has surpassed what was formerly imaginable, and where the light of heaven, now only the sky, shines remorselessly upon the damned, now only on this earth.

Peter Keating has suggested that Gissing's metaphor of the abyss in his social fiction reflects a new fear of the masses in the last decades of the century, and that the metaphor recurs with this connotation in the work of H. G. Wells, C. F. G. Masterman, and E. M. Forster.[95] Just as central to Gissing's writing is the idea of the circle of hell, here secularized in the careful grading of the levels of poverty on each floor of depressing lodging-houses, for example, in the city of the damned. The circular structure of his early novels – *Workers in the Dawn* begins and ends in an abyss, the famous 'Io Saturnalia' chapter in *The Nether World* almost literally revolves around the pawnshop (12) – suggests the vicious circle or downward spiral that we now call the poverty trap. In Gissing's world only a madman could experience an angel visitation, and even this sole angel can offer no hope of transcendence: 'This life you are now leading', it announces to Mad Jack, 'is that of the damned; this place to which you are confined is Hell!' (*The Nether World*, 37).

The haunting portrayal in Gissing's fiction of marriages or liaisons under intolerable pressure, largely for financial reasons, and of the psychological 'hell' in which couples find themselves trapped, reflects the unhappiness of his two disastrous marriages to women of a lower social class than his own. George Meredith's experience was closer to Ruskin's: by June 1857 he knew that his young (and probably sexually frustrated) wife Mary Ellen and the painter Henry Wallis were lovers; less than a year later she had a child by Wallis. The focus of his creative effort at this time is summed up in the subtitle of David Williams's informal biography, *George Meredith: His Life and Lost Love* (1977). First, only two years after he and his wife separated, Meredith published *The Ordeal of Richard Feverel: A History of a Father and Son* (July 1859). With his high style, which is liberally embellished with allegory, classical allusion, and synecdoche (his favourite figure of speech), Meredith is the only novelist who can write at mid-century of hell and the devil in a relaxed and assured manner, treating them figuratively but without sacrificing a sense of the profound moral significance attached to them in European culture. His early work represents the most significant exploration in the Victorian period of our second kind of hell on earth: the secularized version of *poena damni*, in which love is dead or betrayed.

Two of Meredith's most familiar metaphors – the devil and the mask – recur in the key chapter (33) in which Sir Austin Feverel, whose wife ran off with a poet, confronts the fact that the famous educational 'System' which he applied to his son Richard has failed. Meredith himself explained the chapter in a letter to Samuel Lucas, the journalist and reviewer: 'The "System", you see, had its origin not so much in love for his son, as in wrath at his wife, and so carries its own Nemesis.'[96] In what one reviewer called Richard Feverel's 'fall' into the 'perilous regions of the "demi-monde"'[97] in the extraordinary chapter entitled 'An Enchantress' (38), Meredith marshals the forces of the melodrama in order to dramatize his young hero's temptation by the fascinating Bella Mount – herself seduced at sixteen and an experienced woman of the world at twenty-one, and described as receiving 'the devil's wages'. As she moves through a bewildering series of role changes – now masquerading as the dandiacal 'Sir Julius', a raffish member of the fast set and a stock 'gentleman seducer', now as a witch, now as her usual social persona – a 'lurid splendour' glances about her like 'lights from the pit', and Richard, drinking a couple of glasses of champagne in succession, stares about: 'Was he in hell, with a lost soul raving to him?' In the seductress's boldest *coup de théâtre*, when she looks 'beautiful and devilish' in the role of a witch, the chapter's play on the idea of hell comes to a bizarre climax as she spills burning spirits onto the carpet, which catches fire, creating a miniature domestic inferno which Richard extinguishes, but which presages judgment. As the couple finally come together, an intimation of the desolation which is to ensue (after his wife Lucy loses her mind and dies) is conveyed in the language of lost souls and the echo of *Richard III*:

'Lost, Richard! lost for ever! give me up!'
He cried: 'I never will!' and strained her in his arms, and kissed her passion-ately on the lips.
She was not acting now as she sidled and slunk her half-averted head with a kind of maiden shame under his arm, sighing heavily, weeping, clinging to him. It was wicked truth.
Not a word of love between them!
Was ever hero in this fashion won?

'Not a word of love between them': sex without love is one of the most difficult and dangerous areas of an already taboo subject in the mid-Victorian period, and it was one which haunted the cuckolded George Meredith, for whom it seems to have represented hell on earth. Indeed, the close parallels between the satanic language of *Richard Fev-erel* and of *Modern Love*, published three years later, suggest an obsess-ive mind at work. Meredith's description of Bella Mount, for example – 'There was sorcery in her breath; sorcery in her hair: the ends of it stung him like *little snakes*' (my emphasis) – is echoed in the familiar opening lines of the sequence:

> By this he knew she wept with waking eyes:
> That, at his hand's light quiver by her head,
> The strange low sobs that shook their common bed,
> Were called into her with a sharp surprise,
> And strangled mute, like *little* gaping *snakes*,
> Dreadfully venomous to him.   (1; my emphases)[98]

Similarly, the wife in the poem is described as a 'star with lurid beams' which 'seemed to crown / The *pit* of infamy' (II; cf. XXIII), and as a 'devilish malignant *witch*' (IX; my emphases). The tone of the 'Enchant-ress' chapter in *Richard Feverel* is also to be heard in *Modern Love*. Keith Hanley suggests of the husband's expression of feeling towards his wife that in 'a welter of maniacally melodramatic imagery accom-panied by Biblical diction he conveys the moral repulsiveness of his

attraction to this snake-like witch, who brings out in him the demon
and the beast'.[99]

As Hanley also points out, *Modern Love* derives ironically from the
Renaissance sonnet sequence tradition of amatory courtship.[100] That
Petrarchan tradition continued the medieval courtly love convention of
applying the language of divine love to the experience of profane love.
Thus Meredith's description of the death of love as hell represents
another aspect of that ironical relationship between his sonnet sequence
and the tradition upon which it is formally based. In the first phase of
the poem (I–XXVI),[101] 'death' (*thanatos*) and the death wish are closely
associated with 'love' (*eros*) and its breakdown, and the two words
seem increasingly to coil around each other in serpentine movements:

> Like sculptured effigies they might be seen
> Upon their marriage-tomb, the sword between;
> Each wishing for the sword that severs all.   (I)

In later sonnets the husband refers to 'Love's corpse-light' (XVII), and
says, 'Shamed nature, then, confesses love can die' (VI). When in earlier,
happier days he caused her to weep by saying (though not thinking),
'Ah, yes! / Love dies!' (XVI), the 'red chasm' which grew 'among the
clinking coals' proved to be prophetic, for now he gets 'a glimpse of
hell' in guessing that his wife may have something to confess:

> She will not speak. I will not ask. We are
> League-sundered by the silent gulf between.   (XXII)

Traditional biblical imagery relating to the separation of the saved from
the damned, and of man from God (who is love), here conveys a sense
of a secularized and existential *poena damni* – the pain of loss of the
vision and fruition of (profane) love. At Christmas time, the husband's
dream inverts the hope embodied in the incarnation:

> I dreamed a banished angel to me crept:
> My feet were nourished on his breasts all night.   (XXIII)

Love betrayed becomes a 'subtle serpent' with which he is 'cursed'
henceforward (XXVI).

In the second phase, concerning the husband's subsequent affair, the
devil seems kind when 'not a soul' will comfort his distress (XXVII),
and he feels 'the promptings of Satanic power' (XXVIII). In his illicit
relationship with the blonde 'Lady', he is acutely aware of their mortal-

ity – 'But, as you will! we'll sit contentedly, / And eat our pot of honey
on the grave' (XXIX; cf. XXX) – and of the reality of temptation, as he
indicates in his criticism of Raphael's portrayal of a 'too serene' St
Michael conquering the devil:

> 'Oh, Raphael! when men the Fiend do fight,
> They conquer not upon such easy terms.
> Half serpent in the struggle grow these worms.
> And does he grow half human, all is right.'   (XXXIII)

Earlier in the poem he has scorned both those 'miserable males' who
'sniff at vice and, daring not to snap, / Do therefore hope for heaven'
(XX), and the man who 'would burden the poor deuce / With what
ensues from his own slipperiness'. The real moral battle must be fought
out and the repercussions suffered in the here-and-now.

The attempted reconciliation with his wife in the third and final phase
(XL–L) is ill-fated, for his confession of his own affair prompts her to
leave him free to go to his Lady:

> She has gone forth, I know not where.
> Will the hard world my sentience of her share?
> I feel the truth; so let the world surmise.   (XLVIII)

Whether her going forth is a departure, possibly with her lover, or her
death, is unclear until the end of the following sonnet, which Meredith
may have added as an afterthought, together with the final sonnet in
the sequence: the husband 'knows all' when he kisses his wife – 'Lethe
had passed those lips' (XLIX). She has taken poison.

In June 1862 Swinburne defended *Modern Love* in the *Spectator* by
answering those who denigrated the sequence for not preaching the
bourgeois gospel of marriage: the time had come, he argued, for the
age to accommodate itself to a new and bolder species of poetry which
dealt with art rather than morality.[102] Ironically, when Swinburne himself was preparing his *Poems and Ballads* for the press four years later,
it was Meredith, the scourge of Grundyism, who encouraged him to
establish a 'firmly grounded' reputation by expurgating passages from
the volume.[103] In the event the publication of *Poems and Ballads* proved
to be one of the sensations of the decade, deeply offending the conservative majority of readers and commentators, and delighting the younger
generation. (Undergraduates shouted the morally offensive stanzas of
'Dolores' on the pavements of Cambridge, shocking their elders.)[104] Like

the Decadents of the 1890s, several of whom were deeply impressed by *Poems and Ballads* as adolescents, Swinburne's style of life and style of writing were similar: both were outrageously extravagant, and both were frequently associated with the satanic by opponents and supporters alike.

Struggling to come to terms with *Poems and Ballads*, John Morley in his review in the *Saturday Review* itemized features of what sounds like an extreme version of Meredith's psychic melodrama in *Modern Love*:

We are in the midst of fire and serpents, wine and ashes, blood and foam, and a hundred lurid horrors. Unsparing use of the most violent colours and the most intoxicated ideas and images is Mr. Swinburne's prime characteristic.[105]

Swinburne's religious position seemed equally puzzling, and, to some critics, no less lurid. Robert Buchanan announced in a review in the *Athenaeum* that Swinburne had clearly 'never thought at all on religious questions', but imagined that 'rank blasphemy' would be esteemed very clever, while W. M. Rossetti, in his preface to the poems, argued that Swinburne had never 'enacted the act of faith'.[106] In the *London Review*, however, an anonymous reviewer commented that 'the strangest and most melancholy fact in these strange and melancholy poems is, not the *absence* of faith, but the presence of a faith which mocks at itself, and takes pleasure in its own degradation'.[107] Swinburne speaks of a hell, for example, but 'says he would gladly encounter it for one minute's hot enjoyment' ('Les Noyades'). The ambivalence of Swinburne's religious position is reflected in the fact that Henry Morley's reading in the *Examiner* is diametrically opposed to the *London Review*'s, locating in the poetry a 'terrible earnestness':

He sings of Lust as Sin, its portion Pain and its end Death. He paints its fruit as Sodom apples, very fair without, ashes and dust within. In dwelling on their outward beauty he is sensual. Men see that and say that he is a licentious writer. But again and again when he has dwelt as proper folk object to dwell on the desire of the flesh, the beauty drops away and shows the grinning skeleton beneath with fires of hell below.[108]

Swinburne himself stated that he had never mocked what the English held most sacred, unlike Shelley and Byron, and it is worth recalling here that in 1872 Benjamin Jowett was to commission him to assist in the production of a *Children's Bible*.[109] He may have lost his faith as an undergraduate at Balliol, but he never lost his remarkable ability, developed in childhood, to quote extensively from the Bible.[110] That the reviewers found it difficult to judge Swinburne's moral position and to interpret his religious references is hardly surprising. He was pleased with Henry Morley's review while not entirely agreeing with its point of view, yet had himself read Baudelaire in a similar way, claiming in 1861 that

there is not one poem of the *Fleurs du Mal* which has not a distinct and vivid background of morality to it. Only, this moral side of the book is not thrust forward in the foolish and repulsive manner of a half-taught artist . . .[111]

Baudelaire's response to Swinburne's review anticipated Swinburne's response to Morley's: he mildly demurred.[112]

This parallel is particularly striking because *Poems and Ballads* reveals a profound debt to Baudelaire, more in the treatment of sexuality than of urban life. One of the most significant similarities between the poets, however, is in their use of the language of hell and damnation. Baudelaire rejected the liberal position on hell – that it was incompatible with a beneficent creator – and thought of his own life as irredeemably 'damned', from the beginning and for ever. F. W. J. Hemmings argues that 'damnation' can almost be equated with 'vocation' here: in the nineteenth century it was 'almost a commonplace that a vocation for art or poetry was inseparable from moral suffering and only too often entailed desperate material privation as well'.[113] The nature of Baudelaire's damnation

was that he could have said 'yes' to his better promptings, but he could not help constantly saying 'no' or 'not yet'. In this sense, in a purely theological if not Christian sense, he was damned.[114]

In Hemmings's view the clearest example of this sense of damnation is in 'Le Rebelle', a sonnet in which the response of 'the damned' to his good angel – a threateningly powerful figure – remains the same: 'Je ne veux pas.' Another side, however, to Baudelaire's treatment of hell and damnation is typified in the final lines of 'Le Gouffre':

> Plonger au fond du gouffre, Enfer ou Ciel, qu'importe?
> Au fond de l'Inconnu pour trouver *du nouveau*![115]

For Robert Hughes these lines reflect the way in which the imagery of hell shifted into the realm of aesthetics during the nineteenth century, 'thanks to the Satanists and Decadents':

Hell, by their implication, is an antidote to vulgarity. Its terrors exist to produce an unexpected *frisson* for poets and painters; and so they are, in reality, neutralised.[116]

The last part of this statement is too sweeping, as references to hell and Satan, far from being neutral, carried a powerful charge for many English Decadents, from Swinburne to Wilde. Moreover, Swinburne's apparent relishing of the prospect of hell and revulsion from bourgeois ideas of heaven, like Baudelaire's, is often in fact expressed by a dramatized persona, and cannot be read as a personal statement of the poet's. Take, for example, the final stanza of 'Dolores (Notre-Dame des Sept Douleurs)':

> We shall know what the darkness discovers
>   If the grave-pit be shallow or deep;
> And our fathers of old, and our lovers,
>   We shall know if they sleep not or sleep.
> We shall see whether hell be not heaven,
>   Find out whether tares be not grain,
> And the joys of thee seventy times seven,
>   Our Lady of Pain.[117]

Swinburne's defence of his work in *Notes on Poems and Reviews* (1866) is grounded in the statement that 'the book is dramatic, many-faced, multifarious; and no utterance of enjoyment or despair, belief or unbelief, can properly be assumed as the assertion of its author's personal feeling or faith'.[118] Thus 'Dolores' is to be read not as a 'study in the school of realism', but as a 'distinctly symbolic and fanciful' expression of

that transient state of spirit through which a man may be supposed to pass, foiled in love and weary of loving, but not yet in sight of rest; seeking refuge in those 'violent delights' which 'have violent ends', in fierce and frank sensualities which at least profess to be no more than they are.[119]

Swinburne's further observation in the *Notes* that suffering and passion are 'indeed the same thing and the same word' reflects a 'terrible earnestness', but not of the moralizing kind that Henry Morley discerned where 'the beauty drops away and shows the grinning skeleton beneath with fire of hell below'. It is 'Laus Veneris', however – for Morley an exposure of 'rottenness within' – which best illustrates the slipperiness of Swinburne's language of hell and damnation where he investigates the nature of passion/suffering.

One way of approaching this poem is via Swinburne's *Notes on Poems and Reviews*, where he explains his treatment of the Tannhäuser legend:

my first aim was to rehandle the old story in a new fashion. To me it seemed that the tragedy began with the knight's return to Venus – began at the point where hitherto it had seemed to leave off. The immortal agony of a man lost after all repentance – cast down from fearful hope into fearless despair – believing in Christ and bound to Venus – desirous of penitential pain, and damned to joyless pleasure – this in my eyes was the kernel and nucleus of a myth comparable only to that of the foolish virgins and bearing the same burden. The tragic touch of the story is this: that the knight who has renounced Christ believes in him; the lover who has embraced Venus disbelieves in her. Vainly and in despair would he make the best of that which is the worst – vainly remonstrate with God, and argue on the side he would fain desert. Once accept or admit the least admixture of pagan worship, or of modern thought, and the whole story collapses into froth and smoke.[120]

Swinburne's commentary, like his poem, is reminiscent of Browning, whom he admired. 'Laus Veneris' is a dramatic monologue in which an old legend is reworked in its original setting, providing a vehicle for the exploration of the central persona's ambiguous position within a traditional system of belief. Although he has repented, inspired by his love of God, he believes himself to be beyond the means of grace, as an unwilling outcast from the Church whose pontiff holds St Peter's keys of heaven and hell. Yet ironically, in spite of his repulsion from his own lust for Venus, which was at one time love, he finds himself to be once more an insider in her abode: 'Inside the Horsel here the air is hot.' Located in the consciousness of the suffering narrator, the poem moves with disturbing agility between memories, present reality, and an anticipated future state, and blurs the boundary between the orthodox hell of Catholic doctrine and the hellish experience that is the narrator's present experience.

Ambiguous from the start ('Asleep or waking is it?'), the poem's shifting perspective unsettles traditional theological categories. The narrrator speaks of 'the gold bars of the gates', which are suggestive of purgatory, the 'Golden Prison'. Yet although in Swinburne's words 'desirous of penitential pain', he remains unpurged. 'Damned to joyless pleasure', he tries to make Venus and himself believe that they should not envy the saved, 'High up in barren heaven'. It is the language of hell which predominates in the poem, the subject of which – burning lust without love – is an extreme version of the second kind of hell on earth, in which love is dead or betrayed. Yet the narrator's state is less a secularized version of Gehenna than of Hades, or more specifically of the intermediate Prison of the Lost in Hades described in Bickersteth's *Yesterday, To-Day, and For Ever*, published the same year. For 'Laus Veneris', like the parable of the foolish virgins, is about exclusion from the kingdom, and is eschatological in its anticipation of the last judgment. Parallels between the narrator's state and hell are of several kinds, each of which is problematic. First, the hellish quality of the poem's inner, psychic landscape is comparable to *poena sensus*, in its references to fire and heat for example – 'the air is hot', 'the salt burnt sands', 'Night falls like fire', 'the flame shakes' – and in the physicality of the metaphors applied to Venus:

> I dare not always touch her, lest the kiss
> Leave my lips charred. Yea, Lord, a little bliss,
>   Brief bitter bliss, one hath for a great sin;
> Nathless thou knowest how sweet a thing it is.
>
> Sin, is it sin whereby men's souls are thrust
> Into the pit? yet had I a good trust
>   To save my soul before it slipped therein,
> Trod under by the fire-shod feet of lust.
>
> For if mine eyes fail and my soul takes breath,
> I look between the iron sides of death
>   Into sad hell where all sweet love hath end,
> All but the pain that never finisheth.
>
> There are the naked faces of great kings,
> The singing folk with all their lute-playings;
>   There when one cometh he shall have to friend
> The grave that covets and the worm that clings.

The second stanza quoted here is ambiguous, the tenses – 'yet *had* I a good trust / To save my soul before it *slipped* therein' – suggesting on a first reading that the speaker has already been damned, but then, in the light of the vision of hell which follows, suggesting that hell is elsewhere, as is confirmed in later references to the 'fire of hell' and the 'heat of hell'.

Secondly, the narrator's suffering in the poem is akin to that of *poena damni*, as he feels himself to be cut off from what Newman called the 'Vision and Fruition of God'. He sees his former escape from the Horsel as God's saving act:

> So that God looked upon me when your hands
> Were hot about me; yea, God brake my bands
>   To save my soul alive, and I came forth
> Like a man blind and naked in strange lands . . .

His pilgrimage to Rome, however, was abortive, as the Pope refused to accept his penance, thereby precipitating his return to Venus. But the Vicar of Christ, in rehearsing the role of the divine judge on the last day, added what appeared to be an empty limiting clause to the excommunication:

> 'Until this dry shred staff, that hath no whit
> Of leaf nor bark, bear blossom and smell sweet,
>   Seek thou not any mercy in God's sight,
> For so long shalt thou be cast out from it.'

In the original legend the staff breaks into blossom after three days, signifying, presumably, the power of God's grace as revealed most fully in the resurrection. When the Pope tries to recall the knight, however, it is too late: he has returned to the Horsel. Now for Swinburne the tragedy begins here, and therefore the narrator's account of his journey to Rome is introduced only at the end of 'Laus Veneris', the main body of which is devoted to the description of a state approximating to *poena damni*, experienced by a man 'believing in Christ and bound to Venus'. By writing a dramatic monologue in which the protagonist's view is limited to the this-worldly, Swinburne explores the '*immortal* agony of a man lost after all repentance' (my emphasis) within the horizon of an earthly life extended until the end of time. Thus the referential status of the poem's eschatological language remains profoundly ambiguous.

Thirdly, and finally, the narrator's frequently expressed longing for extinction is characteristic of those who suffer the torments of hell.[121] In some of the poem's loveliest lines he yearns to be dead and buried:

> Ah yet would God this flesh of mine might be
> Where air might wash and long leaves cover me,
>   Where tides of grass break into foam of flowers,
> Or where the wind's feet shine along the sea.

The mingling of the elements here, as the air and grass imitate the action of the sea, associate his imagined physical dissolution with a soothing coolness after the heat of the Horsel. For the knight is the sole survivor of Venus's sinister 'little chambers' which 'drip with flower-like red':

> Yea, all she slayeth; yea, every man save me;
> Me, love, thy lover that must cleave to thee
>   Till the ending of the days and ways of earth,
> The shaking of the sources of the sea.
>
> Me, most forsaken of all souls that fell;
> Me, satiated with things insatiable;
>   Me, for whose sake the extreme hell makes mirth,
> Yea, laughter kindles at the heart of hell.

Hell, then, is elsewhere, and death in some distant future, as the poem's final stanzas confirm.

When Rochester contemplates suicide in *Jane Eyre* (1847; 27), arguing that 'there is not a future state worse than this present one' in the 'bottomless pit' that is his married life in Jamaica, Hope prevents him by persuading him to return to England. *Modern Love* (1862), a later realist narrative, ends with a death-wish fulfilled, through suicide. 'Laus Veneris' (1866), however, takes the idea of the death of love as hell on earth to its limit, applying the language of orthodox eschatology, descriptive of an intermediate state of the lost which will be followed by judgment and hell, to the present agony of one who finds himself doomed until the end of time to be outside the community, cut off from God, and enduring the passion/suffering of his lust. Swinburne's inheritors were the late-nineteenth-century Decadents, whose work lies beyond the scope of this study. The story of the man who 'killed the thing he loved' in *The Ballad of Reading Gaol* (1898), with its references to the Tannhäuser legend, its portrayal of the condemned man being watched in case he takes his own life, and its treatment of the other prisoners, 'each in his separate Hell' where 'Hope' is dead and 'all but Lust is turned to dust', probably owes something to Wilde's reading of Swinburne. Like Wilde's, Arthur Symons's life led directly to imprisonment and pain which, as Barbara Charlesworth puts it, 'lies at the end of the mind's darkest passages'.[122] Symons, in his essay on Beardsley (1898), celebrated the fact that evil, 'carried to the point of a perverse ecstasy, becomes a kind of good, by means of that energy which, otherwise directed, is virtue', and went on, in a sentence that would have appealed to Swinburne:

The devil is nearer to God, by the whole height from which he fell, than the average man who has not recognised his own need to rejoice or to repent.[123]

Between the first edition of *Poems and Ballads* and the poetry of the 1890s, however, came James Thomson's masterpiece, *The City of Dreadful Night* (1874), in which a descent from 'fearful hope into fearless despair' is *celebrated* as the means to stoic resistance in a godless universe. Earlier in this chapter it was argued that the question of hell turns upon our idea of hope: does Farrar's 'eternal hope' embrace suicides, for example? It is precisely this theological relation between hope and the doctrine of damnation with which Thomson plays in *The City*, where his critique of hell is closely associated with his secularist rejection of Christianity's 'lively hope'. An atheist with an intimate knowledge of the Bible, Thomson had been brought up in the strictest Presbyterian doctrines, and had not altogether lost his Christian faith when he first began writing.[124] Significantly, however, it was after the death of the young Irish girl whom he hoped to marry – a lock of whose hair is buried with him in the same grave as Austin Holyoake in Highgate Cemetery – that he moved first into a 'doubtful' phase in early adulthood, then into the melancholia and sporadic alcoholism which afflicted him as an army schoolmaster, and finally the declared atheism of his London period.[125] After T. R. Wright had read an adapted version of Holyoake's *Secularist Burial Service* over Thomson's grave, he gave a tribute which included these words: 'it would have given him pleasure to know that his ashes would mingle with those of his old friend and fellow-worker in the great cause of the *redemption* of humanity from the bondage of superstition' (my emphasis).[126] Hatred of that bondage fuels the speaker's 'cold rage' in *The City*, and informs the poem's critique of hell.[127] As in Wright's secularist eulogy, however, the language of that critique cannot finally free itself from the theological categories it denies.

Many of the poem's most striking episodes and images, however, subvert received religious ideas and the conventionalized consolatory strategies of the period. The speaker in the cathedral, for example, states that 'We fall asleep and never wake again; / Nothing is of us but the mouldering flesh', and concludes: 'Lo, you are free to end it when you will, / Without the fear of waking after death' (XIV.51–2, 83–4). This

theme is developed later, in the River of the Suicides section (XIX), where
received ideas of the 'good' death (quietly, in one's own bed) and the
'bad' death (violently, in the river) are deconstructed. Social critics such
as Hood and Dickens had lamented the conditions which caused the
destitute and the 'fallen' to throw themselves into the Thames, while
the churches had taught that suicides were 'lost souls'. Neither view is
expressed here. Rather, the speaker regards suicide as a rational act in
a world of pain, and death as a 'sweet sleep' precisely because it is the
'one best sleep which never wakes again' (34–5). Whereas hope is
invoked in the rescue of both Edward Rochester and Markham Sutherland from the brink of suicide, Thomson's speaker associates hope with
a religion of fear which he denies. Indeed, his strongest argument against
suicide seems to be that stoic resistance is better than escape from a life
that is but 'one brief night of dreary pain' (30).

Thomson liked to think of himself as a Job figure, and Melville called
The City 'the modern Book of Job'.[128] For Thomson, Sheol, as described
in a verse from Job which he thought of using as an epigraph for his
poem, offers no false hope of transcendence, as the despised Christian
scheme does: 'A land of darkness, as darkness itself, and of the shadow
of death; without any order, and where the light is as darkness'.[129] The
speaker's rage is vented in the attempt to express the woe which only
the reader whose 'faith and hope are dead' can understand (Proem, 28).
Like, it could be argued, the very gospel which the poem rejects, 'None
uninitiate by many a presage / Will comprehend the language of the
message' (40–1). Thus the speaker's description of this true opposite of
the City of God[130] reads like a coded anti-gospel: 'Where Death-in-Life
is the eternal king' (III.25); 'And he is verily as if new-born' (V.14);
'Good tidings of great joy for you, for all: / There is no God' (XIV.39–
40); and so on. The denial of the cardinal virtue of hope is dramatized
early in the poem.[131] First, the speaker follows a man who endlessly
revisits the sites of his desolation: 'Perpetual recurrence in the scope /
Of but three terms, dead Faith, dead Love, dead Hope' (II.47–8). Then
the 'stalwart shape' who has come from the desert declaims to the city:
'But I strode on austere; / No hope could have no fear' (IV.14–15, etc.).

A religion of hope, it is argued, is also a religion of fear, so to die
without hope of a future life is a blessing. The speaker says of the City:

> They leave all hope behind who enter there:
>   One certitude while sane they cannot leave,
>   One anodyne for torture and despair;

>   The certitude of Death, which no reprieve
>   Can put off long; and which, divinely tender,
>   But waits the outstretched hand to promptly render
>   That draught whose slumber nothing can bereave.   (1.78–84)

Thomson had a profound respect for Dante, agreeing with Ruskin's estimate that he is 'the central intellect' of the world.[132] In section VI of *The City*, a 'stranger' adopts Dante's triplets in relating to one who was to follow him how a 'demon warder' prevented him from passing through the gates of hell on which is written 'Leave hope behind, all ye who enter here', as he had no hope to leave in the chest which stood open there (25–36).[133] Following this radical revision of the traditional soul-at-heaven's-gate narrative, the couple bemoan their lot in this 'limbo' of an earthly life, and begin looking for 'some minute lost hope' to gain entrance to hell. Through this bitterest of ironic subversions, they find themselves in the ultimate marginal state.

Thomson, then, goes beyond those Victorian writers who describe this life as hell on earth: it is worse than that. Yet both kinds of hell on earth that we have been considering are present in the subtext of the poem – that associated with the Industrial Revolution and the city most consistently, but also the hell of love which is dead. When the orator in section IV states, for example, that 'hell is mild / And piteous' matched with the 'accursed wild' of the desert from which he has come, he is describing the pain experienced in his encounter with a woman, 'Bareheaded and barefooted on that strand', which revived hope that 'travailed with such fear' (65–81). Half of him dies with her, losing all hope and fear; 'But I, what do I here?' (106). In the City a different kind of isolation is experienced, more reminiscent of Engels's analysis of the 'dissolution of mankind into monads' in the urban throng, cited earlier. As in 'some necropolis', each isolated mourner is 'wrapt in his own doom' (1.50–4). On William Sharpe's argument, however, Thomson's poem 'also attempts to overcome the very isolation and despair it so vividly conveys': 'by sharing, though not necessarily in conventional consolations like hope, men can eventually forge identity through unflinching consciousness of their situation'.[134] In contrast to the submissiveness of the damned in Bickersteth's Evangelical epic poem, for example, the several voices of *The City* gradually build up a vague sense of solidarity based upon citizenship. A *polis*, however, with no discernible history and no politics, the City seems to represent a world that is post-holocaust, as well as post-Christian. In revolutionary Paris, as Dickens recalls in *A Tale of Two Cities* (1859), the cemetery gates bore the secularist legend, 'Here is eternal sleep.'[135] Whereas Dickens's second city is a hellish site of conflict and bloody anarchy, Thomson's City is a limbo, an 'insufferable inane', empty of meaning and direction, its permanent public monuments (described in the last two sections of the poem) the sphinx which outfaces the angel, and the massive statue of 'Melencolia'. Its people can endure to the end or, less admirably, take their own lives. The choice marks out the limits of their freedom. A world without God, it is a world without hope (of heaven), without fear (of hell), and without transcendence (through love). One begins to understand how the children who heard Father Furniss preach on hell could say they loved him.

In this chapter the responses of two men of sharply opposed beliefs to the literal interpretation of religious language associated with hell have been cited. First there was James Thomson's friend and fellow secularist, Austin Holyoake, who asked in 1873 how hell could be both within the earth and bottomless. Secondly, there was Archbishop Tait, who stated in the previous year that nobody in the Church of England took the damnatory clauses in the Athanasian Creed in their plain and literal sense. Whereas Holyoake's aim was to expose the illogicalities of traditional religious language to a simple, broadly scientific-materialist critique, Tait's was to remind his audience of the figurative nature of religious, as of all, language. In drawing attention to the limitations of the English translators, churchmen like Maurice and Farrar opened up discussion on the dangers of a literal interpretation of words such as 'everlasting damnation' and 'hell' in the Authorized Version. It is no coincidence that in their apologetical writings, both Maurice and Farrar refer to the poets of their generation – in Farrar's case frequently. For it was the Victorian poets whose writing explored its own metaphorical nature. Thus hell came to be written, by poet and theologian alike, as a state rather than a place, a spiritual condition rather than a physical torment, a theological reality rather than a polemical threat.

Conclusion

For tho' my nature rarely yields
  To that vague fear implied in death;
  Nor shudders at the gulfs beneath,
The howlings from forgotten fields;

Yet oft when sundown skirts the moor
  An inner trouble I behold,
  A spectral doubt which makes me cold,
That I shall be thy mate no more . . .
                    (In Memoriam, 41)[1]

Various sources for Tennyson's 'gulfs' and 'forgotten fields' have been suggested, but the poet himself commented: 'The eternal miseries of the Inferno'.[2] Whereas Tennyson's liberal position on hell was admired by like-minded readers when *In Memoriam* was published in 1850, the Revd F. D. Maurice lost his chair at King's College, London three years later for expressing similar views.[3]

In exercising the comparative freedom of the poetic imagination over the seventeen years following Arthur Hallam's early death in 1833, Tennyson spoke for a whole generation, not only in expressing advanced views on judgment, which anticipated a general decline in belief in the traditional hell of gulfs and forgotten fields, but also in the 'spectral doubt' that touches even the strongest faith. The lyrist's specific doubt – 'That I shall be thy mate no more' – relates to ideas about heaven in lyrics 40–7 which address the question of the nature of heaven, described by Arthur Hallam's uncle as 'that better world for which he was created'.[4] If there is development in heaven (for Tennyson a place of reunion), the lyrist could find himself to be 'evermore a life behind' the friend whose powers and spiritual gifts are such that he can be seen as the 'type' of a future and higher race. F. W. Farrar was not alone, however, in suggesting that Tennyson would be 'remembered by posterity as the poet of "the larger hope"' (lyric 55).[5] Tennyson's son, Hallam, quotes him as saying that he 'would rather know that he was to be lost eternally than not know that the whole human race was to live eternally', and he meant by the larger hope 'that the whole human race would through, perhaps, ages of suffering, be at length purified and saved, even those who now "better not with time"'.[6]

In *In Memoriam*, Tennyson exploits the ambiguities of Victorian consolatory language – of death as sleep (68), the grave as a bed (67), the written word as the spoken voice (95) – with a subtlety and sophistication which makes the poem the finest literary work on death and the future life in the period. In many ways exceptional, it is also typically Victorian, being kept on Queen Victoria's bedside table after the death of Prince Albert. And how typically Victorian is Tennyson's belief, as stated to Bishop Lightfoot, that 'the cardinal point of Christianity is the Life after Death'.[7] Like Maurice, Tennyson looked forward to 'the Christ that is to be' (106). Like Farrar, he longed for the salvation of all mankind. Like Arthur Hallam, he believed that mankind could partake of God's loving nature, and that this was made possible in the incarnation, reflected in the Johannine emphasis of the poem, the importance of the three Christmases, and the comparative neglect of Christ's resurrection as a theme. The better world for which Hallam was created – and here was the final and most fruitful ambiguity associated with his death – is both here and elsewhere. Hallam was taken before the time was ripe from a world he would have made better had he survived, but he represented to Tennyson and his circle a sign of God's loving nature, made in God's image, which gave the poet hope for the future of the race and for continued development after death, for the eventual salvation of the whole world, and, linked with the latter, a broader kind of Christianity, grounded in love.

The heart is the seat of human love, and Tennyson's heartfelt response to Hallam's death is reflected in the pulse or heart-beat that informs the structures of *In Memoriam* at every level of its organization: its lines (in their iambic beat), stanzas (in their diastolic-systolic ABBA construction), lyrics (in their pulsing oppositions), and groups of lyrics (in their similar pattern of opposition and polarity). This use of the heart as the poem's controlling conceit reflects Tennyson's inheritance of his Romantic precursors' respect for the authority of the heart, and, more significantly in relation to our present theme, of a broader tradition of Protestant religious authority. But the authority of the heart has a yet wider reach in the nineteenth century, and of the three other major Victorian writers on the theme of death and the future life who frequently referred to that authority, and to whom brief reference should be made here, two – John Henry Newman and Gerard Manley Hopkins – were Roman Catholics.

The third, Charles Dickens, would have understood Tennyson's thinking on the authority of feeling and the heart in matters of religion, while Tennyson would have been interested in Dickens's treatment of the margins of consciousness and unconsciousness, of day and night, life and death in his later novels. Although much less knowledgeable than Tennyson about science, theology, and philosophy, Dickens read more of the key documents of the early 1860s, such as *Essays and Reviews*, than is generally realized.[8] Tennyson's urbane contribution to Broad Church liberalism was considered to be that of the poet, the intellectual, the reader of Dante in the original, whereas Dickens's populist agenda was that of the Broad Church social reformer. Their positions, however, on the teachings and practices of the Church of England, were not dissimilar. Both longed for a broader Christianity, and they held similar views on a number of major doctrinal issues of the day.

Dickens's emphasis in his novels upon finding Christ in other people, and upon the 'redemptive' role of a few enlightened individuals in society, suggests further parallels with Broad Church theologians, and with Arthur Hallam's ideas on the 'confusion' of our personality with Christ's, which informed Tennyson's thinking in *In Memoriam*. This emphasis is particularly strong in his last completed novel, *Our Mutual Friend* (1864–5), published at a time when, in Owen Chadwick's words, 'the anthropologists confronted religious man with a new kind of conflict – the fall of man versus the rise of man'.[9] Traditional teaching on the fall and on man's prelapsarian state is embodied in the mystical language of the prayer book, which figures in both *Our Mutual Friend* and *In Memoriam*. For the reader of the novel, talk of the fall of man versus the rise of man brings to mind its most powerful symbolic language, so that the river mud at Limehouse Hole and the slippery sides of Plashwater Weir Mill Lock begin to suggest primeval slime.

Our Mutual Friend continues Dickens's exploration in his novels of the 1860s of the inner or spiritual life, and of the hope of salvation and transcendence in a fallen world which threatens to return to its original primeval state, expressed in the novel's insistent symbolism of rising and falling. Bradley Headstone is tormented in a psychological version of the hell that is the absence of love. Whereas in the highly schematized plot of *Hard Times* (1854), Stephen Blackpool, who takes his Christian name from the first Christian martyr, is beatified in his descent into Old Hell Shaft and ascent into heaven (III.6), the descents and ascents of *Our Mutual Friend*, while signifying regeneration, are represented as a *prelude* to the working out of John Harmon's and Eugene Wrayburn's salvation through love in human relationship.

Unlike Tennyson, Dickens disliked speculation on the nature of the heavenly state, although he was equally open-minded on the subject of spiritualism.[10] For Dickens the Christian hope of heaven is associated mainly with peace and with rest. Like little Johnny's death (II.9), Betty Higden's (III.8) is described at the end of a chapter which is immediately followed by Revd Frank Milvey's reading of the burial service. Milvey holds his peace in clerical disputes over the 'sure and certain hope of the Resurrection to eternal life' (II.10) proclaimed in the burial service, and is Dickens's ideal Church of England clergyman, just as Betty is his ideal good-hearted old woman who believes in angels and in heaven. Out of her suffering and death (at 'the foot of the Cross') there comes reconciliation, as the funeral brings John Harmon and Bella to Lizzie, and thus the novel's two main plots together.

In form, subject-matter, and tone, *Our Mutual Friend* and *In Memoriam* could hardly be more different Victorian texts. Even in terms of Christian eschatology, Dickens's idea of heaven is more static than Tennyson's; and whereas the poet emphasizes the incarnation in his treatment of the subject, the novelist stresses the relationship between resurrection and baptism. When the two works are placed together, however, similarities between them prove to be as revealing as their more obvious differences. Both end in marriage, and in a celebration of love that has grown, of light that has come out of darkness. Both affirm the hope of a future life in Christ. Both identify signs of transcendence within the horizon of the present, particularly in the development, through love, of special individuals in a fallen world, and their ability to influence the lot of others for good. Both are Johannine in their theology and symbolism, and reflect a longing for a broader Christianity that can accommodate the findings of science. Both emphasize the importance of touch at the precise points at which language breaks down. Above all, both writers sympathized with Anglican Broad Church opinion on most of the major doctrinal issues of the day, and grounded their writing on the subject of death and the future life in *Our Mutual Friend* and *In Memoriam* on the authority of the heart and a liberal interpretation of scripture. We can now turn, by way of contrast, to Newman and Hopkins, who, while frequently invoking the authority of the heart, based their treatments of purgatory and martyrdom in *The Dream of Gerontius* and *The Wreck of the Deutschland* on the authority and theology of the Roman Catholic Church to which they had converted.

After *In Memoriam*, Newman's *The Dream of Gerontius* (1865) was the best known and most frequently discussed literary work on the subject of death and the future life to be published in the Victorian Age. Both works were welcomed by readers and critics as helpful, and specifically hopeful, religious poetry, and it is possible to discern similarities between them, and between their authors. Tennyson and Newman differed markedly, however, in their ideas on authority, and this is reflected in the formal differences between their works. Mediated through the unifying 'I' of the lyrist, *In Memoriam's* short swallow-flights of song record the heart's events mainly within the limits of this-worldly experience. In contrast, the unique qualities, as well as the limitations, of the *Dream* as a work of devotional literature are closely associated with its heavy reliance on the Roman rite and scripture, and the authority of the Catholic Church. In Newman's verse drama, the immediacy of a form which functions in what was earlier called the 'locutionary present' (see p. 136 above) is exploited in ways which recall the origins of medieval drama in ritual and liturgy. For the drama unfolds not only in the 'horizontal' dimension of chronological time, but also in the 'vertical' dimension of the eternal present, or what Newman called the 'eternal now', in which a larger divine providential scheme for mankind is revealed.

The structure and symbolism of the *Dream* emphasize parallels between two major transitions, or liminal phases: first, the agony and death of Gerontius, and then the particular judgment and entry into purgatory of the Soul. On his deathbed, Gerontius prays to Christ in his 'own agony' (1)[11]; as the Soul approaches the particular judgment, the Fifth Choir of Angelicals sing of Christ's 'double agony' (5). In its forward momentum, and its language of rehearsal, presage, and first-fruits, the poem also enacts a series of returns – through the Choirs' salvation history, for example, the Angel's account of Gerontius's mortal life, and the Soul's references to the sound of the Subvenite being said by those who still kneel around his deathbed. The *Dream* claims our attention not in its power of 'myth-making', as *The Prelude* does, for example,[12] but in its effectiveness as devotional verse, its ability to convey to the reader a sense of the eternal present where the spiritual journey of Everyman towards his God is now. Today the *Dream* is best known through Elgar's oratorio of 1900, in which the composer brilliantly augments Newman's comparatively limited dramatic effects, having first heavily cut the text. Significantly, however, Elgar's handling of the libretto reveals an awareness of, and thus highlights Newman's unique spiritual insight into the nature of death, judgment, and purgatory, and a theology of purgatory based upon Christ's agony in the garden and the ministry of angels.

Like *The Dream of Gerontius*, Hopkins's *The Wreck of the Deutschland* was written by a Catholic for a Catholic readership. Their critical receptions as Catholic poems have, however, been very different. Newman's treatment of purgatory was well received by his contemporaries, including some Protestants, but has been largely neglected in this century outside the Catholic journals. Hopkins's poem, on the other hand, remained unpublished until it appeared in Robert Bridges's edition of the *Poems* (1918), since when it has received an enormous amount of critical attention, much of which focuses upon the poet's technical innovations, and his theories of inscape and instress. The poem's specifically Catholic content has often been treated as a matter of regret, or, more recently, regarded as a means of sublimating frustrated sexual drives. Yet of all the Victorian literature on death and the future life discussed in this study, the *Wreck* articulates most fully a theology of death which is grounded in Christ's own death and passion. Hopkins's thinking on death, and on the 'beauty of suffering' in martyrdom (a stumbling-block for many readers), is rooted in his Ignatian meditations on the passion (part of his training for the Jesuit priesthood), including, as in Newman's *Dream*, the agony in the garden. Whereas in the *Dream*, Gerontius, whose name is generic, is supported by the whole company of the Church triumphant in a work which is full of names from Christian and Jewish tradition, Hopkins's sparing use of names in the *Wreck* reflects a more specifically typological treatment of death and the future life. The treatment of the heroic tall nun in the second part of the poem, where Hopkins's eschatology is externalized and conceived in terms of nature, is read in the light of his invocation of the (wrecked) 'hero of Calvary' in the first part, where the I/ Thou relationship between the poet and his God is described in terms of an eschatology that is internalized.

The poet's meditations in the *Wreck* – on Mary and the nativity, Christ and the passion, St Gertrude as a bride of Christ, the tall nun as a martyr – are drawn together in the final intercessory stanzas. For Hopkins the English convert, writing only a year after moves had begun to beatify the English Catholic confessors and martyrs, and Gladstone had written a 'political expostulation' on the Vatican decrees of 1870,[13] 'us' signifies both the Catholic minority and the majority of unconverted English whose behaviour at the site of the wreck of the Deutschland in December 1875 made the need for conversion seem the more urgent. He prays, however, that Christ's coming may be neither catastrophic, as in premillennialist apocalyptic, nor obscurely painful, as in his nativity, but mediated through grace. Far from being an unsatisfactory ending, it is a fine example of Hopkins's favourite technique of knotting different strands of his poetry together in a richly textured finale:

> Now burn, new born to the world,
>   Double-naturèd name,
> The heaven-flung, heart-fleshed, maiden-furled
>   Miracle-in-Mary-of-flame,
> Mid-numberèd he in three of the thunder-throne!
> Not a dooms-day dazzle in his coming nor dark as he came;
>   Kind, but royally reclaiming his own;
> A released shower, let flash to the shire, not a lightning of fire hard-hurled.

> Dame, at our door
>   Drowned, and among our shoals,
> Remember us in the roads, the heaven-haven of the reward:
>   Our King back, Oh, upon English souls!
> Let him easter in us, be a dayspring to the dimness of us, be
>   a crimson-cresseted east,
> More brightening her, rare-dear Britain, as his reign rolls,
>   Pride, rose, prince, hero of us, high-priest,
> Our hearts' charity's hearth's fire, our thoughts' chivalry's throng's Lord.

In several ways the ending of the *Wreck* is similar to that of *In Memoriam*. Both are affirmative, and expectant of some future revelation. Both draw together threads from earlier parts of the work which are here broadened and universalized. But whereas the Anglican Broad Church

Tennyson ends his *Divina Commedia* with a wedding and the conception of a baby, Hopkins's position is that of the celibate Catholic priest, for whom the type of the mystical marriage of Christ with his Church is the religious in her or his devotions. Whereas Tennyson, like Dickens, tends in Hans Frei's terms to fit the biblical story into another world with another story, Hopkins, like Newman, incorporates that world into the biblical story, as interpreted by the conservative Church of Rome. Both Catholic writers laid great stress on the importance of the human heart in the spiritual life, Newman taking as his motto the words *Cor ad cor loquitur*, and Hopkins being touched in the heart by a reading (in his case of Sister Emmerich's *The Dolorous Passion*), as the lyrist is in the garden in *In Memoriam* (of Hallam's letters). Whereas such movements of the heart, however, are for Newman and Hopkins subordinated to and regulated by those of the sacred heart of Christ, Tennyson and Dickens make them their main authorities in their Romantic treatments of death and the future life.

It was in a letter of 1881 that Hopkins commented adversely on Bridges's poem entitled 'On a Dead Child', and wrote an amusing parody of Victorian treatments of this by now conventionalized and sentimentalized subject (see p. 46 above). In Samuel Butler's Utopian satire, *Erewhon* (1872), the Victorian cult of the dead child is quietly set aside in the Erewhonians' concealment of the fact that a child has died, in a country where illness is a crime:

Should the child unhappily die, a coroner's inquest is inevitable, but in order to avoid disgracing a family which may have been hitherto respected, it is almost invariably found that the child was over seventy-five years old, and died from the decay of nature.   (13)

At the end of *Jude the Obscure* (1894–5), Arabella is inconvenienced by Jude's dying just when she wants to join in the celebrations that are going on in Christminster (VI.11). She decides to leave the body unattended, however, and rejoins the revellers, announcing that Jude is 'sleeping quite sound' and that he 'won't wake yet'. The language of religious consolation – 'Not dead, but sleeping', and 'The dead shall awake' – that is so central to Victorian belief and custom relating to the four last things becomes in Arabella's mouth a casual deception.

Hardy was to write some of the most grotesquely ironical poetry on the subject of death and bereavement in the language, and we will return to this. For the moment, however, an earlier example of a grimly satiric treatment of the Victorian way of death should be cited: part of Mr Herbert's lecture in Mallock's *The New Republic* (1877). Mr Herbert – Mallock's parody of Ruskin – outlines his ideas for the sanitary disposal of the dead in a Utopian city. A 'sincere advocate for cremation', he would have corpses turned into gas, which could be collected in small separate gasometers:

There is not one amongst you who, watching a dead friend flickering for the last time before you in the form of a gas-flame, and seeing how a little while and this flame was with you, and again a little while and it was not with you, would be at all sure whether this was really because, as your hearts would suggest to you, it went to the Father, or because, as your men of science would assert to you, it went simply – out.   (v.1)

Black humour can be therapeutic, and to laugh in death's face was not unknown to the Victorians. The passage quoted culminates in a playful version of the main linguistic feature we considered in Chapter 1, in that two alternative interpretations reflect the two-fold aspect of death: 'went to the Father' or 'went simply – out'. The disposal of the body after death, then, dramatized the antithesis between physical and spiritual interpretations of death as sharply as did the deathbed in the nineteenth century.

Three years before the publication of *The New Republic*, Bishop Christopher Wordsworth of Lincoln preached a sermon in Westminster Abbey entitled 'On Burning of the Body; and on Burial'. Christianity, he argued, had extinguished the flames of the funeral piles which blazed throughout the Roman Empire. If, as was now being proposed in certain quarters, their piles should be rekindled in London and other great cities, popular belief in the resurrection of the body would be weakened. When Bishop Wordsworth turned, however, to the effect on the individual mourner of committing a loved one to the flames, as if for 'penal execution', his defence of Christian burial was grounded in traditional organic symbolism drawn from New Testament eschatology and the Book of Common Prayer:

No, – rather you will consign that beloved form to the bosom of the earth in Christian faith, hope, and love, as the husbandman commits the seed to the ground, in full reliance on God's mercy, and with a joyful foresight of the great day of harvest, when Christ, the Lord of the Harvest, will send His Reapers, the Angels, to gather together His elect from the four winds of heaven.[14]

Other conservative clergymen were to continue the defence of burial and its associated natural eschatological analogies via a rearguard action against cremation, but the arguments of the sanitary reformers could not be set aside. Following a vigorous campaign, supported, incidentally, by Anthony Trollope, cremation was finally legalized in 1885. At the end of the century the Catholic Modernist theologian, George Tyrrell, affirmed in the year in which he wrote his notorious article on hell entitled 'A Perverted Devotion' that the question of cremation was a 'purely disciplinary matter', and that

To try and connect the practice with the doctrine of the Resurrection as though the disintegration and dispersion of our dust presented any greater difficulty in one case than the other, is too ridiculous to think of. There would be more faith – more intelligent faith, in cremation, from that point of view. Custom and the sentiment founded on it, is doubtless the root-reason.[15]

Interestingly, however, he added that for himself he liked the idea of 'quietly mouldering away under the green sod in some quiet Catholic Churchyard with those *qui dormiunt in somno pacis*' (in the event he was refused a Catholic burial), and considered that there was something 'violent and unrestful' in the mechanics of cremation. The only argument for cremation to which Tyrrell would listen was 'the sanitary one', and even Christopher Wordsworth had acknowledged in his sermon of 1874 that the danger to public health of overcrowded burial grounds could not be ignored. 'The Burial of the Dead', he observed, 'ought never to be the cause of injury to the living.'[16]

While the cremation question opened up a rift between the modern rational arguments of the sanitary reformers and old-fashioned sentiment inherited from traditional 'Christian' practice, Thomas Hardy's poetry probed the conventions of that sentimental tradition and its inscription in Victorian consolatory verse. The final stanza of 'In Tenebris I' is characteristic:

> Black is night's cope;
> But death will not appal
> One who, past doubtings all,
> Waits in unhope.[17]

Like Swinburne, Hardy makes the hallowed ground of God's acre a space in which he can explore death's little ironies. In 'The Levelled Churchyard', dated 1882, the dead cry out to the passing 'passenger', complaining that they are 'Half stifled in this jumbled patch / Of wrenched memorial stones!':

> Here's not a modest maiden elf
> But dreads the final Trumpet,
> Lest half of her should rise herself,
> And half some sturdy strumpet!

Whereas earlier Victorian writers tried to reconcile the physical reality of death and the Christian hope of resurrection, Hardy deconstructs the other-worldly language of transcendence by inserting it into the jocular this-worldly language of the popular lyric. 'In Death Divided', a poem of the 1890s, denies that most common Victorian hope of reunion after death by limiting the subject to the topographical. The lovers of the poem are buried in different graveyards:

> The simply-cut memorial at my head
>   Perhaps may take
> A rustic form, and that above your bed
>   A stately make;
> No linking symbol show thereon for our tale's sake.

Perhaps the most painful poems, however, are those in which Hardy examines the human need, strongly felt in the nineteenth century, to honour the dead by visiting the grave. Mothers squabble over their children's graves in 'In the Cemetery' ('Satires of Circumstance in Fifteen Glimpses', v; 1911), ignorant of the fact that the gravediggers have 'moved the lot' to make way for a new main drain. In the familiar 'Ah, Are You Digging on My Grave', which ends with the dead woman's dog admitting that he had simply buried his bone here, but had 'quite forgot' it was her 'resting-place', we have come a long way from the breathless solemnity of Bowler's *The Doubt: 'Can These Dry Bones Live?'* Only a few years later the war that was to end all wars in fact precipitated the West into a new way of thinking about death in the mass. And for the British war poets the challenge was to be a new one: to write meaningfully of death in the trenches, in a hellish landscape far from the green churchyards of home and the consolations associated with the Victorian graveyard tradition.

Notes

Place of publication is London, unless otherwise stated. For ease and economy of reference, and where there are no significant variants, locations of quotations from novels and from some well-known poetry are given in the main text (by chapter number and section/line numbers as appropriate), rather than by page number in these references. Both in the main text and in the end-matter, obvious and insignificant printers' errors have been silently corrected.

Introduction

1 Compare Hopkins's 'Fresh-firecoal chestnut-falls' ('Pied Beauty') with the last lines of 'The Windhover', also completed in the summer of 1877 '. . . and blue-bleak embers, ah my dear, / Fall, gall themselves, and gash gold-vermillion.' Hopkins wrote in his journal, 'Chestnuts as bright as coals or spots of vermillion': see *The Poems of Gerard Manley Hopkins*, fourth edition, edited by W. H. Gardner and N. H. MacKenzie (Oxford, 1967), p. 269. The analogy of the butterfly, fly, or winged insect of the spirit emerging from the chrysalis (or mortal flesh) at the moment of death is an ancient one. See, for example, Dante's *Purgatory*, x. Also compare the first chapter of Butler's *Analogy of Religion* (p. 18 above). For nineteenth-century examples see Paley's *Natural Theology* (1802), in *The Works of William Paley*, 4 vols (Edinburgh, 1823), 1, 383; Keble's Twenty-third Sunday after Trinity, in *The Christian Year*, p. 257; Mrs Gilman's 'Mother, What is Death?', in *Sacred Poems for Mourners*, [selected by Priscilla Maurice], introduced by R. C. Trench (1846), p. 151; [Elizabeth Stone], *God's Acre; or, Historical Notices Relating to Churchyards* (1858), p. 107; Stone, p. 107; Ellice Hopkins, 'Life in Death' (1883), in *The Penguin Book of Victorian Verse*, edited by George MacBeth (Harmondsworth, 1969), p. 275.

2 See *The Complete Poems of Christina Rossetti*, Variorum Edition, edited by R. W. Crump, 2 vols. (Baton Rouge and London, 1979–86), 1, 74.

3 T. S. Eliot, 'In Memoriam' (1936), in *Selected Essays*, third edition (1951), p. 336.

4 Jerome Buckley, *Tennyson: The Growth of a Poet* (Cambridge, Mass., 1960), p. 127.

5 Frederic Harrison, *Tennyson, Ruskin, Mill, and Other Literary Estimates* (London and New York, 1899), p. 11.

6 For a full discussion of *In Memoriam, Our Mutual Friend, The Dream of Gerontius*, and *The Wreck of the Deutschland* from this perspective, see Michael Wheeler, *Death and the Future Life in Victorian Literature and Theology* (Cambridge, 1990), pp. 221–366.

7 *The Poems of Gerard Manley Hopkins*, p. 60.

8 See Elisabeth W. Schneider, *The Dragon in the Gate: Studies in the Poetry of Gerard Manley Hopkins* (Berkeley and Los Angeles, 1968), p. 29.

9 Tom Paulin, 'On the Rampage', *TLS*, 14 August 1987, p. 863.

10 Hans Frei, *The Eclipse of Biblical Narrative: A Study in Eighteenth and Nineteenth Century Hermeneutics* (New Haven and London, 1974), p. 130.

11 See J. H. A. Hart, 'The First Epistle General of Peter', in *The Expositor's Greek Testament*, edited by W. Robertson Nicoll, 5 vols. (1897–1910), V, 41–2.

12 See Geoffrey Rowell, *Hell and the Victorians: A Study of the Nineteenth-Century Theological Controversies Concerning Eternal Punishment and the Future Life* (Oxford, 1974), pp. 19–20. Cf. the debate between the 'orthodox' in the early church, who preached the bodily resurrection of Christ, and the gnostics, who denied it and were denounced as 'heretics': Elaine Pagels, *The Gnostic Gospels* (1980), p. 101.

13 See Stephen H. Travis, *Christian Hope and the Future of Man*, Issues in Contemporary Theology series, edited by I. H. Marshall (Leicester, 1980), pp. 96–7. Travis adds, however: 'the doctrines of "resurrection" and "immortality" are not as opposed to each other as is commonly believed'. Cf. also Maurice Wiles, *The Remaking of Christian Doctrine* (1974), pp. 125–46, on immortality.

14 See Travis, pp. 13–14.

15 Rudolf Bultmann and Karl Heinrich Rengstorf, *Hope*, Bible Key Words series, 12 (1963), p. 38. On 'realized' and 'inaugurated' eschatology, see also A. T. Hanson, 'Eschatology', in *A New Dictionary of Christian Theology*, edited by Alan Richardson and John Bowden (1983), pp. 183–6.

16 See Patrick Sherry, *Spirits, Saints and Immortality*, Library of Philosophy and Religion, edited by John Hick (1984), pp. 51–63.

17 See Travis, pp. 13, 19–23, 63ff.

18 Cf. Sherry, pp. 62–3.

19 Ruskin quotes these verses when commenting approvingly on Veronese's portrayal of hope as aged and assured, rather than young and joyous, in *Modern Painters*, vol. v (1860), pt. IX, ch. 3, para. 20: *The Works of John Ruskin*, edited by E. T. Cook and Alexander Wedderburn, Library Edition, 39 vols. (1903–12), VII, 291.

20 See Andrew Lincoln, *Paradise Now and Not Yet: Studies in the Role of the Heavenly Dimension in Paul's Thought with Special Reference to his Eschatology*, Society for New Testament Studies Monograph series, edited by R. McL. Wilson and M. E. Thrall, 43 (Cambridge, 1981).

21 See, e.g., Stewart D. F. Salmond, *The Christian Doctrine of Immortality* (Edinburgh, 1895), p. 294. Henry Cadbury's helpful analysis of the question is cited in John Hick, *Death and Eternal Life* (1976), p. 181.

22 See S. G. F. Brandon, *The Judgment of the Dead: An Historical and Comparative Study of the Idea of a Post-Mortem Judgment in the Major Religions* (1967), pp. 100–1.

23 *In Memoriam* (1850), lyric 31: Tennyson, *In Memoriam*, edited by Susan Shatto and Marion Shaw (Oxford, 1982), p. 63.

24 See, e.g., Frank Kermode, *The Genesis of Secrecy: On the Interpretation of Narrative*, The Charles Eliot Norton Lectures, 1977–1978 (Cambridge, Mass. and London, 1979), pp. 23–7, 47.

25 *The Great Texts of the Bible: Revelation*, edited by James Hastings (1915), p. 291.

26 Salmond, pp. 423–5.

27 Northrop Frye, *The Great Code: The Bible and Literature* (1983), p. 135.

28 Friedrich Schleiermacher, *The Christian Faith*, edited by H. R. Mackintosh and J. S. Stewart (Edinburgh, 1928), p. 702.

29 See Arthur Stuart Duncan-Jones, 'The Burial of the Dead', in *Liturgy and Worship: A Companion to the Prayer Books of the Anglican Communion*, edited by W. K. Lowther Clarke (London and New York, 1932), p. 616; Ulrich Simon, *Heaven in the Christian Tradition* (1958), pp. 218–19.

30 Many Methodists, for example, used the Book of Common Prayer in their worship, and were buried by the Church of England incumbent. Nonconformists who objected to the burial service of the established church often maintained silence in the churchyard. The question of nonconformist burials became increasingly contentious until the Burials Act was passed in 1880. The prayer book service could now be replaced by other suitable forms. See Owen Chadwick, *The Victorian Church*, second edition, 2 vols., Ecclesiastical History of England, edited by J. D. Dickinson, vols. VII–VIII (1970), I, 370–1; II, 202–7. Roman Catholic

prayers for the dead are discussed in Wheeler, *Death and the Future Life,* pp. 315–24.

31 See Duncan-Jones, p. 623.

32 Edward Henry Bickersteth, *The Shadowed Home, and the Light Beyond* (1875), p. 179.

33 *Sacred Poems for Mourners* [selected by Priscilla Maurice], introduced by R. C. Trench (1846), p. 123.

34 *The Illustrated Book of Sacred Poems*, edited by Robert H. Baynes (London and New York, 1867), p. 130.

35 On *Our Mutual Friend,* see Wheeler, *Death and The Future Life*, pp. 273–4 above. The British Library Catalogue lists twenty-seven tracts and books on liturgical reform published between 1859 and 1863 by individual named authors alone. Church reports, etc., must be added to this list.

36 Charles John Vaughan, *Revisions of the Liturgy: Five Discourses* (Cambridge and London, 1860), pp. 73–4.

37 *The Stones of Venice*, vol. II *(1853)*, *ch. 8, para. 85: Works*, X, 399.

38 *Hymns Ancient and Modern, For Use in the Services of the Church; With Accompanying Tunes* [edited by Henry Williams Baker, *et al.*], Standard Edition (1916), p. 236. Cf. also Bishop Christopher Wordsworth's 'Gracious Spirit, Holy Ghost', p. 219.

39 *Hymns Ancient and Modern*, p. 242.

40 Bernard Ramm, *The Pattern of Religious Authority* (Grand Rapids, Mich., 1957), pp. 20, 63, 28, 29.

41 See John Henry Newman, *Lectures on the Prophetical Office of the Church, Viewed Relatively to Romanism and Popular Protestantism* (London and Oxford, 1837), pp. 152–201.

42 See Stephen Neill, *The Interpretation of the New Testament, 1861–1961*, The Firth Lectures, 1962 (1966), p. 31.

43 See James C. Livingston, *Modern Christian Thought: From the Enlightenment to Vatican II* (New York and London, 1971), p. 96.

44 Samuel Taylor Coleridge, *Confessions of an Inquiring Spirit*, edited by H. St J. Hart, Library of Modern Religious Thought (1956), p. 64.

45 Ibid., p. 59.

46 Benjamin Jowett, 'On the Interpretation of Scripture', in *Essays and Reviews*, seventh edition (1861), pp. 377, 383.

47 See Rowell, *Hell and the Victorians*, p. 121.

48 See Chadwick, II, 69.

49 Ibid., II, 74–5.

50 See Neill, pp. 33–60.

51 Matthew Arnold, *Dissent and Dogma*, edited by R. H. Super, Complete Prose Works, 11 vols. (Ann Arbor, Mich., 1960–77), VI, 362, 161.

52 Ibid., pp. 143–6.

53 Matthew Arnold, *God and the Bible*, edited by R. H. Super, Complete Prose Works, 11 vols. (Ann Arbor, Mich., 1960–77), VII, 350–1.

54 Ibid., pp. 371–2.

55 Arnold, *Dissent and Dogma*, p. 237.

56 Arnold, *God and the Bible*, p. 244.

57 *Lux Mundi: A Series of Studies in the Religion of the Incarnation*, edited by Charles Gore, eighth edition (1890), pp. 325–6.

58 Ibid., p. 357.

59 See, e.g., Chadwick, II, 100–11.

60 F. W. Farrar, *The Bible: Its Meaning and Supremacy*, second edition (1901), pp. 42, 98, 136.

61 Ibid., pp. 203–6.

62 Ibid., p. 214.

63 Ibid., p. 199.

64 Ibid., p. 52.

65 Chris Brooks, *Signs for the Times: Symbolic Realism in the Mid-Victorian World* (1984), pp. 3, 14. Like Brooks, W. David Shaw in his masterly study on Victorian poetics discusses the Victorian 'recovery of analogy' in terms of typology, in Keble's conservative hermeneutics and the poetry of Hopkins and Christina Rossetti, for example, but does not discuss the influence on these writers of Joseph Butler: see *The Lucid Veil: Poetic Truth in the Victorian Age* (1987), chapter 6. See also George P. Landow, *Victorian Types, Victorian Shadows: Biblical Typology in Victorian Literature, Art, and Thought* (1980).

66 On Butler's *Analogy*, see p. 62 above.

67 *The Works of Joseph Butler*, edited by W. E. Gladstone, 2 vols. (Oxford, 1896), I, 19–24.

68 James Buchanan, *Analogy, Considered as a Guide to Truth, and Applied as an Aid to Faith* (Edinburgh and London, 1864), p. 354.

69 Ibid., p. 124.

70 S. T. Coleridge, *Aids to Reflection in the Formation of a Manly Character on the Several Grounds of Prudence, Morality and Religion*, edited by Thomas Fenby, New Universal Library (London and New York, [1905]), pp. 181–2.

71 Austin Farrer, *The Glass of Vision*, Bampton Lectures (1948), pp. 42, 109, 136.

72 Ibid., p. 74.

73 Ibid., p. 110.

74 See Michael Wheeler, 'Austin Farrer's *Glass of Vision*: A Literary and Theological Debate', *National Conference on Literature and Religion Newsletter*, 6 (April 1985), 14–21.

75 John MacQuarrie, *God-Talk: An Examination of the Language and Logic of Theology* (1967), p. 228.

76 Ibid., pp. 194–5.

77 F. W. Dillistone, *Christianity and Symbolism* (1955), p. 161.

78 Sallie McFague, *Metaphorical Theology: Models of God in Religious Language* (1983), p. 38.

79 Dillistone, p. 160.

80 McFague, p. 19.

81 Michael Edwards, *Towards a Christian Poetics* (London and Basingstoke, 1984), pp. 4–5.

82 Ibid., pp. 5–6.

83 Arnold, *God and the Bible*, p. 350.

84 Bickersteth, *Shadowed Home*, pp. 4–5.

85 During his time as Bishop of Exeter (1885–1900), however, Bickersteth acknowledged the role of biblical criticism 'when serious and reverent', and claimed that the Church of England stood on 'a far higher level than those who unconvinced, are compelled to submit, if not to subscribe, to the recent encyclical letter from the Vatican': Francis Keyes Aglionby, *The Life of Edward Henry Bickersteth, D.D., Bishop and Poet* (1907), p. 73.

86 Bickersteth, *Shadowed Home*, pp. 14–15.

87 James Beattie, *Elements of Moral Science*, 2 vols. (Edinburgh, 1790–3), II, 467.

88 John Hutchison, *Our Lord's Signs in St. John's Gospel: Discussions Chiefly Exegetical and Doctrinal on the Eight Miracles in the Fourth Gospel* (Edinburgh, 1892), p. 153.

89 Frederick Denison Maurice, *The Gospel of St. John: A Series of Discourses* (Cambridge, 1857), p. 306.

90 F. D. Maurice, *Death and Life: A Sermon Preached in Lincoln's Inn Chapel on the 25th March, 1855* (Cambridge and London, [1855]), pp. 9–11. Maurice intimated to his wife that his brother-in-law, Julius Hare, who had died only two months previously, was more 'present' to him than the man of whom he was more directly preaching: *The Life of Frederick Denison Maurice, Chiefly Told in his Own Letters*, edited by Frederick Maurice, 2 vols. (1884), II, 259.

91 David Friedrich Strauss, *The Life of Jesus, Critically Examined*, translated by Marian Evans, 3 vols. (1846), II, 371. Rudolf Bultmann argues, however, that the misunderstanding is not 'Johannine', for it 'has nothing to do with the confusion of the heavenly and earthly. Rather a primitive artificial device of the source lies behind this (cp. Mk.5.39)': *The Gospel of John: A Commentary*, translated by G. R. Beasley-Murray (Oxford, 1971), p. 399, n. 6; cf. p. 135, n. 1. Bultmann's position was in turn challenged by Cullmann: see *Theological Dictionary of the New Testament*, edited by Gerhard Kittel, translated and edited by Geoffrey W. Bromiley, 10 vols. (Grand Rapids, Mich., 1964–76), VIII, 555, n. 73.

92 Strauss, II, 383.
93 Cf. Edwyn Clement Hoskyns, *The Fourth Gospel*, edited by Francis Noel Davey, second edition (1947), p. 401.
94 *Theological Dictionary of the New Testament*, VIII, 555.
95 Arnold, *God and the Bible*, p. 171.
96 Ibid., p. 299.
97 Ibid., pp. 350–1.
98 Ibid., p. 350.
99 Cf. Bultmann and Rengstorf, p. 38. On 'realized' and 'inaugurated' eschatology, see also A. T. Hanson, 'Eschatology', in *A New Dictionary of Christian Theology*, edited by Richardson and Bowden, pp. 183–6.

1 Death

1 *The Poetical Works of William Wordsworth*, edited by E[rnest] de Selincourt and Helen Darbishire, 5 vols. (Oxford, 1940–9), V, 171. All further quotations from Wordsworth's poetry are taken from this edition.
2 See, for example, John R. Reed, *Victorian Conventions* (Athens, Ohio, 1975), chapter 7; A. O. J. Cockshut, *Truth to Life: The Art of Biography in the Nineteenth Century* (1974), chapter 3; Garrett Stewart, *Death Sentences: Styles of Dying in British Fiction* (Cambridge, Mass. and London, 1984), chapters 1–3. The best discussion on doctrinal questions related to deathbed conventions is Elisabeth Jay's in *The Religion of the Heart: Anglican Evangelicalism and the Nineteenth-Century Novel* (Oxford, 1979), chapter 3.
3 See, for example, the titles of poems in the collected works of Anna Barbauld (1743–1824), Felicia Hemans (1793–1835), Elizabeth Barrett Browning (1806–61) and Christina Rossetti (1830–94). See also Eric Smith, *By Mourning Tongues: Studies in English Elegy* (Ipswich and Totowa, N.J., 1977).
4 See John Morley, *Death, Heaven and the Victorians* (1971); James Stevens Curl, *The Victorian Celebration of Death* (Newton Abbot, 1972); Chris Brooks, *et al.*, *Mortal Remains: The History and Present State of the Victorian and Edwardian Cemetery* (Exeter, 1989); Sylvia M. Barnard, *To Prove I'm not Forgot: Living and Dying in a Victorian City* (Manchester, 1990); Julian Litten, *The English Way of Death: The Common Funeral since 1450* (London, 1991).
5 'Archangel. Behold there, Death! / . . . his scythe, / Still wet out of its bloody swathe, one hand / Tottering sustains . . .': Philip James Bailey, *Festus: A Poem*, ninth edition (1875), p. 560.
6 Charlotte Brontë to W. S. Williams, 16 March 1850, in *The Brontës: Their Lives, Friendships & Correspondence*, edited by Thomas James

Wise and John Alexander Symington, 4 vols., The Shakespeare Head
Brontë (Oxford, 1932), III, 82; [John Henry Newman], *Verses on Various
Occasions*, second edition (1869), p. 315.

7 *The Poems of Tennyson*, edited by Christopher Ricks, Longman
Annotated English Poets, general editor F. W. Bateson (1969), p. 1,648.
All further quotations from Tennyson's poems, other than *In Memoriam*
(see note 82 below), are taken from this edition.

8 [Elizabeth] Stone, *God's Acre; or, Historical Notices Relating to
Churchyards* (1858), p. 31. A nice cultural contrast to Mrs Stone's book
in our own time is Francesca Greenoak's *God's Acre: The Flowers and
Animals of the Parish Churchyard* (1985), a study of the churchyard as
an 'unofficial nature reserve'. Whereas 'hell' is now often taken to be a
metaphor of a metaphor, in this case the metaphoric has been emptied
of significance and a 'natural' literalism has reclaimed the site.

9 *The Poor Man's Friend*, *Punch*, 8 (Jan.–June 1845), 93.

10 Following the burial of his eldest child, Philip Henry, the
seventeenth-century nonconformist divine, wrote: 'My dear child, now
mine no longer, was laid in the cold earth, not lost, but soon to be raised
again a glorious body, and I shall go to him, but he shall not return to
me. A few days after his dear friend, Mr. Lawrence . . . buried a
daughter, that was grown up and very hopeful, and gave good evidence
of a work of grace wrought upon her soul, how willing, saith he, may
parents be to part with such when the Lord calls; they are not *amissi* but
praemissi.' Matthew Henry, *The Life of the Rev. Philip Henry, A. M.,
with Funeral Sermons for Mr. and Mrs. Henry*, collected and enlarged
by J. B. Williams (1825), p. 111. The saying which the Victorians turned
into a cliché – 'Not lost, but gone before' – figured on many gravestones
of the period, and was often used in popular books on the subject of
death and the future life. See, for example, [Robert Bickersteth] *et al.*,
The Recognition of Friends in Heaven (1866), pp. iv, 179, 250, 254–5.
For an example of the convention of the 'heavenly birthday', which is as
old as Christianity itself, as we know from inscriptions in the Roman
catacombs and from the Roman Martyrology, see 'The Three Birthdays'
(1861) in Edward Henry Bickersteth, *The Two Brothers, and other
Poems*, second edition (1872), pp. 211–13. The poem is dedicated to the
memory of 'one who, in blindness and suffering, but in the full assurance
of faith, said, a few hours before her death, that she had always heard
that three birthdays were ours: – our natural birthday, our spiritual
birthday, and our birthday into glory: and that she was sure the last was
the brightest and the best'.

11 See, for example, *The Collected Letters of Thomas and Jane Welsh
Carlyle*, Duke-Edinburgh Edition, general editor Charles Richard

Sanders, 7 vols. (Durham, N.C., 1970–7), III, 34; and the painting entitled *The Bourne from which no Traveller Returns*, attributed to John Martin in Morley, plate 117, but not listed in William Feaver, *The Art of John Martin* (Oxford, 1975).

12 'Yet sometimes / The veil is lifted by His high behest / Who separates eternity from time, / And spirits have spoken unto men . . .' (1.630–3): Edward Henry Bickersteth, *Yesterday, To-Day, and For Ever: A Poem, in Twelve Books*, eighth edition (1873), p. 23. Tennyson adopts the traditional metaphor in *In Memoriam* (1850), 56: 'Behind the veil, behind the veil'. George Eliot subverts it in her short story 'The Lifted Veil' (1859).

13 A. O. J. Cockshut, *Truth to Life: The Art of Biography in the Nineteenth Century* (1974), p. 41.

14 Frederick W. Robertson, *Sermons, Preached at Trinity Chapel, Brighton*, third series (1857), p. 184.

15 Frederick Denison Maurice, *The Gospel of St. John: A Series of Discourses* (Cambridge, 1857), p. 307.

16 See *The Life of Frederick Denison Maurice, Chiefly Told in his Own Letters*, edited by Frederick Maurice, 2 vols. (1884), II, 640. Quoted in Cockshut, pp. 49–50.

17 Cf. Victorian genre paintings – Christopher Wood, *Victorian Panorama: Paintings of Victorian Life* (1976), chapters 13–14.

18 Cf. Victor W. Turner, *The Ritual Process: Structure and Anti-Structure* (1969), pp. 94–5. See also Arnold van Gennep, *The Rites of Passage*, translated by Monika B. Vizedom and Gabrielle L. Caffee (Chicago, 1960), pp. 10–13, 146–65.

19 [Richard Whateley], *A View of the Scripture Revelations Concerning a Future State: Laid Before his Parishioners, by a Country Pastor* (1829), pp. 246–9.

20 'A priest is never more thoroughly a priest than in the chamber of death' (97). Charles Reade, *The Cloister and the Hearth: A Tale of the Middle Ages*, Everyman's Library (London and New York, 1906), p. 694.

21 [A. M. H. W.], *Glimpses of a Brighter Land* (1871), pp. 122–3.

22 For discussion on *The Way of all Flesh*, see Chapter 2, p. 112.

23 F. W. Farrar, *Mercy and Judgment: A Few Last Words on Christian Eschatology with Reference to Dr. Pusey's 'What is of Faith?'* (1881), pp. 159–61.

24 Henry Nutcombe Oxenham, *Catholic Eschatology and Universalism: An Essay on the Doctrine of Future Retribution*, second edition (1878), p. 45. (First edition, 1876.)

25 Owen Meredith [E. R. B. Lytton], 'Last Words', *Cornhill Magazine*, 2 (July–Dec. 1860), 513–17.

26 Frederic Rowland Marvin, *The Last Words (Real and Traditional) of Distinguished Men and Women, Collected from Various Sources* (Troy, N.Y., 1900), p. 76. Last words are also regarded as being of critical importance in Christian manuals on holy dying. See, for example, [Timothy East], *Death Bed Scenes; or, The Christian's Companion; On Entering the Dark Valley* (1825).

27 See J. A. Symonds, 'Death', in *The Cyclopaedia of Anatomy and Physiology*, edited by Robert B. Todd, 5 vols. (1835–9), I, 803.

28 [Priscilla Maurice], *Prayers for the Sick and Dying* (1853), p. 185.

29 Stone, p. 404.

30 Edward Henry Bickersteth, *Yesterday, To-Day, and For Ever: A Poem, in Twelve Books*, eighth edition (1873), pp. 4–5. Further references in the text are by book and line numbers.

31 Sex is idealized in the memory, and described in biblical terms:

> And then the plucking of the tree of life,
> With its ambrosial fruitage and fresh flowers,
> Upon our bridal day. We took and ate
> And lived – God's smile upon us.   (I.143–5)

32 Philippe Ariès, *Western Attitudes Toward Death: From the Middle Ages to the Present*, translated by Patricia M. Ranum (Baltimore and London, 1974), chapter 3. See also Ariès's more detailed study, *The Hour of Our Death*, translated by Helen Weaver (1981); Elisabeth Bronfen, *Over Her Dead Body: Death, Femininity and the Aesthetic* (Manchester, 1992).

33 See Eric Smith, *By Mourning Tongues: Studies in English Elegy* (Ipswich and Totowa, N.J., 1977), chapters 1 and 4.

34 Morley, illustrations 25 and 30.

35 *The Complete Works of Robert Browning*, edited by Roma A. King, Jr, et al. (Athens, Ohio, 1969–), IV, 189. All further quotations from Browning's poetry are taken from this edition.

36 'Bishop Blougram's Apology'.

37 John Henry Newman, *Parochial and Plain Sermons*, new edition, 8 vols. (1868), I, 4–7. See also pp. 134–5 above.

38 *The Complete Poetical Works of Thomas Hood*, edited by Walter Jerrold (1906), p. 444. Cf. D. G. Rossetti's 'My Sister's Sleep', written in 1847 and published in 1850.

39 'Worldliness and Other-Worldliness: The Poet Young', in *Essays of George Eliot*, edited by Thomas Pinney (New York and London, 1963), pp. 377, 375.

40 Garrett Stewart believes that Jane's question ('Are you going home?') is disingenuous, and that in the inscription on Helen's tombstone 'it is as if the heroine herself, in a dead language recharged with feeling, has

retrospectively engraved the tense of her own resurrection': Stewart, p. 104. The first comment is questionable; the second is more interesting, but takes no account of the fact that the mature Jane respects Helen's position on death and eternal life, and that the language of resurrection is not 'dead' to her.

41 For Stewart, Rochester's response again brings us back to writing and the limits of narrative: 'His ironic mistaking of her temporal grammar plays not only upon her supposed supernatural gifts but implicitly on her role as a narrator, harrowing death so as to strengthen her autobiographical record against recurrent instances of human closure.' Stewart, p. 31.

42 Augustus J. C. Hare, *Memorials of a Quiet Life*, 3 vols. (1872–6), II, 223. Bunsen's idea that spring is a 'type of the revival of the spirit after death' is quoted in the *Memorials*, II, 39. Augustus Hare's biographer, Malcolm Barnes, portrays Maria Hare as a warped and wilful woman who, even in the moment of death, could 'organise the proper gesture': *Augustus Hare* (1984), p. 115.

43 Hare, II, 236. Malcolm Barnes is scornful of such writing, and argues that 'the deeper their misery the more the Hare women resorted to pretentious clichés': Barnes, p. 95.

44 Hare, II, 293.

45 *The Letters of Gerard Manley Hopkins to Robert Bridges*, edited by Claude Colleer Abbot (1935), p. 122.

46 *Poetical Works of Robert Bridges, Excluding the Eight Dramas*, Oxford Edition (1914), pp. 267–8.

47 Peter Coveney, *The Image of Childhood, the Individual and Society: A Study of the Theme in English Literature*, revised edition (Harmondsworth, 1967), pp. 179, 182.

48 Ibid., p. 184.

49 *Catharine and Crauford Tait, Wife and Son of Archibald Campbell, Archbishop of Canterbury: A Memorial*, edited by William Benham (1879), pp. 302–3. For the full text of Thomas Bilby's hymn, see for example *Methodist Free Church School Hymns* (1888), no. 288. The hymn is sung by the Durbeyfield children, who learnt it 'at the Sunday-school': Thomas Hardy, *Tess of the d'Urbervilles* (1891; 51).

50 Hymns mentioned in Catharine Tait's narrative include 'Behold a stranger at the door', 'Jesus, Saviour, Son of God', 'Brother, thou art gone before', 'Away, thou dying saint, away', and 'How fair the day has been'. Consolatory hymns are also sung in F. W. Farrar's novels, for example: 'There is a calm for those who weep' (*Eric*, II.13); 'Nearer, my God, to Thee', 'Jerusalem the Golden', 'O for a closer walk with God', 'Rock of Ages', and 'My God, my Father, while I stay' (*St Winifred's*,

1.19). The spirit and themes of Victorian consolatory hymns for children are conveyed visually in the memorial window dedicated to the memory of the Taits' children in Carlisle Cathedral.

51 *Catharine and Crauford Tait,* pp. 344–5.

52 Ibid., pp. 357–8.

53 Ibid., pp. 311–12.

54 Ibid., p. 372.

55 Randall Thomas Davidson and William Benham, *Life of Archibald Campbell Tait, Archbishop of Canterbury,* 2 vols. (London and New York, 1891), I, 192.

56 Ibid., I, 202.

57 See Francis Keyes Aglionby, *The Life of Edward Henry Bickersteth, D.D., Bishop and Poet* (1907), pp. 26, 117, 198.

58 See Whateley, pp. 246–9.

59 *Poetical Works of Wordsworth,* v, 449–50.

60 See Mary Moorman, *William Wordsworth, A Biography: The Later Years, 1803–1850* (1965), p. 183.

61 See Stephen Prickett, *Romanticism and Religion: The Tradition of Wordsworth and Coleridge in the Victorian Church* (Cambridge, 1976), chapter 3, *et seq.* Prickett does not discuss the main text of *The Excursion* in his study.

62 See Kenneth R. Johnston, *Wordsworth and 'The Recluse'* (New Haven and London, 1983), p. 286.

63 Ibid., p. 286.

64 Having quoted the passage, J. A. Froude can identify it simply by referring to 'the poet's churchyard visitor': 'The Spirit's Trials', in Zeta [James Anthony Froude], *Shadows of the Clouds* (1847), p. 92.

65 See *Encyclopaedia Britannica,* fifth edition, 20 vols. (Edinburgh, 1817), XI, 295–7; *Cyclopaedia of Anatomy,* I, 803–8; Curl, pp. 177–9.

66 *The Complete Works of Algernon Charles Swinburne,* edited by Edmund Gosse and Thomas James Wise, Bonchurch Edition, 20 vols. (1925; rpt. New York, 1968), II, 42.

67 J[oseph] Furniss, *The House of Death,* Books for Children and Young Persons, 7 (Dublin, 1860), pp. 16–17.

68 Austin Holyoake, *A Burial Service,* Secular Ceremonies [1870], p. 4.

69 *Poems and Some Letters of James Thomson,* edited by Anne Ridler (1963), p. 180. Further references in the text are by book numbers.

70 S. T. Coleridge, *Aids to Reflection,* sixth edition, edited by Henry Nelson Coleridge (1848), I, 245. Cf. J. M. Neale's Easter hymn, 'The foe behind, the deep before': 'No longer must the mourners weep, / Nor call departed Christians dead; / For death is hallow'd into sleep, / And ev'ry grave becomes a bed.' *Hymns Ancient and Modern, For Use in the Services of*

the Church; With Accompanying Tunes, [edited by Henry Williams Baker, *et al.*], Standard Edition (1916), pp. 590–1. It was recorded that at Gladstone's burial, earth from the Garden of Gethsemane was mixed in with his native soil: *Black and White*, 4 June 1898, p. 743.

71 Stone, p. 52.

72 [Mrs Cecil Frances Alexander], *Hymns for Little Children* (1848), pp. 33–4.

73 [John Keble], *The Christian Year: Thoughts in Verse for the Sundays and Holydays Throughout the Year*, second edition (Oxford, 1827), p. 2.

74 Ibid., p. 354.

75 *Hymns Ancient and Modern*, p. 304.

76 Stone, p. 109.

77 Buchanan, p. 368. The literary critic R. P. Blackmur argues that 'collateral or analogical form is as near as we are likely to come to the organic' and that for poetry 'only in analogy are the opposites identical': *A Primer of Ignorance*, edited by Joseph Frank (New York, 1967), pp. 42–3.

78 Rudolf Bultmann, *Life and Death*, Bible Key Words series, 14 (1965), pp. 86–7.

79 *The Works of Joseph Butler*, edited by W. E. Gladstone, 2 vols. (Oxford, 1896), I, 19–24.

80 See *The Pre-Raphaelites*, pp. 139–41. (Millais may have been inspired to paint such a scene after helping to sweep up and burn leaves during a visit to the Tennysons at Farringford.)

81 Ibid., pp. 175–7.

82 See Tennyson, *In Memoriam*, edited by Susan Shatto and Marion Shaw (Oxford, 1982), p. 180.

83 Charlotte Yonge's mentor, Keble, believed that the Church of England, the Church of Rome and the Orthodox Church 'are really one, though divided externally'. See Prickett, *Romanticism and Religion*, p. 102.

84 *Poems of Arnold*, edited by Kenneth Allott, second edition, edited by Miriam Allott, Longman Annotated English Poets, general editors F. W. Bateson and John Barnard (London and New York, 1979), pp. 427–8. All further quotations from Arnold's poetry are taken from this edition.

85 Ibid., p. 422.

86 Matthew Arnold, *God and the Bible*, edited by R. H. Super, Complete Prose Works, 11 vols. (Ann Arbor, Mich., 1960–77), VII, 350–1.

2 Judgment

1 Victor W. Turner, *The Ritual Process: Structure and Anti-Structure* (1969), pp. 94–5.

2 See S. G. F. Brandon, *The Judgment of the Dead: An Historical and*

Comparative Study of the Idea of a Post-Mortem Judgment in the Major Religions (1967), pp. 114–15.

3 See Victor Turner and Edith Turner, *Image and Pilgrimage in Christian Culture: Anthropological Perspectives* (New York, 1978), p. 115.

4 E. H. Bickersteth, *The Blessed Dead: What Does Scripture Reveal of their State before the Resurrection?*, second edition, revised (1863), p. 5.

5 Ibid., p. 12.

6 Ibid., pp. 14–15. Bickersteth here draws upon 1 Peter 3.18–19 and Article III of the Church of England, 'as first published': 'That the body of Christ lay in the grave till his resurrection, but his spirit which He gave up was with the spirits which are detained in prison, or in hell, and preached to them, as the place in St. Peter testifieth.' Cf. Bickersteth's *Yesterday, To-Day, and For Ever: A Poem in Twelve Books,* eighth edition (1873), pp. 387–9.

7 These words are cited at the end of *The Cloud of Unknowing.* See *The Cloud of Unknowing and Other Works*, translated by Clifton Wolters (Harmondsworth, 1978), p. 152. On Bultmann's analysis of the *eschaton*, see p. 7 above.

8 Frank Kermode, *The Sense of an Ending: Studies in the Theory of Fiction* (1967), pp. 46–7. For contrasting New Testament usages see, e.g., Revelation 1.3 and 10.6: 'the time (*kairos*) is at hand'; 'there should be time (*chronos*) no longer'. Kermode, however, cites James Barr, Biblical Words for Time (1962), in which the *kairos–chronos* distinction in the work of J. Marsh (1952), J. A. T. Robinson (1950) and others is strongly challenged. Kermode argues that 'the best one can hope for is that the words, in New Testament Greek, maintain a certain polarity' (p. 49). See also the article on 'time' in *The New International Dictionary of New Testament Theology*, edited by Colin Brown, 3 vols. (Exeter, 1978), III, 826, where the distinction is upheld.

9 See John Hick, *Death and Eternal Life* (1976), p. 12.

10 Kermode, *Sense of an Ending,* p. 25.

11 Brandon, p. 109.

12 See Brandon, pp. 110–11. For a Tractarian treatment of the parable and of Christ's words on the cross as evidence for an intermediate state, see Herbert Mortimer Luckock, *After Death: An Examination of the Testimony of Primitive Times Respecting the State of the Faithful Dead, and their Relationship to the Living*, second edition (1880), pp. 26–31. See also notes 40 and 41 below.

13 Frederick Denison Maurice, *Theological Essays*, second edition (Cambridge, 1853), p. 468.

14 Frederic W. Farrar, *Eternal Hope: Five Sermons Preached in Westminster Abbey, November and December, 1877* (1904), p. xxii.

15 Ibid., pp. xxxiii–xxxv.

16 Ibid., pp. xxi–xxii.
17 See Geoffrey Rowell, *Hell and the Victorians: A Study of the Nineteenth-Century Theological Controversies Concerning Eternal Punishment and the Future Life* (Oxford, 1974), p. 181.
18 Ibid., p. 196.
19 Friedrich Schleiermacher, *The Christian Faith*, edited by H. R. Mackintosh and J. S. Stewart (Edinburgh, 1928), p. 701.
20 Farrar, *Eternal Hope*, p. xxii.
21 Jacques Le Goff, *The Birth of Purgatory*, translated by Arthur Goldhammer (1984), p. 226.
22 Ibid., p. 306.
23 Ibid., p. 293.
24 See, for example, A. Dwight Culler, *The Poetry of Tennyson* (New Haven and London, 1977), pp. 14–15.
25 See Elisabeth Jay, *The Religion of the Heart: Anglican Evangelicalism and the Nineteenth-Century Novel* (Oxford, 1979), pp. 84–5.
26 Farrar, *Eternal Hope*, p. xxi.
27 See Schleiermacher, p. 722, where he argues that the final 'universal restoration of all souls' deserves an equal claim to the 'ordinary view' of heaven and hell. See also Brandon, p. 118, and Hick, pp. 200, 208–10.
28 See F. W. Farrar, *Mercy and Judgment: A Few Last Words on Christian Eschatology with Reference to Dr. Pusey's 'What is of Faith?'* (1881), p. 7.
29 See Rowell, *Hell and the Victorians*, pp. 139–52.
30 See W. E. Gladstone, *Studies Subsidiary to the Works of Bishop Butler* (Oxford, 1896), p. 199.
31 John Henry Newman, *An Essay on the Development of Christian Doctrine* (1920), p. 48.
32 Edmund Gurney, *Tertium Quid* (1887), cited in Alan Gauld, *The Founders of Psychical Research* (1968), p. 158.
33 See Farrar, *Eternal Hope*, pp. xxxvi–xxxviii.
34 Ibid., p. xii.
35 Ibid., p. 88; cf. Farrar, *Mercy and Judgment*, pp. 11, 59, 158–75.
36 Henry Bristow Wilson, 'Séances Historiques de Genève – The National Church', in *Essays and Reviews*, seventh edition (1861), pp. 145–206 (p. 206).
37 Luckock, p. 36.
38 See John Morley, *The Life of William Ewart Gladstone*, 3 vols. (1904), I, 131, and Gladstone, pp. 253–4. The church had, in Gladstone's view, condemned the 'sleep of the soul' (*psychopannychia*) as unscriptural.
39 See Francois Wendel, *Calvin: The Origin and Development of his Religious Thought*, translated by Philip Mairet (London and New York, 1965), p. 287; cited in Brandon, p. 132.

40 H. P. Liddon, *Passiontide Sermons* (London and New York, 1891), p. 278–9.

41 See Edward Henry Bickersteth, *The Shadowed Home, and the Light Beyond* (1875), p. 195.

42 See Stewart D. F. Salmond, *The Christian Doctrine of Immortality* (1895), p. 350.

43 Rowell, *Hell and the Victorians*, pp. 215–16.

44 Norman Cohn, *The Pursuit of the Millennium: Revolutionary Millenarians and Mystical Anarchists of the Middle Ages* (1970), p. 13.

45 See Ernest R. Sandeen, 'Millennialism', in *The Rise of Adventism: Religion and Society in Mid-Nineteenth-Century America*, edited by Edwin S. Gaustad (New York, 1974), pp. 104–18 (p. 107); Cohn, pp. 108–10; M. H. Abrams, *Natural Supernaturalism: Tradition and Revelation in Romantic Literature* (New York and London, 1971), p. 58; Marjorie Reeves and Warwick Gould, *Joachim of Fiore and the Myth of the Eternal Evangel in the Nineteenth Century* (Oxford, 1987).

46 See Turner, *Ritual Process*, pp. 111–12.

47 J. F. C. Harrison, *The Second Coming: Popular Millenarianism, 1780– 1850* (London and Henley, 1979).

48 See, for example, Bickersteth, *Yesterday*, pp. 94–5, 103–4.

49 See E. P. Thompson, *The Making of the English Working Class* (1963; rpt. Harmondsworth, 1968), pp. 52–5, 127–30, 420–31, 877–83.

50 See Sandeen, p. 111.

51 See Owen Chadwick, *The Victorian Church*, second edition, 2 vols., Ecclesiastical History of England, edited by J. D. Dickinson, vols. VII– VIII (1970), I, 7–47.

52 Sandeen, p. 109.

53 See John O. Waller, 'Christ's Second Coming: Christina Rossetti and the Premillennialist William Dodsworth', *Bulletin of the New York Public Library*, 73 (1969), 465–82 (pp. 476–7).

54 Bickersteth, *Yesterday*, p. v.

55 William Ker, *'The Things which must Shortly come to Pass': A Series of Discourses on the Prophecies of 'The Last Days,' Delivered in the Parish Church of Tipton, Staffordshire* (Dudley, 1868), discourses XI and XII.

56 Cf. Frank Kermode, 'Lawrence and the Apocalyptic Types', *Critical Quarterly*, Tenth Anniversary Number (1968), 26–35; extract reprinted as '*Middlemarch* and *Apocalypse*', in *George Eliot, 'Middlemarch': A Casebook*, edited by Patrick Swinden, Casebook series, general editor A. E. Dyson (London and Basingstoke, 1972), pp. 131–43.

57 Edmund Gosse, *Father and Son: A Study of Two Temperaments*, popular edition (1909), pp. 327–8.

58 Christina G. Rossetti, *The Face of the Deep: A Devotional Commentary on the Apocalypse* (1892).

59 Mackenzie Bell, *Christina Rossetti: A Biographical and Critical Study* (1898), pp. 244, 180–1.

60 *The Complete Poems of Christina Rossetti: A Variorum Edition*, 2 vols., edited by R. W. Crump (Baton Rouge and London, 1979), I, 68–9. See also Waller's article, cited in note 53 above.

61 See William Feaver, *The Art of John Martin* (Oxford, 1975), pp. 173–4, 181, 196.

62 See Morton D. Paley, *The Apocalyptic Sublime* (New Haven and London, 1986).

63 *The Poetical Works of Robert Southey*, 10 vols. (1837–8), X, 213–14.

64 See, for example, A. D. Harvey, *English Poetry in a Changing Society, 1780–1825* (1980), pp. 17–43.

65 See p. 41 above.

66 *Lord Macaulay's Essays, and Lays of Ancient Rome*, popular edition (1899), p. 132.

67 *The Miscellaneous Writings and Speeches of Lord Macaulay*, popular edition (1891), pp. 443–4.

68 Robert Pollok, *The Course of Time: A Poem*, Illustrated Edition (1857), pp. xvii–xviii.

69 Ibid., pp. 142–3.

70 Ibid., p. 174.

71 Ibid., pp. 176–84.

72 Ibid., p. 186.

73 Ibid., pp. 188–9.

74 Ibid., p. 190.

75 Ibid., p. 192.

76 Ibid., p. 205.

77 Ibid., pp. 221–2.

78 Ibid., p. 228.

79 Ibid., p. 317.

80 Ibid., p. 331.

81 Ibid., p. 334.

82 Ibid., p. 351.

83 Ibid., p. 357.

84 Ibid., pp. 358–9.

85 Francis Keyes Aglionby, *The Life of Edward Henry Bickersteth, D.D., Bishop and Poet* (1907), p. 112.

86 See p. 35 above.

87 Bickersteth, *Yesterday*, pp. 362f., 429–30.

88 Extract from a review in *The Standard*, cited in 'Opinions of the Press', p. 1, printed after the main text of Bickersteth's *Yesterday, To-Day, and For Ever*.

89 Aglionby, p. 109.

90 In Elizabeth Gaskell's novel *North and South* (1854–5), for example, Margaret Hale exclaims: 'I begin to understand now what heaven must be – and, oh! the grandeur and repose of the words – "The same yesterday, today, and for ever"' (46).

91 [Hallam Tennyson], *Alfred Lord Tennyson: A Memoir* (1899), p. 269.

92 See John O. Waller, 'Tennyson and Philip James Bailey's *Festus*', *Bulletin of Research in the Humanities*, 82 (1979), 105–23.

93 See Robert Birley, *Sunk Without Trace: Some Forgotten Masterpieces Reconsidered*, The Clark Lectures, 1960–1961 (New York, 1962), pp. 173–6.

94 Philip James Bailey, *Festus: A Poem*, ninth edition (1875), p. 65. This passage first appeared in the second edition of 1845: see Birley, p. 184.

95 See Waller, 'Tennyson and *Festus*', p. 111.

96 Bailey, pp. 56, 60.

97 Ibid., p. 65.

98 Ibid., e.g. pp. 6, 8, 16, 63, 71, 75, 78, 165, 211, 212, 288, 290, 403, 503, 555.

99 Ibid., p. 507.

100 Ibid., p. 555.

101 Ibid., p. 557.

102 Ibid., pp. 560–1, 572.

103 Ibid., pp. 573–7.

104 Ibid., p. 578.

105 Ibid., p. 579.

106 Ibid., p. 582. In the first edition Lucifer is not restored.

107 Ibid., p. 585.

108 See, e.g., Michael Mason, 'Browning and the Dramatic Monologue', in *Robert Browning*, edited by Isobel Armstrong, Writers and their Background series, edited by R. L. Brett (1974), pp. 231–66.

109 [John] Bunyan, *The Pilgrim's Progress, Grace Abounding and A Relation of his Imprisonment*, edited by Edmund Venables, second edition, revised by Mabel Peacock (Oxford, 1900), p. 302.

110 Abrams, chapter 2.

111 See Michael Wheeler, *Death and the Future Life in Victorian Literature and Theology* (Cambridge, 1990), pp. 253–5.

112 Thomas Carlyle, *Sartor Resartus; On Heroes and Hero Worship*, Everyman's Library, 278 (London and New York, 1908), pp. 124–7.

113 The anonymous reviewer in *The Leader* compared Browning's mingling of 'the ludicrous with the intensely serious' in *Christmas-Eve and Easter-Day* with Carlyle: *Robert Browning: The Critical Heritage*, edited

by Boyd Litzinger and Donald Smalley, Critical Heritage series, general editor B. C. Southam (1970), p. 140.

114 Augustine describes his own sorrow on the death of his mother, Monica, in the *Confessions* (IX. 12).

115 On Browning's sympathy towards Dissent and Evangelicalism see, e.g., William O. Raymond, *The Infinite Moment and Other Essays in Robert Browning* (Toronto, 1950), p. 24; Philip Drew, *The Poetry of Browning: A Critical Introduction* (1970), p. 222; William Irvine and Park Honan, *The Book, the Ring, and the Poet: A Biography of Robert Browning* (1975), p. 263.

116 His statement that 'This sight was shown me, there and then, — / Me, one out of a world of men' (405–6), for example, is reminiscent of Dame Julian of Norwich. On the distinction between the theophanic and the epiphanic see Ashton Nichols, *The Poetics of Epiphany: Nineteenth-Century Origins of the Modern Literary Movement* (Tuscaloosa and London, 1988), pp. 27–9.

117 Drew, pp. 205, 206, 223–4, and 'Browning and Philosophy', in *Browning*, ed. Armstrong, pp. 104–7. (Drew believes that there is no evidence of influence on either side.)

118 William Clyde DeVane, *A Browning Handbook*, second edition (New York, 1955), p. 203.

119 Newman, *Essay on Development*, p. 114.

120 Cf. Abrams's definition of apocalypse as 'a vision in which the old world is replaced by a new and better world': Abrams, p. 41. (*Easter-Day* also conforms to what Abrams identifies as the characteristically circular structure of the Romantic journey narrative, of which Coleridge's 'The Ancient Mariner' is the paradigm.)

121 On ambiguity, see Phyllis J. Guskin, 'Ambiguities in the Structure and Meaning of Browning's *Christmas-Eve*', *Victorian Poetry*, 4 (1966), 21–8.

122 See, e.g., Ian Jack, *Browning's Major Poetry* (Oxford, 1973), pp. 133–4; Irvine and Honan, p. 266. Philip Drew is a notable exception in this respect.

123 Litzinger and Smalley, p. 144.

124 Cf. John Fowles's critique of the Victorian novel in *The French Lieutenant's Woman* (1969), chapters 12–13.

125 See pp. 31–2 above.

126 E. P. Whipple, writing in the *North American Review*, described Heathcliff thus: 'He is a deformed monster ... to whom Dante would hesitate in awarding the honour of a place among those whom he has consigned to the burning pitch.' *The Brontës: The Critical Heritage*, edited by Miriam Allott, Critical Heritage series, general editor B. C. Southam (London and Boston, 1974), p. 248.

127 Charles F. S. Warren, *The Dies Irae: On this Hymn and its English Versions*, Part I, The Hymn (1897), pp. xii–xv.

3 Heaven

1 *Hymns Ancient and Modern, For Use in the Services of the Church; With Accompanying Tunes* [edited by Henry Williams Baker, *et al.*], Standard Edition (1916), p. 170.

2 Edward Gordon Selwyn, *The First Epistle of St. Peter* (1946), p. 124.

3 Edward Henry Bickersteth, *A Practical and Explanatory Commentary on the New Testament* [1868], p. 373.

4 See John Hick, *Death and Eternal Life* (1976), p. 202.

5 In a major survey of the history of heaven in the West, published after work on this chapter was completed, Colleen McDannell and Bernhard Lang show how medieval courtly love and a Renaissance conflation of the Christian and the pagan generated an anthropocentric heaven, the apex of which was to come in the nineteenth century: *Heaven: A History* (New Haven and London, 1988), pp. 353–8.

6 See, for example, George Eliot's *Felix Holt* (1866; 30). For Feuerbach, theology is in reality anthropology, and religion is 'the relation of man to his own nature . . . but to his nature not recognised as his own'; 'God is heaven spiritualised, while heaven is God materialised, or reduced to the forms of the senses': Ludwig Feuerbach, *The Essence of Christianity*, translated by Marian Evans, second edition, English and Foreign Philosophical Library, 15 (1881), pp. 197, 172. On Marx's response to Feuerbach, see Robert C. Tucker, *Philosophy and Myth in Karl Marx* (Cambridge, 1961), pp. 95–105; Arend Th. van Leeuwen, *Critique of Heaven* (1972), pp. 151, 174, 177–8.

7 See Hick, p. 206.

8 See Alan Gauld, *The Founders of Psychical Research* (1968) and Janet Oppenheim, *The Other World: Spiritualism and Psychical Research in England, 1850–1914* (Cambridge, 1985); John Morley, *Death, Heaven and the Victorians* (London and Pittsburgh, 1971), chapter 9.

9 Ulrich Simon, *Heaven in the Christian Tradition* (1958), pp. 31–2. Andrew Lincoln, author of a rigorous work of biblical scholarship in the area, considers that Simon provides in his broad overview 'some interesting, though often fanciful, insights': *Paradise Now and Not Yet: Studies in the Role of the Heavenly Dimension in Paul's Thought with Special Reference to his Eschatology*, Society for New Testament Studies Monograph series, edited by R. McL. Wilson and M. E. Thrall, 43 (Cambridge, 1981), p. 6.

10 Simon, p. 34.

11 See Introduction, note 28 above.

12 See, for example, William E. Addis and Thomas Arnold, *A Catholic Dictionary, Containing some Account of the Doctrine, Discipline, Rites, Ceremonies, Councils, and Religious Orders of the Catholic Church* (1884), pp. 736, 776, 853.

13 See Simon, pp. 52–5.

14 Gerhard von Rad, '*ouranos*', in *Theological Dictionary of the New Testament*, edited by Gerhard Kittel and Gerhard Friedrich, translated and edited by Geoffrey W. Bromiley, 10 vols. (Grand Rapids, Mich., 1964–76), V, 509.

15 See, e.g., Northrop Frye, *The Great Code: The Bible and Literature* (1982), p. 175.

16 In *Kerygma and Myth*, edited by H. W. Bartsch (New York, 1961), p. 4; quoted in Lincoln, *Paradise Now and Not Yet*, p. 4, where he records that 'volumes could be and have been written on this'.

17 See, e.g., *Science and Religion in the Nineteenth Century*, edited by Tess Cosslett (Cambridge, 1984).

18 Simon, p. xii.

19 Lincoln, p. 79.

20 Ibid., p. 80; also cf. Simon, pp. 44–5.

21 See, e.g., Max F. Schulz, *Paradise Preserved: Recreations of Eden in Eighteenth- and Nineteenth-Century England* (Cambridge, 1985).

22 See, e.g., Oriel's description of Eden before the fall as 'heaven's miniature' in *Yesterday, To-Day, and For Ever: A Poem in Twelve Books*, eighth edition (1873), p. 153.

23 John Henry Newman, *Parochial and Plain Sermons*, new edition, 8 vols. (1891), III, 374.

24 See Lincoln, pp. 77–80. On Lincoln's own argument the third heaven cannot simply be equated with paradise, and Paul is granted an experience of an aspect of heaven which 'anticipates both 'the intermediate state' and the glory of the final consummation'.

25 See, e.g., Arthur Penrhyn Stanley, *The Epistles of St. Paul to the Corinthians*, fourth edition (1876), p. 538. E. H. Bickersteth, who in *Yesterday, To-Day, and For Ever* clearly separates Paradise from the 'Many Mansions' of Heaven, takes a different line on 'paradise' in 2 Corinthians 12 in his commentary on the New Testament, where he argues that it 'may here well describe the region of celestial glory': *The Holy Bible*, with a Devotional and Practical Commentary by R. Jamieson and E. H. Bickersteth, 3 vols. (London and New York, 1861–5), III, 299.

26 See C. K. Barrett, *A Commentary on the Second Epistle to the Corinthians* (1973), p. 309. Cf. also Christopher Rowland, *The Open Heaven: A Study of Apocalyptic in Judaism and Early Christianity* (1982), pp. 378–86.

27 See Lincoln, p. 77.

28 See, e.g., Lincoln, p. 82; Simon, p. 46.

29 Karl Ludwig Schmidt, '*basilea*', in *Theological Dictionary of New Testament*, I, 582.

30 Addis and Arnold, pp. 776, 853.

31 Frederick Denison Maurice, *The Kingdom of Christ; or, Hints to a Quaker Respecting the Principles, Constitution and Ordinances of the Catholic Church*, edited by Alec R. Vidler, 2 vols. (1958), I, 256–7.

32 Cf. Stephen Prickett, *Romanticism and Religion: The Tradition of Coleridge and Wordsworth in the Victorian Church* (Cambridge, 1976), p. 142. On the 'secularization of the kingdom idea in terms of notions of progress, development, evolution and material prosperity', for which Kant's, Schleiermacher's and Ritschl's view of the kingdom 'as the realm of ideal human relations on earth' prepared the ground, see Eric J. Sharpe, 'Kingdom of God', in *A New Dictionary of Christian Theology*, edited by Alan Richardson and John Bowden (1983), p. 317.

33 Frederick Denison Maurice, *Lectures on the Apocalypse; or, Book of Revelation of St. John the Divine*, second edition (Cambridge and London, 1865), pp. 302–4.

34 See Anon., 'Spirits and Spirit-Rapping', *Westminster Review*, NS 13 (1858), 29–66.

35 A. M. H. W., *Glimpses of a Brighter Land* (1871), p. vii. The book is dedicated to Mary Howitt. See also the *Christian Spiritualist*, a weekly newspaper published by the Society for the Diffusion of Spiritual Knowledge in the middle of the nineteenth century. The Churches' Fellowship for Psychical and Spiritual Studies, founded in 1953, is still active today. Its president, Revd Dr Martin Israel, and chairman, The Venerable Michael Perry, have both published widely in the area.

36 See Gauld, p. 21.

37 Addis and Arnold, p. 394.

38 John Angell James, *Heaven; or, The Church Triumphant in its State of Celestial Repose* (1859), p. 6. Bailey had taken up the theme in Festus, where Lucifer states that

> Heaven is no place;
> Unless it be a place with God, allwhere.
> It is the being good – the knowing God –
> The consciousness of happiness and power.

Philip James Bailey, *Festus: A Poem*, ninth edition (1875), p. 36. (This passage first appeared in the second edition of 1845: see Robert Birley, *Sunk Without Trace: Some Forgotten Masterpieces Reconsidered*, The Clark Lectures, 1960–1961 (New York, 1962), p. 184.) A banal piece of Spasmodic theologizing, the passage hints at the poem's universalism but is difficult to reconcile with Bailey's placing of the action in the Skies, the Heaven of Heavens, Angel World, and so on. Such locations are suggestive of 'place', and for Bailey's *dramatis personae* to have some kind of identity, these locations have to be inhabited by beings who can speak a language of this world.

39 [William Branks], *Heaven our Home* (Edinburgh, 1861).

40 See Geoffrey Rowell, *Hell and the Victorians: A Study of the Nineteenth-Century Theological Controversies Concerning Eternal Punishment and the Future Life* (Oxford, 1974), pp. 9–10.

41 [Robert Bickersteth] et al., *The Recognition of Friends in Heaven* (1866), p. 5.

42 The author himself, who is not identified, later writes of the everlasting blessedness of heaven as a state: R. Bickersteth, p. 8.

43 Ibid., pp. 6–8.

44 E. H. Bickersteth, *The Risen Saints: What does Scripture Reveal of their Estate and Employments?* (1865), p. 54.

45 E. H. Bickersteth, *Yesterday*, p. 387.

46 Austin Holyoake, *Heaven & Hell: Where Situated?: A Search after the Objects of Man's Fervent Hope & Abiding Terror* [1873], p. 2. Cf. Feuerbach's question, 'Where is the space in which individuals will live in the life after death?': see William B. Chamberlain, *Heaven Wasn't his Destination: The Philosophy of Ludwig Feuerbach* (1941), p. 89.

47 See, e.g., Newman, *Parochial and Plain Sermons*, III, 368.

48   But peace – still voice and closed eye
            Suit best with hearts beyond the sky,
            Hearts training in their low abode,
         Daily to lose themselves in hope to find their God.
[John Keble], *The Christian Year: Thoughts in Verse for the Sundays and Holydays Throughout the Year*, second edition (Oxford, 1827), II, 82.

49 See Rowell, *Hell and the Victorians*, pp. 70–5.

50 Thomas Erskine, *The Unconditional Freeness of the Gospel: In Two Essays*, fourth edition (Edinburgh, 1831), pp. 24, 9.

51 Frederic W. Farrar, *Eternal Hope: Five Sermons Preached in Westminster Abbey, November and December, 1877* (1904), p. 19.

52 Ibid., pp. 21, 25. Cf. the contemporary theologian Hans Küng, who argues that the 'heaven of faith is not a place, but a mode of being; the infinite God cannot be localized in space, cannot be limited by time': *Eternal Life?*, translated by Edward Quinn (1984), p. 182.

53 Cf. also William Alger, an American Unitarian, who argued in 1878 that belief in a future life was possible and necessary in spite of the

'incongruous medley of physical imagery and gross imaginative pictures' that were to be found in the doctrine of some Christian believers. This whole 'suppositious mass' of 'mere poetry or superstition' is to be dismissed in favour of a 'calm confronting of the mystery of the future in its confessed secrecy as it is, and a peaceful resignation to the will of God in conscious ignorance and trust'; William Rounseville Alger, *The Destiny of the Soul: A Critical History of the Doctrine of a Future Life*, tenth edition (New York, 1878), pp. 727, 732.

54 See, e.g., Bailey, p. 73; R. W. Church, *Dante and Other Essays* (London and New York, 1901), p. 83.

55 Branks, *Heaven our Home*, p. 59.

56 [Robert Weaver], *Heaven: A Manual for the Heirs of Heaven; Designed for the Satisfaction of the Inquisitive, as well as for Assistance to the Devout. Also, on Angels and their Ministry* (1837), p. 34.

57 *The Complete Poems of Christina Rossetti*, Variorum Edition, 2 vols., edited by R. W. Crump (Baton Rouge and London, 1979–86), I, 221–2. All further quotations from Christina Rossetti's verse are taken from this edition.

58 See pp. 50–4 above.

59 Tennyson's Enoch Arden (1864) contains a famous example. Having looked for a sign in the Bible and found the words 'Under the palm-tree', Enoch's wife has a dream which leads her to believe that he must be in heaven, rather than shipwrecked, as in fact he is:

> When lo! her Enoch sitting on a height,
> Under a palm-tree, over him the Sun:
> 'He is gone,' she thought, 'he is happy, he is singing
> Hosanna in the highest. . .'   (496–9)

Tennyson completed the set of associations in a description of Enoch's paradisal tropical island that Hopkins considered to be inspired: 'The mountain wooded to the peak, the lawns / And winding glades high up like ways to Heaven' (568–9).

60 One of the finest Victorian applications is H. F. Lyte's in 'Abide with me', where he conflates the fall of evening and the ebbing of the tide – two traditional analogies for death: 'Abide with me; fast falls the eventide; / The darkness deepens, Lord, with me abide'; 'Swift to its close ebbs out life's little day': *Hymns Ancient and Modern*, p. 26. For an excellent detailed account of the hymn, see J. R. Watson, *The Victorian Hymn*, Inaugural Lecture, 1981 (Durham, 1981), pp. 9–12. Where images of sea and shore become mere detached tokens, as so often in popular consolatory writing, the effect is banal sentimentalism. W. D. Smith's Minstrel ballad, 'Ring the Bell Softly', for example, has these immortal lines: 'Someone has gone to the bright golden shore, / Ring the bell softly,

there's crape on the door': *The Parlour Song Book: A Casquet of Vocal Gems*, edited by Michael R. Turner (London and Sydney, 1972), p. 313.

61 See, e.g., E. H. Bickersteth, *Yesterday*, pp. 374–5.

62 See Eduard Lohse, 'Sion', in *Theological Dictionary of New Testament*, VII, 317.

63 See Augustine, *The City of God*, translated by Marcus Dods, introduced by Thomas Merton, Modern Library (New York, 1950), pp. 736–7.

64 E. H. Bickersteth, *Yesterday*, p. 431.

65 Examples include E. H. Bickersteth, *The Master's Home-Call: A Memoir of Alice Frances Bickersteth* (1872) and *The Shadowed Home, and the Light Beyond* (1875). E. H. Bickersteth wrote of his own daughter, who died at the age of nineteen, 'She always spoke of death as going home': *Master's Home-Call*, p. 31. Keble's *The Christian Year* (1827) contains numerous references to the 'eternal home above', the 'endless home', and so on. F. D. Maurice described the 'sleep in Jesus' as 'the rest of one who has . . . reached his home after long wanderings': 'Death and Life', in *Christmas Day, and Other Sermons*, second edition (1892), p. 397. One of Christina Rossetti's most significant poems is 'From House to Home' (see pp. 161–2 above). Numerous examples from deathbed scenes in nineteenth-century fiction include *Jane Eyre* (see p. 41–2 above), The Revd Legh Richmond's *The Dairyman's Daughter* (1810), and F. W. Farrar's *Eric; or, Little by Little* (1858). Markham Sutherland in J. A. Froude's *The Nemesis of Faith* (1849) relates the idea to people's desire to be buried where they first worshipped and were brought up: 'We call heaven our home, as the best name we know to give it': *The Nemesis of Faith*, *Victorian Fiction: Novels of Faith and Doubt* (New York and London, 1975), pp. 101–2.

66 [Isaac Taylor], *Physical Theory of Another Life* (1836), pp. 181–2. On analogy he wrote: 'If once we relinquish the principle of analogy, as applicable to the divine operations and government, we abandon all means of extending our knowledge, and are left in a state of distressing incertitude, in relation to the most momentous subjects': p. 181.

67 Branks, *Heaven our Home*, p. 159.

68 'What we, when face to face we see', in *The Poems of Arthur Hugh Clough*, edited by A. L. P. Norrington (1968), p. 62.

69 Immanuel Kant, *Lectures on Philosophical Theology*, translated by Allen W. Wood and Gertrude M. Clark (Ithaca and London, 1978), p. 110.

70 Robert Pollok, *The Course of Time: A Poem*, Illustrated Edition (1857), p. 169.

71 *Catharine and Crauford Tait, Wife and Son of Archibald Campbell, Archbishop of Canterbury: A Memoir*, edited by William Benham (1879), p. 173.

72 *In Memoriam*, 41; see p. 244 above.
73 See Simon, pp. 217–18; Hick, p. 204; McDannell and Lang, pp. 217, 229, 257–64.
74 R. Bickersteth, p. 178.
75 See, e.g., A. Midlane's 'There's a Friend for little children', in *Hymns Ancient and Modern*, p. 381, and Mrs Cecil Frances Alexander's 'Once in royal David's city', in her *Hymns for Little Children* (1848), p. 31.
76 See, e.g., R. Bickersteth, pp. 32, 181–2.
77 Julius Hare held that consolation for the loss of friends 'lies in the thought, that, blessed as it is to have friends on earth, it is still more blessed to have friends in heaven': [Julius and Augustus Hare], *Guesses at Truth* (1867), p. 175. The young Thomas Carlyle wrote in a letter to Jane Welsh in 1823, 'With the hope of meeting in a brighter scene of existence, I look on Death as the most inestimable privilege of man': *The Collected Letters of Thomas and Jane Welsh Carlyle*, Duke-Edinburgh Edition, general editor Charles Richard Sanders, 7 vols. (Durham, N.C., 1970–7), II, 446. Froude records in the *Life* that, after the death of his wife, Carlyle spoke 'of a life to come, and the meeting of friends in it as a thing not impossible': James Anthony Froude, *Thomas Carlyle: A History of his Life in London, 1834–1881*, new edition, 2 vols. (1897), II, 347.
78 See Rowell, *Hell and the Victorians*, pp. 5–6, n. 19.
79 Taylor, p. 170.
80 Branks, p. iv.
81 Elizabeth Stuart Phelps, *The Gates Ajar*, edited by Helen Sootin Smith, John Harvard Library, edited by Bernard Bailyn (Cambridge, Mass., 1964).
82 A. Dean, *'The Gates Ajar' Critically Examined* (1871). See also Mark Twain's parody of the novel, entitled *Extract from Captain Stormfield's Visit to Heaven* (New York and London, 1909).
83 Keble, II, 195.
84 Frederick Denison Maurice, *The Gospel of St. John: A Series of Discourses* (Cambridge, 1857), p. 318.
85 See p. 23 above.
86 Pollok, p. 29.
87 Mackenzie Bell, *Christina Rossetti: A Biographical and Critical Study* (1898), p. 179.
88 Newman, *Parochial and Plain Sermons*, IV, 174–5.
89 Ibid., IV, 207.
90 Ibid., IV, 210.
91 Ibid., IV, 204.
92 Ibid., I, 5.

93 Ibid., I, 7, 3–4.
94 J. A. James, for example, argued that heaven, which is closed against the unpardoned, 'could in fact be no heaven to them; every view of the glory of 'Him that sitteth upon the throne,' that was attended with the consciousness that He had not forgiven their sins, and that they did not stand spotless before Him, would fill the mind with intolerable anguish': *Heaven*, pp. 9–10. Nelly Dean in *Wuthering Heights* (1847), declares that 'all sinners would be miserable in heaven' (9).
95 Maurice, *Lectures on Apocalypse*, pp. 63–4.
96 Thomas Carlyle, *Past and Present* (1843), book III, chapter 14.
97 Maurice, *Lectures on Apocalypse*, p. 65.
98 See, e.g., Adelaide Procter's 'The Lost Chord', with music by Arthur Sullivan (1877), in M. R. Turner, p. 239.
99 Although Victorian hymnody often described a static, theocentric heaven, the popular hymns of late-nineteenth-century revivalists such as Moody and Sankey were more anthropocentric in their emphasis on the heavenly home: see McDannell and Lang, pp. 288–9.
100 See Lincoln, note 9 above.
101 *Hymns Ancient and Modern*, p. 378.
102 See *The English Hymnal* (Oxford and London, 1906), p. 81.
103
    I need Thy Presence every passing hour;
    What but Thy grace can foil the tempter's power?
    Who like Thyself my guide and stay can be?
    Through cloud and sunshine, Lord, abide with me.
See also note 61 above.
104 *Hymns Ancient and Modern*, p. 249.
105 Ibid., p. 323.
106 *Historical Companion to 'Hymns Ancient & Modern'*, edited by Maurice Frost, new edition (1962), p. 284.
107 Lincoln, p. 61.
108 *Hymns Ancient and Modern*, p. 257.
109 *Historical Companion*, p. 276.
110 *Hymns Ancient and Modern*, p. 793.
111 *Historical Companion*, p. 282.
112 *Hymns Ancient and Modern*, p. 839.
113 Ibid., p. 369.
114 Ibid., p. 257.
115 Ibid., p. 255.
116 Ibid., p. 495.
117 Ibid., p. 334.
118 Ibid., p. 154. See also pp. 151, 152, 153, 159.
119 Ibid., p. 150.

120 Ibid., p. 155.

121 Ibid., p. 157.

122 See [Hallam Tennyson], *Alfred Lord Tennyson: A Memoir (1899)*, p. 754.

123 *The New International Version Interlinear Greek-English New Testament*, The Nestle Greek Text with a Literal English Translation by Alfred Marshall (Grand Rapids, Mich., 1976), p. 969.

124 *Hymns Ancient and Modern*, p. 170.

125 Günther Bornkamm, '*presbys*', in Kittel, ed., *Theological Dictionary of the New Testament*, VI, 668.

126 D. M. R. Bentley has called Hall Caine's often quoted reminiscence in question: '"The Blessed Damozel": A Young Man's Fantasy', *Victorian Poetry*, 20 (1982), 31–43 (p. 31).

127 *Collected Works of Edgar Allan Poe*, edited by Thomas Ollive Mabbott, 3 vols. (Cambridge, Mass., 1969–78), I, 364–5. All further quotations from the poem are taken from this edition.

128 For discussion of parallels between this aspect of 'The Raven' and Rossetti's poem see Paul Lauter, 'The Narrator of "The Blessed Damozel"', *Modern Language Notes*, 73 (1958), 344–8.

129 Item 19a in Virginia Surtees, *The Paintings and Drawings of Dante Gabriel Rossetti (1828–1882): A Catalogue Raisonné*, 2 vols. (Oxford, 1971), I, 4. *Surtees's description of the sketch ('A man sitting by a table rises from a chair and gazes at the face of an angel; other angels, behind and in front') ignores the fact that the female figure who leans towards the man is not winged.*

130 Bentley, p. 43.

131 Ibid., p. 42.

132 Ibid., p. 43. Cf. David G. Riede, *Dante Gabriel Rossetti and the Limits of Victorian Vision* (Ithaca and London, 1983), p. 21.

133 See Dante Gabriel Rossetti, *The Blessed Damozel: The Unpublished Manuscript, Texts and Collation*, edited by Paull Franklin Baum (Chapel Hill, 1937). All quotations from the poem are taken from Baum. Unless otherwise stated, the 1856 version (*Oxford and Cambridge Magazine*) is quoted (pp. 17–21). Bentley argues that these changes reflect Rossetti's 'urge to secularize his early poems', and that the poem 'assumed the burden of his wish-fulfilment fantasies': Bentley, p. 33. David G. Riede's disagreement with Bentley's view that Rossetti displayed genuine religious belief in the early version of the poem is based on comparisons he draws between it and a roughly contemporary elegy by Rossetti: "A 'Juvenile Affair": D. G. Rossetti's "Sacred to the Memory of Algernon R. G. Stanhope"', *Victorian Poetry*, 20 (1982), 187–98 (pp. 195–8). Cf. Reide, *Rossetti*, p. 53.

134 Bentley explains this as empathy on the part of the 'percipient': Bentley,
    p. 40. Schulz believes that in the poem 'Rossetti appears to be fusing the
    spiritual message of divine love related to the *hortus conclusus* with the
    guilty tale of carnal love enacted in Eden': Schulz, p. 251.

135 The two stanzas at this point in the 1850 version in *The Germ* are less
    ambiguous and less dramatic in effect. The earthly lover bemoans the
    isolation of the damozel in heaven, and wonders whether he himself could
    worship in heaven:

> (Alas! to *her* wise simple mind
>   These things were all but known
> Before they trembled on her sense, –
>   Her voice had caught their tone.
> Alas for lonely Heaven! Alas
>   For life wrung out alone!
>
> Alas, and though the end were reached? . . .
>   Was *thy* part understood
> Or borne in trust? And for her sake
>   Shall this too be found good? –
> May the close lips that knew not prayer
>   Praise ever, though they would?)

136 See Surtees, I, 142.

137 Cited in Surtees, I, 58.

138 Ibid.

139 Cf. Peter and Linda Murray, *The Art of the Renaissance* (1963), p. 217.

140 See *Blessed Damozel*, ed. Baum, p. xiii.

141 See Joan Rees, *The Poetry of Dante Gabriel Rossetti: Modes of
    Self-Expression* (Cambridge, 1981), p. 169.

142 See Christina Rossetti, *The Face of the Deep: A Devotional Commentary
    on the Apocalypse*, sixth edition (1911), e.g. pp. 539–51.

143 See p. 135 above.

144 See Jerome J. McGann, 'Rossetti's Significant Details', *Victorian Poetry*,
    7 (1969), 41–54 (pp. 48–52).

145 See J. C. Reid, *The Mind and Art of Coventry Patmore* (1957), p. 91.

146 'Homo' (XIX), in *The Rod, the Root and the Flower*, edited by Derek
    Patmore (1950), p. 124. The first edition of *The Rod* was published in
    1896.

147 *The Rod*, p. 125.

148 See Reid, pp. 81, 90.

149 Ibid., p. 36.

150 Cf. Antony H. Harrison, *Christina Rossetti in Context* (1988).

151 See Rod Edmond, 'Death Sequences: Patmore, Hardy, and the New Domestic Elegy', *Victorian Poetry*, 19 (1981), 151–65. Patmore's first wife brought up their children to anticipate having a step-mother one day, and in her will left her wedding ring to the second wife, with her 'love and blessing': see Basil Champneys, *Memoirs and Correspondence of Coventry Patmore*, 2 vols. (1900), I, 133–4.

152 Cf. Reid, p. 167.

153 See 'Departure', *The Unknown Eros* (I.VIII), in Coventry Patmore, *Poems*, edited by Basil Champneys (1906), p. 284. All further quotations from Patmore's verse are taken from this edition.

154 See Champneys, *Memoirs and Correspondence*, I, 146.

155 Compare the following words and phrases from the poem with verses from Luke: 'body' (23.55), 'vows of faith' (22.32, 48, 60); 'as, Lord, Thou wilt' (22.42); 'agony' (22.44), 'crucify' (23.33), 'treason' (23.2), 'devotion' (23.55–6), 'grace ... in a fair stranger' and 'thy delusive likeness' (24.13–31), 'chilly dawn' (24.1), 'I lived again' (24.1–53). Also see the use of the Johannine post-Resurrection experiences in 'Vesica Piscis' (I.XXIV).

156 See Reid, p. 161.

157 Ibid., p. 5.

158 Ibid., pp. 21, 29.

159 See Brigid M. Boardman, *Between Heaven and Charing Cross: The Life of Francis Thompson* (London and New Haven, 1988), p. 171.

160 'Paganism Old and New', in *The Works of Francis Thompson*, edited by Wilfrid Meynell, 3 vols. (1913), III, 38–51 (p. 48).

161 *Poems of Francis Thompson*, edited by Terence L. Connolly, revised edition (New York, 1941), p. 77. All further quotations from Thompson's verse are taken from this edition.

162 Cf. R. L. Mégroz, *Francis Thompson, The Poet of Earth in Heaven: A Study in Mysticism and the Evolution of Love-Poetry* (1927), pp. 153f.

163 For an alternative reading, which sees the ending as more open, see Boardman, p. 139.

164 Cited in Boardman, p. 140.

165 Ibid., p. 120.

166 Ibid., pp. 124, 308.

167 Ibid., p. 306.

168 See p. 134 above.

4 Hell

1 [John Keble], *The Christian Year: Thoughts in Verse for the Sundays and Holydays throughout the Year*, second edition (Oxford, 1827), p. 88 (Second Sunday in Lent).

2 The standard work on hell in the period is Geoffrey Rowell's *Hell and the Victorians: A Study of the Nineteenth-Century Theological Controversies Concerning Eternal Punishment and the Future Life* (Oxford, 1974).

3 Robert Pollok, *The Course of Time*: A Poem, Illustrated Edition (1857), p. 15.

4 E. H. Bickersteth, 'Milton's "Paradise Lost"', in *Companions for the Devout Life: Seven Lectures Delivered in St. James's Church, Piccadilly, A.D. 1876*, St James's Lectures, second series (1876), pp. 89–110 (p. 104).

5 See W. E. Gladstone, *Studies Subsidiary to the Works of Bishop Butler* (Oxford, 1896), p. 206, and Rowell, p. 212; David Lodge, *How Far Can You Go?* (Harmondsworth, 1981), p. 113.

6 Robert Hughes, *Heaven and Hell in Western Art* (London, 1968), p. 281.

7 Mark Pattison, *Memoirs* (1885), p. 249.

8 See D. P. Walker, *The Decline of Hell: Seventeenth-Century Discussions of Eternal Torments* (1964), pp. 3–4.

9 St Chrysostom, *Homilies*, iii, cited in Henry Nutcombe Oxenham, *Catholic Eschatology and Universalism: An Essay on the Doctrine of Future Retribution*, second edition (1878), pp. 80–1.

10 J[oseph] Furniss, *The Sight of Hell*, Books for Children and Young Persons, 10 (Dublin, 1861), p. 27.

11 A figure of over four million copies of Furniss's booklets is recorded in *The Catholic Encyclopedia*, edited by Charles G. Herbermann, *et al.*, 15 vols. (1907–12; rpt. New York, 1913), vi, 324.

12 Coffin's translation of Liguori's *The Eternal Truths* was published in 1857. (See Rowell, pp. 154–7.) Liguori's 'considerations' on 'The Pains of Hell' and 'The Eternity of Hell' clearly influenced Furniss's tract entitled *The Sight of Hell*.

13 Furniss, pp. 13–14.

14 Ibid., pp. 18–21.

15 Pollok, p. 18.

16 On the *Spiritual Exercises* of St Ignatius, see Michael Wheeler, *Death and the Future Life in Victorian Literature and Theology* (Cambridge, 1990), pp. 344–6).

17 Furniss, *Sight of Hell*, p. 24.

18 Ibid., p. 18.

19 See S. G. F. Brandon, *The Judgment of the Dead: An Historical and Comparative Study of the Idea of a Post-Mortem Judgment in the Major Religions* (1967), p. 116.

20 E. B. Pusey, *What is of Faith as to Everlasting Punishment?: In Reply to Dr. Farrar's Challenge in his 'Eternal Hope,' 1879*, second edition (Oxford and London, 1880), p. 19.

21 See Harold Begbie, *Life of William Booth: The Founder of the Salvation Army*, abridged edition, 2 vols. (1926), I, 183–4.

22 See Chapter 2, note 74.

23 See Chapter 6, note 47.

24 *Poems and Ballads,* in *The Complete Works of Algernon Charles Swinburne*, edited by Edmund Gosse and Thomas James Wise, Bonchurch Edition, 20 vols. (1925; rpt. New York, 1968), I, 298.

25 E. H. Bickersteth, *The Second Death; or, the Certainty of Everlasting Punishment: A Paper Read before the London Clerical Conference, in the Vestry Room of St. Giles-in-the-Fields* (1869), pp. 6, 12. On Tennyson and Swinburne, see pp. 56–7 above.

26 Furniss, p. 9. Cf. Liguori, p. 252.

27 Austin Holyoake, *Heaven & Hell: Where Situated?: A Search after the Objects of Man's Fervent Hope & Abiding Terror* [1873], p. 8.

28 Frederic W. Farrar, *Eternal Hope: Five Sermons Preached in Westminster Abbey, November and December, 1877* (1904), p. 120.

29 See above, p. 16.

30 Matthew Arnold, *Culture and Anarchy, with Friendship's Garland and Some Literary Essays*, edited by R. H. Super, Complete Prose Works, 11 vols. (Ann Arbor, Mich., 1960–77), V, 186.

31 Oxenham, p. xxxvii.

32 Gladstone, pp. 199–206.

33 J. B. Mozley, 'Professor Maurice's Theological Essays' (January 1854), in *Essays Historical and Theological*, 2 vols., third edition (1892), II, 297.

34 See pp. 75–6 above.

35 Cf. Robert Lee Wolff, *Gains and Losses: Novels of Faith and Doubt in Victorian England* (1977), p. 227.

36 *See Irish Ecclesiastical Record,* 8 (1872), 245, cited in Rowell, *Hell and the Victorians*, p. 173.

37 Cited in F. W. Farrar, *Mercy and Judgment: A Few Last Words on Christian Eschatology with Reference to Dr. Pusey's 'What is of Faith?'* (1881), p. 31.

38 Gladstone, p. 205.

39 See Wheeler, *Death and the Future Life*, Chapter 6, notes 45 and 76.

40 A. C. Charity, *Events and their Afterlife: The Dialectics of Christian Typology in the Bible and Dante* (Cambridge, 1966), p. 210.

41 Frederick Denison Maurice, *Theological Essays*, second edition (Cambridge, 1853), pp. 455, 473.

42 [Hallam Tennyson], *Alfred Lord Tennyson: A Memoir* (1899), pp. 719–20.

43 Hans Kung, *Eternal Life?*, translated by Edward Quinn (1984), p. 179;

John Bowker, 'The Human Imagination of Hell', *Theology*, 85 (1982), 403–10 (pp. 407–8).

44 See Furniss, *Sight of Hell*, p. 3.

45 See Holyoake, *Heaven and Hell*, p. 4.

46 *Catholic Encyclopedia*, VII, 207.

47 Catherine Crowe, for example, argued that 'it is a vulgar notion to imagine that Heaven and Hell are places; they are states; and it is in ourselves we must look for both': *The Night Side of Nature; or, Ghosts and Ghost Seers*, 2 vols. (1848), I, 370.

48 Bickersteth, *The Second Death*, p. 4.

49 Ibid., p. 9.

50 Ibid., p. 10.

51 Ibid., p. 11.

52 Ibid., p. 13.

53 Ibid., pp. 13, 16.

54 Robert Hughes prefers to relate hell as the 'image of total injustice' to the totalitarian atrocities of the twentieth century: see Hughes, p. 42.

55 James Anthony Froude, *The Nemesis of Faith*, Victorian Fiction: Novels of Faith and Doubt *(New York and London, 1975), p. 15.*

56 Ibid., p. 19.

57 Ibid., p. 205.

58 Ibid., p. 216.

59 Ibid., p. 160.

60 Randall Thomas Davidson and William Benham, *Life of Archibald Campbell Tait, Archbishop of Canterbury*, 2 vols. (London and New York, 1891), II, 129.

61 Ibid., II, 126.

62 Anthony Trollope, *Clergymen of the Church of England*, introduction by Ruth apRoberts (Leicester, 1974), p. 126.

63 See Davidson and Benham, II, 133, 140.

64 Ibid., II, 142.

65 Ibid., II, 160–1.

66 Bickersteth, *The Second Death*, pp. 20–1.

67 Ibid., p. 29.

68 Wilfrid Ward, *The Life of John Henry Cardinal Newman: Based on his Private Journals and Correspondence*, 2 vols. (1912), II, 46.

69 Trollope, p. 124.

70 *The Brontës: Their Lives, Friendships and Correspondence*, edited by Thomas James Wise and John Alexander Symington, 4 vols., Shakespeare Head Brontë (Oxford, 1932), II, 166. Cited in Arthur Pollard, 'The Brontës and their Father's Faith', *Essays and Reviews*, NS 37 (1984), 46–61 (p. 61).

71 *The Traveller's Guide, from Death to Life*, edited by Mrs Stephen Menzies (n.d.), p. 53.

72 Gladstone, p. 207.

73 [Richard Whateley], *A View of the Scripture Revelations Concerning a Future State: Laid Before his Parishioners, by a Country Pastor* (1829), p. 53.

74 Farrar, *Eternal Hope*, pp. xxxviii–xli.

75 Bickersteth, *The Second Death*, pp. 16–17.

76 Ibid., pp. 19–20.

77 Farrar, *Eternal Hope*, pp. 78–9; also cf. pp. 197–202.

78 Maurice, p. 450.

79 Farrar, *Mercy and Judgment*, p. 1.

80 Stewart D. F. Salmond, *The Christian Doctrine of Immortality* (1895), p. 376.

81 G. Somers Bellamy, *Essays from Shakspeare* (1879), pp. 15–16.

82 *Notes on Poems and Reviews, in Works of Swinburne*, XVI, 365.

83 Francis D. Klingender, *Art and the Industrial Revolution* [1947], edited and revised by Arthur Elton (1972), p. 109.

84 Thomas Balston, *John Martin, 1789–1854: His Life and Works* (1947), p. 236.

85 [William] Booth, *In Darkest England and the Way Out* [1890], p. 13. For further examples see *Into Unknown England, 1866–1913: Selections from the Social Explorers*, edited by Peter Keating (Glasgow, 1976).

86 See Gustave Doré and Blanchard Jerrold, *London: A Pilgrimage* (1872), e.g. facing pp. 30, 138, 148.

87 Frederick Engels, *The Condition of the Working-Class in England, From Personal Observation and Authentic Sources* (German, 1845; English, 1892), introduction by Eric Hobsbawm (1969), p. 58.

88 Engels, p. 86.

89 Alexis de Tocqueville, *Journeys to England and Ireland*, translated by George Lawrence and K. P. Mayer, edited by J. P. Mayer (1958), p. 107.

90 Alexander Welsh, *The City of Dickens* (Oxford, 1971), p. 65; S. E. Finer, *The Life and Times of Sir Edwin Chadwick* (1952), p. 315.

91 Booth, pp. 13–14.

92 See, e.g., Alfred Hall, *The Beliefs of a Unitarian* (1932), p. 35; Rowell, pp. 32–61.

93 For more detailed discussion on biblical allusion in *Mary Barton* see Michael Wheeler, *The Art of Allusion in Victorian Fiction* (London and Basingstoke, 1979), pp. 50–7.

94 Theophilus Lindsey, *Sermons, with Appropriate Prayers Annexed*, 2 vols. (1810), I, 507.

95 See *Into Unknown England*, pp. 20–2.

96 *The Letters of George Meredith*, edited by C. L. Cline, 3 vols. (Oxford, 1970), I, 48.

97 *Meredith: The Critical Heritage*, edited by Ioan Williams, Critical Heritage series, general editor B. C. Southam (1971), p. 76; cf. also pp. 74–5.

98 *The Poems of George Meredith*, edited by Phyllis B. Bartlett, 2 vols. (New Haven and London, 1978), I, 116. (All further quotations from *Modern Love* are taken from this edition.) Cf. also: 'By stealth / Our eyes dart scrutinizing snakes' (XXXIV).

99 George Meredith, *Selected Poems*, edited by Keith Hanley (Manchester, 1983), p. 20.

100 Ibid., p. 105.

101 Ibid., p. 106; the three phases are those suggested by Norman Friedman.

102 Williams, pp. 97–9.

103 See Donald Thomas, *Swinburne: The Poet in his World* (1979), p. 114.

104 See Thomas, p. 130.

105 *Swinburne: The Critical Heritage*, edited by Clyde K. Hyder, Critical Heritage series, general editor B. C. Southam (1970), p. 26.

106 Ibid., pp. 33, 67.

107 Ibid., p. 36.

108 Ibid., pp. 42–3.

109 See *Works of Swinburne*, XVI, 354–5.

110 See Thomas, p. 15.

111 *Works of Swinburne*, XIII, 423.

112 See Hyder, p. 42.

113 F. W. J. Hemmings, *Baudelaire the Damned: A Biography* (1982), pp. vii–viii.

114 Ibid., p. x.

115 Charles Baudelaire, *Les Fleurs du Mal* (Montreal, 1950), p. 158.

116 Hughes, pp. 42, 155.

117 *Works of Swinburne*, I, 298. (All further quotations from Swinburne's verse are taken from this edition.)

118 Ibid., XVI, 354.

119 Ibid., XVI, 360.

120 Ibid., XVI, 365.

121 See, for example, Bickersteth, *Yesterday, To-Day, and For Ever: A Poem In Twelve Books*, eighth edition (1873), III, 573.

122 Barbara Charlesworth, *Dark Passages: The Decadent Consciousness in Victorian Literature* (Madison and Milwaukee, 1965), p. 119.

123 Arthur Symons, 'Aubrey Beardsley', *Fortnightly Review*, NS 58 (1898), 752–61 (p. 757).

124 See H[enry] S. Salt, *The Life of James Thomson ('B.V.'), with a Selection*

from his Letters and a Study of his Works (1889), p. 295. The poet's mother, Sarah Kennedy, was a 'deeply religious woman of the Irvingite faith, whose nature, unlike that of her husband, seems to have been of a somewhat melancholy cast' (Salt, p. 1).

125 Ibid., pp. 182, 297.

126 Ibid., p. 184.

127 *The City of Dreadful Night*, Proem, line 8: *Poems and Some Letters of James Thomson*, edited by Anne Ridler (1963), p. 177. (All further quotations from *The City* are taken from this edition.)

128 See William Sharpe, 'Learning to Read *The City*', *Victorian Poetry*, 22 (1984), 65–84 (p. 81).

129 *Poems of Thomson*, ed. Ridler, p. 271.

130 Cf. Sharpe, p. 82.

131 See also *The City*, I.78; II.24; IV.15; VI.15; VII.21f.; IX.19; XI.7; XIV.35; XXI.48, 60.

132 See Salt, p. 287. For further Dante echoes and parallels see *The City*, II.2, 11–12, 45; IV.25–33; IX–XI.

133 The first of the three epigraphs finally chosen by Thomson was from the *Inferno*, in the Italian (III.1: 'Through me you pass into the city of woe').

134 See Sharpe, pp. 66, 75.

135 See Charles Dickens, *A Tale of Two Cities*, edited by Andrew Sanders, World's Classics (Oxford and New York, 1988), pp. 388, 518.

Conclusion

1 Alfred Lord Tennyson, *In Memoriam*, edited by Susan Shatto and Marion Shaw (Oxford, 1982), p. 70. All quotations from the poem are taken from this edition; numbers given in the text refer to lyrics. For an extensive discussion of *In Memoriam*, *Our Mutual Friend*, *The Dream of Gerontius*, and *The Wreck of the Deutschland*, see Michael Wheeler, *Death and the Future Life in Victorian Literature and Theology* (Cambridge, 1990), pp. 221–366.

2 See Shatto and Shaw, p. 206.

3 See Geoffrey Rowell, *Hell and the Victorians: A Study of the Nineteenth-Century Theological Controversies Concerning Eternal Punishment and the Future Life* (Oxford, 1974), pp. 76–89.

4 [Hallam Tennyson], *Alfred Lord Tennyson: A Memoir* (1899), p. 89.

5 F. W. Farrar, *Mercy and Judgment: A Few Last Words on Christian Eschatology with Reference to Dr. Pusey's 'What is of Faith?'* (1881), p.v.

6 H. Tennyson, *Memoir*, p. 269.

7 Ibid.

8 See, for example, *The Letters of Charles Dickens,* edited by Walter Dexter, Nonesuch Edition, 3 vols. (1938), III, 352.

9 Owen Chadwick, *The Victorian Church,* second edition, 2 vols., Ecclesiastical History of England, edited by J. D. Dickinson, vols. VII-VIII (1970), II, 33.

10 See Andrew Sanders, *Charles Dickens, Resurrectionist* (London and Basingstoke, 1982), p. XI.

11 [John Henry Newman], *Verses on Various Occasions,* second edition (1869), p. 320.

12 Cf. Stephen Prickett, *Romanticism and Religion: The Tradition of Coleridge and Wordsworth in the Victorian Church* (Cambridge, 1976), p. 208.

13 See Chadwick, II, 419.

14 Chr[istopher] Wordsworth, *On Burning of the Body; and on Burial: A Sermon Preached in Westminster Abbey on Sunday July 5th, 1874* (Lincoln, 1874), p. 14.

15 *Letters from a 'Modernist',* edited by M. J. Weaver (1981), pp. 20–1.

16 C. Wordsworth, p. 8.

17 *The Complete Poems of Thomas Hardy,* edited by James Gibson, New Wessex Edition (1976), p. 167. (Further quotations from Hardy's verse are taken from this edition.)

Index